WITH THE
GERMAN
GUNS

WITH THE
GERMAN
GUNS

FOUR YEARS ON THE WESTERN FRONT

BY
HERBERT SULZBACH

WITH A FOREWORD BY TERENCE PRITTIE
TRANSLATED FROM THE GERMAN *ZWEI LEBENDE MAUERN*
BY RICHARD THONGER

Pen & Sword
MILITARY

First published in Germany in 1935
First published in Great Britain in 1973
and reprinted in 1998 by Leo Cooper
Republished in 2003 by Pen & Sword Military Classics

Reprinted in this format in 2012 by
PEN & SWORD MILITARY
An imprint of
Pen & Sword Books Ltd
47 Church Street
Barnsley
South Yorkshire
S70 2AS

ISBN 978 1 84884 864 1

Printed and bound in England
By CPI Group (UK) Ltd, Croydon, CR0 4YY

Pen & Sword Books Ltd incorporates the Imprints of Pen & Sword Aviation,
Pen & Sword Family History, Pen & Sword Maritime, Pen & Sword Military,
Pen & Sword Discovery, Wharncliffe Local History, Wharncliffe True Crime,
Wharncliffe Transport, Pen & Sword Select, Pen & Sword Military Classics,
Leo Cooper, The Praetorian Press, Remember When,
Seaforth Publishing and Frontline Publishing

For a complete list of Pen & Sword titles please contact
PEN & SWORD BOOKS LIMITED
47 Church Street, Barnsley, South Yorkshire, S70 2AS, England
E-mail: enquiries@pen-and-sword.co.uk
Website: www.pen-and-sword.co.uk

CONTENTS

CONTENTS

ILLUSTRATIONS

Foreword

HERBERT SULZBACH

A MEMOIR
by
Terence Prittie

IN the 1930s a novel was published called *Bretherton. Khaki or Field Grey?* It told the story of a British officer in the First World War, who was passed through the lines in German uniform in place of a dead German who was his double, served with the latter's Prussian regiment, returned by plane through the lines, and was eventually killed on his second spy-mission with the Kaiser's army. On his first, he had identified completely with an enemy whom he could no longer regard as such, and his last thoughts when dying fluctuated between the dual loyalties and personalities which had become interwoven.

Herbert Sulzbach's story has this in common with that of the mythical Bretherton. He served in the First World War as a German citizen, totally loyal to his German Fatherland. He served in the Second World War in the British Army, against Nazi Germany, and is—as far as I know—the only man in the country who was commissioned in World War I by Kaiser Wilhelm II and in World War II by King George VI. Yet he remained, although this may sound paradoxical, as loyal as before to his *true* fatherland, the Germany which has outlived conquerors and tyrannies. In putting on khaki in place of field-grey, he believed that he had one immediate, overriding duty; in his own words it was 'to help to destroy Hitler'. He had, in addition, a longer-term aim—to work for the reconciliation of two nations which he loved and to which he felt that he belonged. He was able to begin doing this even before the end of the war.

So much for the broad outline of his life. There have been a great many significant episodes in it. Here are some, at least, of its relevant details:

He was born in February, 1894, into a wealthy and respected Jewish family of Frankfurt-on-Main. His grandfather, Rudolf, was the founder in 1855 of the Sulzbach private bank (*Bankhaus Gebrüder Sulzbach*), one of the founders of the *Deutsche Bank*— today one of the 'Big Three' German commercial banks—as well as a partner in a number of other major industrial undertakings. He was offered a title of nobility by Kaiser Wilhelm II, but refused it. Herbert's father, Emil, inherited the family business which was recently taken over by the banking firm of Oppenheim. He died in 1932, on the eve of the Nazi seizure of power. Frankfurt named a street '*Emil Sulzbach-Straße*' in gratitude for his contribution to Frankfurt's cultural life.

Herbert Sulzbach volunteered for military service at the outbreak of war in 1914 and was accepted in the 63rd (Frankfurt) Field Artillery Regiment on 8 August. Four weeks later he was on his way to the Western Front. He was to stay there, but for one short spell of service against the Russians, for the next four years.

He won the Iron Cross, second class, in the Battle of the Somme in 1916, and the Iron Cross, first class, after the bloody battle of Villers-Cotterets in 1918. He received the '*Frontkämpfer Ehrenkreuz*' (Front-line Cross of Merit) from Field Marshal Paul von Hindenburg, later to become President of the 1919–33 Weimar Republic. Among his war-mementoes is a letter from Field-Marshal Ludendorff, with photograph, thanking him for his zeal in discovering the wreckage of his dead stepson's aeroplane. Years later, in 1935, his own wartime diaries were published under the title of *Zwei lebende Mauern* (Two Living Walls). The book received enthusiastic reviews, even from Nazi newspapers and journals—whose editors must surely have been unaware that the author came from a Jewish family and therefore a supposed and proclaimed enemy of the German race. The Berlin publishers, Bernard and Graefe, included *Two Living Walls* in a prospectus of three specially recommended books. Ironically, the other two were profusely illustrated short biographies of Hitler and Mussolini.

Only two years after his book was published, Herbert Sulzbach had to leave Germany. Nazi persecution of the Jews was already under way, and it would have been dangerous, even suicidal, for him to have stayed on. Indeed, his name may already have been on the Nazi Black List—the so-called 'Fahndungsliste' drawn up by the Central Security Office of the Reich (Reichssicherheits-Hauptamt). Certainly his name appears as No. 147 of the British section of the Black List, found at the end of the war and published in The Last Ditch (p. 194), a book written by David Lampe. In 1932 Herbert Sulzbach had written a letter bitterly critical of the Nazis to the Berlin paper Der Tag. A man who alleged that he was a member of the paper's staff, but who was too cowardly to sign his name, wrote back in brutal and vicious terms. In his letter was the sinister and significant sentence: 'Your name has been noted down.' In any case, Herbert Sulzbach was never a man to mince his words or hide his feelings.

He had to leave, and he chose to go to Britain. One reason—in spite of having fought for four years against the British, he had an admiration and even a feeling of affection for them and their country. And, a more mundane consideration, he had built up a firm in a Berlin suburb, making fancy paper for box coverings and book-bindings and doing a busy trade with Britain. A branch of the firm was opened in Slough, offering at least the chance of a living.

In 1938 he returned to Berlin to fetch his wife, Beate, niece of Prof Otto Klemperer, the great conductor, and her sister—a highly risky undertaking. At Bremerhaven, where he landed, he had to stand waiting while a passport official checked his name against the list held below desk-level, but found nothing. He brought the two women, both Jewish, safely to Britian but to a life which was to be far from easy. First, the Slough branch of his firm failed. He was deprived of his German nationality by Nazi decree, thus becoming stateless, and was unable to recover assets left in Germany. Then, with the outbreak of the Second World War, he became, technically, an enemy alien. He and his wife had to leave their home in North London and were interned on the Isle of Man—in spite of his having volunteered for service in the British Army. Life on the Isle of Man, with Nazis and anti-Nazis gathered in together, must have been nightmarish. Perhaps the only fortunate circumstance was that neither Herbert nor Beate was in their home when it was flattened by a Luftwaffe bomb during a raid in November, 1940. But the loss of their small home, coming after the loss of country, possessions and livelihood, could hardly have seemed an unmitigated blessing at the time.

Just before this, Herbert Sulzbach had in fact been accepted for military service; his desperate efforts to volunteer had at last been taken at face value. He joined the Pioneer Corps as a private and spent much of the next four years building defences against possible German landings from sea or air—a strange contrast indeed to his four years of fighting on the Western Front from 1914 to 1918! As the chances of German landings became ever more remote, his work became increasingly unrewarding. With ever larger numbers of Germans being taken prisoner-of-war, he decided to offer his services as an interpreter; and at the end of 1944 he was transferred to the 'Interpreters Pool' and posted as a staff sergeant to Comrie P.O.W. camp in Scotland in January, 1945. At the age of over 50, the most productive period of his life had begun.

He made it his business to talk and reason with the 4,000 men in his charge. Many of them were red-hot Nazis; quite a few were members of the Nazi fighting-elite, the '*Waffen S.S.*', an organization proscribed as criminal by the Nuremberg War-Crimes Tribunal after the war. The task which he undertook was daunting; he discharged it with immense and infectious enthusiasm, with great patience and with an absolute belief in the virtues of the democratic way of life which he made it his duty to explain. His success at Comrie was aptly illustrated by what took place on Armistice Day, November 11, 1945. A day or two earlier he explained to the German prisoners the meaning of 'poppy day', read them John McCrae's poem *In Flanders Fields*, and proposed in these words how they should celebrate the occasion:

If you agree with my proposal, parade on November 11 on your parade ground and salute the dead of *all* nations—your comrades, your former enemies, all murdered fighters for freedom who laid down their lives in German concentration-camps—and make the following vow:

'Never again shall such murder take place! It is the last time that we will allow ourselves to be deceived and betrayed.

It is not true that we Germans are a superior race; we have no right to believe that we are better than others. We are all equal before God, whatever our race or religion. Endless misery has come to us, and we have realized where arrogance leads ... In this minute of silence, at 11 a.m. on this November 11, 1945, we swear to return to Germany as good Europeans, and to take part as long as we live in the reconciliation of all people and the maintenance of peace ... !'

Out of the 4,000 German P.O.W.'s only about a dozen stayed, like Ajax, sulking in their huts. On a raw November morning the remainder stood to attention on the football field, while the 'Last Post' was played. Herbert Sulzbach's own comment: 'Nazism could be fought, and beaten as early as 1945.'

Already commissioned Lieutenant, he moved on early in 1946 to Featherstone Park Camp in Northumberland, where he was promoted Captain in March. He helped to organize a camp newspaper, radio service, orchestra, theatre, art gallery; he worked away with redoubled vigour on the political re-education of the prisoners. An article in the *Manchester Guardian* in May paid tribute to his achievement—the paper's correspondent noted that a German-Jewish refugee, who might have been treated with disdain, was 'universally liked and trusted. I have seen some of the letters received in his daily post-bag from former prisoners who have been released to Germany, and have therefore nothing to gain by courting his favour. They leave one in no doubt whatever as to his influence as an apostle of democratic thought and as a political confessor.'

A succinct comment came from Major Herbert Christiansen of the S.S. in a letter written years later—'We were all the more astonished that you did not exclude us members of the S.S., who should inevitably have been your enemies to the death.' Equally revealing was the 'conversion' of the high-ranking S.S. officer (*Standartenführer*), Günther d'Alquen, a man who had in 1938–39 published a 'death sentence' and an 'obituary' on Czechoslovakia in the paper of the S.S. Führer, Heinrich Himmler, *Schwarze Korps*. D'Alquen, who had been a dedicated Nazi, told Sulzbach: 'You have cured me of certain preconceptions.' Many hundreds of other Germans could have said the same.

The Featherstone Park Camp newspaper *Die Zeit am Tyne* (*Time on the Tyne*) was to publish a farewell message from Herbert Sulzbach, when he left towards the middle of 1948. The camp was already due to be closed down and its inmates repatriated. The farewell message paid tribute to the editors of the paper, who had already returned one by one to Germany. It pointed out that during the two years of the paper's life not a single sentence had been censored; Germans, who had mostly forgotten, were given the chance of learning what freedom of the press meant. The farewell message concluded with an appeal to all German prisoners to go home believing in tolerance, rejecting bitterness, determined to restore Germany to a position of real greatness, as a centre of thought and knowledge in the heart of Europe. Three thousand ex-prisoners, in fact, wrote letters of thanks after they had returned home, a strange and unique fan-mail for Herbert Sulzbach.

Twelve years later he founded a 'Featherstone Park Group' in Düsseldorf, and for a very good reason. In the intervening years the Federal German Republic had established outstandingly good relations with two out of the three Western Powers with special responsibilities in Germany: the United States and France. This was in large part the result of the efforts of the Adenauer governments in Bonn, and of Konrad Adenauer's personal belief that the solid backing of the U.S.A. was indispensible and that Franco-German friendship was a necessary basis for the creation of a new, united Europe. Britain was left on the sidelines; Adenauer did not regard Anglo-German friendship as a priority, while the British people—slow to anger, but slow to forgive or forget—were in no hurry to take the initiative. The essential purpose of the 'Featherstone Park Group' was to foster Anglo-German relations on a personal level, by mobilizing the feelings of sympathy, even of gratitude to Britain of the ex-prisoners who had passed through Herbert Sulzbach's hands.

A couple of years later, Lord Birdwood had this to say in a House of Lords debate, having referred to the hostile attitude towards Germany of a section of the British press: 'In contrast, my Lords, I shall tell a rather different sort of story. Twenty-five thousand German officers and men passed through a prisoner-of-war camp, the Featherstone Park Camp in Northumberland, during the war. They received better and more imaginative treatment that is usually given to prisoners in such circumstances. They were allowed to print their own newspaper. They were treated well in the countryside where they worked. When the tide of Anglo-German relations started to flow the wrong way a year or two ago, they formed in Germany their own association, the Featherstone Park Group, with membership stretching to places as far apart as Hamburg and Munich. They are now dedicated to doing just this, to combating this evil thing—for that is what it is—the encouragement and perpetuation of hate between peoples who should be thinking, surely, in relation to the international situation ... of imperative unity in Europe.'

The Featherstone Park Group, holding meetings, sending sons and daughters to Britain, promoting Anglo-German relations by letters to the press of both countries as well as through personal contact, has done sterling work for the past twelve years. Its activities have been only a small part of Herbert Sulzbach's work. As a cultural affairs officer in the German Embassy in London since 1955 he has been untiring in his own field and in that of public relations, dealing with German and British students, bearing his message of goodwill, mutual interest and understanding over the length and breadth of the British Isles. At 86, his age when these lines were written, he is on the point of retiring from his job as an able and persistent promoter of international friendship. On being pressed for an answer, he agreed that he had a 'message' for people in both Britain and Germany. For the British, it is that a new, democratic Germany is indeed in being and is taking root ever more strongly; that the German people is re-finding itself and is on the way back to the positive and productive traditions of the past; and that a country which elects Willy Brandt as its Chancellor has come to terms with the evil memory of the Nazi era. For the Germans, his thoughts are that Britain even after losing an empire, has much to offer—tolerance, moderation, commonsense and an instinct for practical democracy.

To his Iron Crosses of the First World War, Herbert Sulzbach has added the German Cross of Merit 1st class and recently, the Grand Cross of the German Order of Merit to wear alongside his British medals of the Second World War. In October 1978 he was awarded the Croix de paix de L'Europe, a Franco-German peace decoration. Granted British citizenship in 1947, he was given back German nationality, filched from him by Hitler, in 1952. For the last two decades he has had two 'fatherlands' and his love of both has reinforced his belief in the future of Europe. The man who has worn both khaki and field-grey has come a long way; his war diaries are a major episode on a road which he has trod with great good humour and honest courage.

In a personal tribute on his 80th birthday Sir Bernard Braine said 'We British and Germans owe more to Herbert Sulzbach than we can ever repay, for he led the way in Anglo-German relations.'

Terence Prittie

Translator's Note

HERBERT SULZBACH and I had known each other for fourteen years when he offered me his book for translation. I have attempted, while following the original with all possible fidelity, to give the English reader some insight into the thought of a young, kindly, observant war volunteer who soldiered through the fifty months of mud and death, his resolution enriched and unshaken, recording his impressions faithfully in the notebooks which he now treasures. We sat together for many hours to extract the last ounce from the faded handwriting as well as from the Gothic print of the 1935 edition.

Our principle addition to the 1935 text was the replacement of the initials used for most of the people mentioned by their full names—which we felt would be of particular interest to German readers whose relatives fought on the Western Front, as well as to English readers with an interest in German families.

German ranks have generally been translated into the nearest English equivalent rank: lance-corporal or lance-bombardier for *Gefreiter*, corporal or bombardier for *Unteroffizier*, sergeant for the infantry or artillery *Feldwebel* or the cavalry *Wachtmeister*, sergeant-major for *Offizierstellvertreter*, officer cadet for *Fahnenjunker*, second lieutenant or 2/Lt for *Leutnant*, lieutenant or Lt for *Oberleutnant*, captain for *Hauptmann* or the cavalry rank *Rittmeister*, *Major* unchanged, colonel for *Oberst*, and so on with higher ranks; a naval captain's rank for *Kapitän*; and the nearest possible equivalents for the German flying ranks prefixed *Flieger-*, such as *Fliegerhauptmann*. The nearest suitable equivalents have been sought for the names of German units, and atlases have been combed for the usual English spelling of the many place-names particularly those occurring in reports of action in Eastern sectors.

I have done what I can to translate the pieces of verse which Herbert Sulzbach quotes, giving the German original in each case.

Research in contemporary newspapers has provided at least the approximate wording of the occasional passages recorded by the author in German translated from an English original. French passages quoted have been given in the original and translated.

My sternest attempts at a true rendering were devoted to the passages expressing Herbert Sulzbach's personal feeling: his lively reports of military action; his respect and affection for his friends, indeed for all his comrades; his vivid sketches of scenes and places; and his deep, uncomplicated, front-line soldier's patriotism.

R.T.

Prologue

IT is a very strange and proud feeling for me that my diaries of World War I—published as a book in Germany nearly forty years ago—are now being re-issued again by Leo Cooper under the Warne imprint. In 1937 I offered my book to Putnam's but the clouds of another war were hanging above us and the publishers could not then take the risk. Yet I cannot forget the words of Stanley Went, the late Director of Putnam's London: 'I was fascinated to read that for many years we were trying to kill each other—I am glad we did not succeed.'

Mr Went was, of course, on 'the other side' of the 'Wall'! My first major battle in October, 1914, was against my English friends, near Armentières and I shall never forget the first sight of dead Tommies in Flanders.

For our generation the Great War is still so near to us, nearer than 1939–45. Names like Lille and Armentières, Ypres and Péronne, St Quentin, the Somme and the Chemin des Dames, recall memories mixed with melancholy and an indescribable longing. It was, as I wrote on 4 August, 1964, in *The Northern Echo*, the 'last knightly war ever fought'.

Also in 1934 a book was published in Germany called *Der Baum von Cléry* (*The Tree of Cléry*) (Cléry was a village on the Somme) by Joachim von der Goltz. To me it is the most moving book written about the Great War. In one chapter von der Goltz describes a chat between two German soldiers during the first battle of the Champagne, in February, 1915; the infantryman says to his comrade in the mud, dirt and permanent gunfire:

> ... and then I felt that I loved this country [France]—this poor, trampled-down French earth.

19

*(da spürte ich dass ich sie liebte-diese arme, zertretene franzö-
sische Erde.)*

This field-grey comrade was speaking for all of us, describing
our feelings, mixed with sorrow, sadness, love and nostalgia for
something seemingly lost forever.

My late friend and comrade of 1914, Benno Reifenberg, who
received the Goethe Prize in Frankfurt after the last war, reviewed
von der Goltz' book in 1934 in the old *Frankfurter Zeitung* and
his article on the book was as moving and as beautiful as *Der
Baum von Cléry* itself:

> ... this poetic work was born from war diaries. Can you see
> the notebook? A thin, black diary, worn, slightly bulging,
> as it was worn for months under the tunic near a soldier's
> breast. Can you see the writing? Pale, evenly written, sud-
> denly broken off, rising again, storming ahead, in immense
> excitement, still to be able to make notes, still to be able to
> keep firm what made your heart beat strongly seconds ago.
> That is how these war diaries came into existence—the true
> prayer books of the soldiers.

Benno Reifenberg may have seen me making notes in Flanders
in October, 1914, when English bullets were coming across us
endlessly. Some fifty years later—on the occasion of a certain
birthday—he sent me a telegram in which he recalled our days
in Flanders:

> When we were so unbelievably young and thought ourselves
> to be immortal in spite of the thousandfold death around
> us.

We believed in the justice of our cause, were filled with idealism,
as your soldiers were in the trenches over there in the Allied living
wall. My thirteen notebooks, saved even during the Blitz in 1940–
41, are still my most precious belongings, though today my heart
beats for Europe.

H. Sulzbach
1981

I

1914

Frankfurt-am-Main, 28 June, 1914: Archduke Francis Ferdinand has been murdered, with his wife (the Duchess of Hohenberg), by two Serbs at Sarajevo. What follows from this is not clear. You feel that a stone has begun to roll downhill and that dreadful things may be in store for Europe.

I am proposing on 1 October to start my military service instead of going to Hamburg as a commercial trainee. I'm twenty, you see, a fine age for soldiering, I don't know a better.

14 July: I travel to Würzburg, report to the 2nd Bavarian Field Artillery Regiment and get accepted.

Böhm, the German airman, has scored a world record with 24½ hours of continuous flight.

23 July: Ultimatum delivered to Serbia by Austria-Hungary. No strong action by Austria appeared to have been taken since the assassination on 28 June until suddenly this note was presented, containing ten demands which among other things were supposed to allow Austria herself to take action on Serbian soil against activities hostile to Austria. Serbia has to accept the ultimatum within 48 hours, otherwise Austria reserves the right to take military action. A world war is hanging by a thread.

25 July: Unbelievably large crowds are waiting outside the newspaper offices. News arrives in the evening that Serbia is rejecting the ultimatum. General excitement and enthusiasm, and all eyes turn towards Russia—is she going to support Serbia?

The days pass from 25 to 31 July. Incredibly exciting; the whole world is agog to see whether Germany is now going to mobilize. I've hardly got enough peace of mind left to go to the bank and do my trainee job. I play truant as though it were school and stand about all day outside the newspaper offices, feeling that war is inevitable.

Friday, 31 July: State of war declared and total mobilization announced in Austria-Hungary.

Saturday, 1 August: 6.30 p.m. The Kaiser orders mobilization of the Army and Navy. That word 'mobilize', it's weird, you can't grasp what it means. First mobilization day is 2 August.

Try as I may I simply can't convey the splendid spirit and wild enthusiasm that has come over us all. We feel we've been attacked, and the idea that we have to defend ourselves gives us unbelievable strength.

Russia's dirty intrigues are dragging us into this war; the Kaiser sent the Russians an ultimatum as late as 31 July. You still can't imagine what it's going to be like. Is it all real, or just a dream?

My brother-in-law travelled to Wilhelmshaven on 3 August. He's a staff medical officer on the Naval Reserve. I put my name down on the nominal roll, as a war volunteer, of course; I'm hoping to get into our 63rd. I go to the barracks and try my luck. A lot going on there, and people very enthusiastic; some tearful good-byes too, as the regiment of regulars is pulling out.

I visit my nice motherly friend Martha Dreyfus and get given a lucky penny. My brother is in London and means to be here in four days' time, or six at the most.

Berthold, who has been our manservant for quite a time, is joining his regiment, and our dear friend Captain Rückward has already pulled out of barracks. Very rapidly, you might almost say in a few hours, nearly all the men one knows have disappeared from civilian life. My sister and all her married women friends are left alone—their husbands have joined the colours.

The first enemy aircraft is reported to have flown over Frankfurt.

4 August: I think I'll certainly be able to get into the 63rd. All of us who have reported as war volunteers are enduring hours of anxiety in case there won't be room for us.

Mobilization is going as smoothly as you please, and people feel a terrible hatred for the Russians and the French. England's attitude is ambiguous.

Reports are coming in of the first clashes on the frontier. There's a huge spy-hunt going on inside Germany, and notices in foreign languages are disappearing from the shops. And a curfew at 11 o'clock.

My friends who have already completed their year of military service are all off now, and our beautiful Adler car has been 'called up' too.

The German Army has a huge job on its hands: war on two fronts. We can only hope that Providence will stand by us.

At home our first officer is billeted on us, O.W., second lieutenant, Army Reserve, from Herborn.

On 4 August, in the evening, news that England has declared war.

7 August: My brother has landed at Hamburg, so he got away from England all right. My last day in civvy street.

News in the evening that Liège has been taken by assault.

8 August: I am a soldier at last. Everybody so friendly, most touching. The girls are all most concerned, getting very motherly.

Incidentally, I've been unbelievably lucky to have got into the 63rd, because no fewer than 1,500 war volunteers applied there in the first few days, and only 200 were taken; many of my school friends are in the same artillery battalion.

My brother-in-law is in the S.M.S. *Ariadne*.

9 August: My brother has arrived.

10 August: We are allowed out into the town in our fatigue uniforms: it is not very easy for us, since we can't even salute properly yet, but we manage it without being too glaringly conspicuous.

The next few days are given over to training; the old drivers take particular pleasure in making us do 'stables', so that we get to know this aspect of military life. It isn't easy at first to muck out the stalls, water the horses, feed them and groom them. We start having instruction periods on shooting technique.

10 August: We hear about the victorious battle at Mulhouse in Alsace; also news of the battle of Lagarde.

My brother has not been accepted by the Hanau Uhlans.

When Liège was taken, a Zeppelin went into action giving air support for the first time.

11 August: Montenegro declares war on us, after previously declaring war on Austria-Hungary.

13 August: France and England declare war on Austria-Hungary.

Japan is still keeping neutral, but seems unfortunately to have an alliance with England.

Our Zeppelin, the *Viktoria Luise*, comes here every day to do practice bombing.

The German battleship *Goeben* is unfortunately stuck in the Mediterranean.

Mobilization is gradually finishing off. It went marvellously. There are still a lot of military transports coming through.

20 August: Brussels has surrendered without firing a shot (Ghent did too, on 23 August). We need to occupy Belgium before we can be happy about advancing into France, because otherwise the French, whom the Belgians would certainly have let through, would have attacked us from the rear.

20–22 August: Great victorious battle in Lorraine, after which the French go into general retreat, more like a rout. Huge number of prisoners. It's the biggest battle so far, on a 300-kilometre front. The Crown Prince of Bavaria has been in command. In Paris the people seem to be very depressed.

23 August: My sister has arrived from Kissingen with her small child. My brother is with the 9th Hussars at Strasburg.

Japan's ultimatum to us over Kiauchau not replied to: that means war with Japan as well. The few thousand Germans over there won't be a match for the superior weight of Japanese forces, but they'll fight like heroes until they are killed or taken prisoner.

Victorious action by the Crown Prince's army at Longwy.

24 August: Big victory celebration here under a wonderful summer night sky.

25 August: Namur falls.

26 August: Longwy falls.

26 August: We are sworn in.

26 August: Captain Rückward has been wounded and is back from the front, also Ottomar Starke and other people I know.

27 August: Our Reserve Battalion is ready to march. Wild enthusiasm.

28 August: Belgium has been completely occupied, and the French Army bulletins are beginning to admit that France is on the defensive.

Big victory at St Quentin against the British and French.

29 August: Big victory against the Russians in East Prussia. General von Hindenburg in command.

Terrible news: the *Ariadne* has been sunk in a sea-battle off Heligoland. And my brother-in-law was in the *Ariadne.* I am just beginning to say good-bye to my parents and my sister, and at the very same moment my sister has had news that her husband has died a hero's death: he went down with the *Ariadne.* It is nearly impossible to say good-bye to her because she finds the sight of me in uniform too painful.

Morale at the barracks is terrific, and I'd be just as happy and enthusiastic if this terrible misfortune hadn't happened to us; even the sympathetic telegram from the captain of the *Ariadne* is not able to bring us any comfort. The death of my brother-in-law is also honourably mentioned in naval despatches.

The victory in East Prussia which I have already noted

seems to have had a decisive effect, since the Russians who had pushed into East Prussia are pouring back in full retreat across their own border. Down in Galicia a battle is raging between Austrians and Russians.

We've been ready to march since 28 August, the very day my brother-in-law was killed in action.

On 1 September we had more shooting with live ammunition at Bergen.

In the evening news that 70,000 Russians have been taken prisoner in East Prussia, a huge victory, while the gigantic battle between the Austrians and the Russians seems to have ended in a draw after six days.

2 September: Reveille at 3.45 a.m.; then a solemn church parade, and at 8 o'clock the long-awaited march-off after a bare four weeks' training. We are among the first few volunteers to reach the front. We entrained at the goods station, and I was seized by a strange feeling, a mixture of happiness, exhilaration, pride, the emotion of saying good-bye, and the consciousness of the greatness of the hour. We were three batteries, and marched in close order through the town to the cheers of the inhabitants. We travelled away through the country I love, past Boppard, Coblenz and on past all those enchanting villages and little towns along the Rhine. We were given our rations at Mehlem.

We hear that Turkey is mobilizing against Russia.

The journey continues. The horses stand quietly in their vans, and we lie between them. It is an idyllic picture; the men are cheerful.

The first night, with a wonderful full moon, makes you feel a bit melancholy. You lie there in your fatigue uniform and try to sleep.

Among my fellow war service volunteers are many acquaintances and friends from my schooldays. I know my bombardier; he was a hairdresser. On 2 September, that is the day we marched off and the anniversary of Sedan, overwhelming victory by the German Army against the French Army at Verdun. Apart from that, the Germans are only forty kilometres from Paris. If we could only be up there ourselves!

The Austrians are having another hard fight against the Russians at Lemberg.

3 September: Aachen. We got breakfast on the station. Many convoys travelling west, but strangely enough, three Army Corps as well, travelling from the west to Russia.

Last German railway station: Herbesthal. We get very ample rations, and the horses have oats, hay and straw in plenty.

At Herbesthal again, more and more military trains, and I see the first trainload of prisoners, Frenchmen and Englishmen. Poor chaps, all dirty and untidy. I gave them as much to eat as I could find. At Herbesthal our convoy train stood still for hours, and fresh German convoys kept passing in both directions. We moved off towards Brussels. Our train stopped often on the way, and you saw the first ruined villages and country mansions; we saw our first carrier-pigeon in flight. During the night, a very long halt. At first it was eerie, but then we were reassured by a beautiful full moon shining down on a ruined mansion, like a scene in a fairy-tale.

The men are relaxed and cheerful. On *4 September* the picture changes. You see sentries everywhere, guarding railway crossings and bridges. It doesn't look so peaceful.

Towards evening we get an order to stop looking out of the train and to shut the doors. Then we get an order to harness the horses in the train—not very easy for us.

On *5 September* at 2 a.m., in the fortress at Namur, taken a few days before, we moved into the Belgian Uhlans' barracks and stables. At daybreak we snatched a few hours' sleep on the straw. Next day begins with 'stables', just the same as in barracks at home. Then we can go out and look at the town, sit in the cafés and fancy ourselves!

We hear that the German cavalry is within a few kilometres of Paris.

There are a lot of German troops in the town: Stolpe Hussars, Mainz Dragoons, Hanau Uhlans.

Strolling round the town, I see the first signs of artillery fire: houses in ruins and sad-faced inhabitants. The effects of bombardment made a very deep impression on us. In the town itself, all private houses have to be shut up by 9 p.m.

You get back at last to the habit of washing yourself properly.

We hear of fresh resounding victories in the East, and here in the West the French seem to be desperate.

At my barracks is a Belgian prisoner, who attacked a German officer and knocked him about and is now going to be shot tomorrow. I talk to him and feel overwhelmed by this event—having a man in front of you who is going to be executed next day.

On many doors in the town you see the proof of our troops' good nature. You are always finding messages chalked up, saying 'Be nice, chaps, and look after the people in this house', followed by the name of a unit.

The days in Namur passed quickly. We had barrack duties, went outside the town to do exercises, and in our free time we could sit in cafés and restaurants; the first close friendships were struck up between comrades. The peaceful days were interrupted from time to time by air-raid warnings. On our exercises outside the town and near the forts of Namur we saw signs of serious fighting, and the terrible effects of artillery fire: houses levelled to the ground, forests mown down, barbed-wire entanglements, trenches, packs thrown away by Belgians or Germans, earth piled up by bursting shells. In the park of a beautiful château, more graves than you could count of Germans, Frenchmen, Belgians, all killed in action—war!

We keep noticing inscriptions on the doors of houses and cottages, even in the villages, 'Very nice people, please treat them kindly. Sergeant X', sometimes written in English and French as well.

We hear that Maubeuge has fallen (40,000 prisoners, including three generals).

The best hours of these days in Namur are when you are on guard duty at night. You feel your responsibility and apart from that you have peace and quiet to think, encouraged by the fabulous summer night sky.

We war volunteers get high praise from our Commanding Officer and from 2/Lt Reinhardt.

We are in a sweat to get to the front at last.

Now and then convoys of prisoners come through, and when

they do I sometimes manage to talk to a prisoner and hear what he thinks. They are all glad to be coming to Germany and to have the war behind them. This is something we can't figure out.

Rumours of the most nonsensical declarations of war: some —not all, unfortunately—are untrue. I receive sad news of the deaths of many of my acquaintances and friends, especially from our sister regiment, the 81st. Who, out of all my friends and acquaintances, is going to follow them?

At last, on *25 September*, warning order to prepare to march. So the days at Namur are over at last, and in great excitement we saddle up, harness our horses and move off in field marching order. Off we go, passing near the battlefield of Waterloo. It's a cold night, but all the same you fall asleep from time to time on your horse. I am the middle driver on No. 2 gun. On *26 September* we go through a pretty district, and hear gunfire from Antwerp way. We pass two villages, Braine-Le Comte and Enghien.

The closest friend I've made so far is Kurt Reinhardt, who is a regular officer cadet and my Lieutenant's brother. As a soldier he is just as hard-working and keen as he is an intelligent and sensitive human being.

On *28 September* things get more exciting. We pull away from our billets in the dark and seem to have been formed into a detachment. 2,000 men are marching with us, from the 76th Rostock, the 87th Mainz *Landwehr*, Sappers and Ulm Uhlans. One troop of my Battery, under 2/Lt Reinhardt (including my own No. 2 gun), is in the lead. For the first time we move up to firing positions at a quick trot. In the excitement, doing a gallop over a trench, we broke a wheel, the No. 1 driver's horses stumbled and both mine fell over them; I was hanging between them, but it all went very smoothly, we replaced the limber and on we went. On this first advance I actually met a man I knew from Frankfurt. We fired four whole rounds, but there was no sign of the enemy. The position is getting more ticklish, and at last we seem to be coming properly into the firing line.

Again and again, when we are passing, the windmills start to turn—suspiciously; it looks as though this is a sign from mill to mill that the Germans are coming. I have no notion where the front runs or how far away our armies are.

Billeted in a tiny, poverty-stricken village—Welle.

On the 29th an awful disappointment: our unit is ordered back to Namur. On the 30th, to our great joy, we are heading west once more. In our billets at Ath we have for the first time a room with a bed—unbelievable luxury, because generally you sleep on the ground or in a stable and don't wash.

On 1 October we march off towards Tournai. The first section, the one containing my gun, is in the lead again today. Twelve kilometres short of Tournai our Uhlans are fired on once again; Tournai seems to be still occupied. The detachment commander is General Wahnschaffe.

At mid-day our advance party is ordered back into the Battery. At 2 o'clock we all go into position in front of Tournai. There is British artillery beyond Tournai; since we are not strong enough, we are ordered to pull back, unfortunately; and we had such an ideal position! It's boiling hot. An enemy airman is given a dose of rifle-fire by ourselves and the infantry, without success. Just this side of Leuze an unmanned locomotive was launched full steam ahead by the enemy towards our Sappers' train; we fired at the locomotive but unfortunately did not hit it. We heard later that it didn't destroy our Sappers' train because they managed to divert it to another siding.

On the march through Leuze we see many inhabitants with frightened faces. The houses have all their window-curtains drawn. The unit which last marched through Leuze seems to have been fired on by the civilian inhabitants, so we all ride through this 'pleasant' village revolver in hand. Next day I become the No. 1 driver on No. 2 gun. We pull back again and after two hours head west once more. An aircraft is sighted, but we see the Iron Crosses under his wings in time—so he's a German.

A cavalry patrol rides towards us; they are not our Uhlans, but Hussars from another unit. Six regiments are supposed to be advancing, including the 13th Hussars from Diedenhofen and artillery as well. And a whole corps is supposed to be coming up as well to support us. They seem to be preparing for a battle. One of the Hussars was wearing the Iron Cross

Second Class; this was the first time I had seen it. We get back to billets in Ath for the third time. This everlasting marching to and fro appears to have the higher purpose of misleading the enemy.

Now it's October—and how very different I had thought this season would be, just a few months ago: first I wanted to take a trainee job with an export firm in Hamburg, then I decided to start doing my military service year on 1 October.

There seems to be an endless amount of cavalry near here.

3 October: Our section is the advance party again. Tournai has been evacuated by the enemy; we march through the town and get stared at by the inhabitants as though we were sea-monsters—not very amiably.

We go into position outside the town, dig ourselves in and spend a pretty cold night in the straw beside the horses. Full moon again. While the sun is rising, the moon is sinking in the west: what a picture! The first Sunday properly in the field. At 9.20 a.m. we cross the Franco-Belgian border. We are in France! At 1 o'clock we are in Helemmes, a *faubourg* of Lille. No. 1 gun had just fired on a windmill, so that No. 2 gun —mine—was in front. Only twenty or thirty men of the 76th in front of us, and the main body behind. The buglers sound 'Fix bayonets for assault'. It was incredible hearing the signal to go into action; you couldn't help thinking of the poem we had at school, *The Bugler of Vionville*. A terrible street battle began. We were right up at the front; the first barricades had been put up in front of a railway embankment, and the infantry swarmed over them all with bayonets fixed, and now a dreadful fire was directed at us, a hail of shots from every window, cellar-opening and skylight. We unlimber, firing into these narrow *faubourg* streets; it rumbles and crackles like hell, and we stand with our horses only ten paces behind the guns, so that it is nearly impossible to hang on to the wildly rearing animals; but hold them we must, for very soon the guns will have to be taken forward or back by these very horses. There's no question of retreat with our guns! The façade of one house collapses, mounted patrol horses tear along the streets, and the first dead and wounded are lying about. You can't see at all where the firing is coming from. I stand, or rather hang, on the reins between my two horses: No. 2 gun keeps on firing and firing. Fires are starting in several places. The hellish noise makes it almost impossible to communicate with the command posts, so that our section has to beat a retreat with the infantry out of this dreadful street, and in so doing we encounter the main body, which has meanwhile also started street fighting. The jam of vehicles and men in this street is unimaginable, and in a few minutes it has accumulated to a scene of real devastation.

After we had reassembled outside the town, we tried to get into Lille by another route, but were met by further fire, especially from machine-guns, and had a number of wounded in the new position. We went back once more, bivouacked in a meadow and lay in the straw recuperating from our generous baptism of fire.

5 *October:* We move into a new position above another Lille suburb, dig the guns in and open fire. Enemy artillery fire replies, but is ineffective. As we limber up from this position we come under heavy infantry fire, and we only manage to move to a new position by using the greatest skill and repeatedly throwing ourselves flat on the ground. The city is brought under continuous fire.

Once more, we are passed by an exceptionally large quantity of German cavalry. We spend 6 *October* in our bivouac and sleep between the horses. The horses have had their tack on for days; so have we, in our peace-time uniforms! At 5 a.m. we move into a new position and dig the guns in once more. Then we witness an unforgettable scene: one cavalry regiment after another rides past us. The 23rd and 24th Dragoons from Darmstadt, mounted chasseurs from Trier, regiments from Metz, Karlsruhe, Bruchsal, Mulhouse and Cassel; they trot past us for hours and hours; they look terrific with their lances, and you feel that something very big is going to happen. You are actually there to see military units advance and take up their appointed places, you feel that a great battle is in preparation and you are suffused with hope and excitement. I saw quite a number of people I knew among the men moving past.

How strange that people should meet on this gigantic front, pretty well on the field of battle.

It is fine to have found a friend like Officer Cadet Reinhardt —he has the same views and ideas as I have; we chat as we walk together to fetch water for the horses, and as we chat we forget the war.

We also foraged on our own account and found some marvellous wine in a deserted château; but the château itself looked terrible, everything broken and smashed to pieces—the owner will never see his fine mansion again in the state in which he left it.

I make notes for my journal, lying beside the horses. You are gradually growing a beard, and you can swear and grumble like an old soldier. You still feel it is something wonderful to be one of the millions who are able to join in the fighting, and you feel it is really necessary.

A few quiet days follow in the same position. Our first casualties, killed on 4 October, are buried. We are quite near a village bearing the pretty name of Baisieux. At night, in the open, it is getting fairly cold.

I am proud to have been praised by my Captain for my conduct on 4 October.

One is only just beginning to realize now what kind of situation we were in at the street battle on 4 October: it was providential that we got out of that fearful mouse-trap; we had not expected our baptism of fire to be so thorough. The enemy had fixed it up in such a cowardly way—he didn't let us fight properly, man to man, he just fired on us out of a snug hiding-place!

10 October: The sun is out and we are just seeing to our horses, when we receive a warning order: the Wahnschaffe Detachment is to occupy the citadel of Lille, which has been evacuated by the enemy. After a six-hour ride we get to the outskirts of Lille at about 6 o'clock; the civilians greet us, outwardly polite and nervous. Strangely, the trams are running, as though there weren't any war! We move in, and along comes a report that our Uhlans have been fired on again. Two batteries move into position, and our troop is the advance party again. On into Lille in the mist and darkness; we shoot into a cul-de-sac and can't get any further. Suddenly we get the order 'About turn, march!', since once again a volley of rapid fire is opened on us with rifles and hand-grenades from all the houses, and the situation is worse because it is night; some Uhlans' horses come back riderless, and we sit hunched up on our horses, as though you wouldn't get hit so much if you were near the horse! By some miracle we get our guns out without any casualties and camp in the open. It's an icy cold night and foggy as well. The horses are kept harnessed up, as every moment we expect the enemy to make a sortie out of Lille. You couldn't think of getting any sleep, and for the first time we are hungry. We are worried and silent; even more than on 4 October, you have the feeling that you're not going to get out of this dead end alive.

Antwerp has fallen.

11 October: Today is my nephew Herbert's birthday, today he's a year old and has never consciously seen his father, who was killed in the first action at sea on 28 August—the terrible fate that has now happened to thousands!

We make our third attempt at getting into Lille and are fired on for the third time in doing so. We now discard all consideration for the inhabitants of Lille and open heavy fire on the city centre. We are not strong enough, and have to go back again; we expect reinforcements and camp near Chereng. Our morale is not good, our minds are full of the horrors of 10 October. We found a farm near by, had our first good meal and bought some wine and jam, which our comrades much appreciated. For some days we had been sleeping in a stable and had a roof over our heads, but we didn't get much sleep— along would come the well-known warning order: March for Lille! Icy cold night, dead tired, you're half asleep on foot or on your horse. At 3.30 we went into firing positions, and the sound of firing around us became louder. We had a blanket of heavy, damp fog over us. After this disagreeable night, on *12 October* the stepped-up artillery attack on Lille began. You could see a huge fiery glow: Lille was burning. We hadn't intended this destruction, but after those street battles (where the heavy fire came not only from the military enemy but from civilians) it was unavoidable. 12 October draws to its close after we have been firing into Lille, with a few breaks, all day.

13 October: We enter Lille, our detachment from one side and part of the 19th Army Corps, which came to support us, from the other side. Now there is no more firing in the streets, and with cheerful hearts and high spirits we march in to the tune of *Die Wacht am Rhein*. We halt in front of the citadel; the 19th A.C. men have already brought out the prisoners, more than 4,000 French and Arabs.

Parts of Lille are still burning. More and more regiments are marching in with bands playing, and some of them march on immediately; apart from the regiments of the 19th (Saxon) Army Corps, Württemberg regiments are coming through as well; and in a staff motor-car, the Crown Prince of Bavaria. At 2 o'clock we occupy the citadel, and a few French soldiers are still sitting about inside it. I have a long talk with them: we should all have been done for on 4 and 10 October if we had risked going any further into the city, and how incredibly lucky we were that they didn't spring that awful trap behind us!

The citadel itself was in an unbelievably scruffy condition; but all the same we found 500 Arab horses, rather thin, which our officers and N.C.O.'s were glad to take on. We move our own horses into dirty stables by the *manège*. The experience of marching into the city and thinking of our own first well-fought victory gives each one of us complete satisfaction. I have another long talk with my friend Kurt Reinhardt and we get on to the subject of civilian life, talk about our childhood; all the things which you used to take for granted when they happened to you seem now idyllically beautiful. 2/Lt Reinhardt has been busy all evening on a job for the High Command, drafting a proclamation in French to the inhabitants of Lille: it is to be posted everywhere tomorrow. 2/Lt Reinhardt was also commissioned to speak to the city councillors of Lille, telling them they were to comply with regulations made by the High Command and would be well treated by us provided they did so.

The French are putting the blame for not being able to hold Lille on to the British. A short while ago Lille was still not occupied by the enemy and apparently it was a British suggestion that the city was in fact put into a state of defence.

14 October: We look after our horses and have quiet duties. We are not allowed out into the town yet. The civilians are supposed to be very much embittered, all the shops are said to be closed. A number of the prisoners have not yet been evacuated, and I talk once more to some of them, also to an Englishman who gives his anger at France an airing. We hear once more from the prisoners what incredible luck we had on 4 October, since the enemy intended to let us advance right up to the citadel and then to cut off our retreat. Only the premature firing at Helemmes saved us from this fate.

14 October was a day of rejoicing, since we received our first mail—no fewer than thirty letters for me, and lovely parcels of things to eat as well.

15 October: We move from the citadel into a barracks.

16 October: Parade.

17 October. We are allowed out into the town for the first time. We ate at a restaurant on the Grande Place. The city is swarming with German military. The whole 6th Army is supposed to be gathered here. I gaze wonderstruck at many cavalry officers and other ranks all wearing the Iron Cross. The cavalry must have been doing sterling work in the last few days. You see Hussars, Dragoons, Uhlans, chasseurs and *chevaulegers*, the light cavalry. I met several school-friends; one keeps on finding it strange to meet people one knows in the middle of a war as though one were in the Goethestrasse at Frankfurt.

19 October: Warning order, but it is cancelled in the evening.

20 October: Warning order! After our few quiet days we pull out of Lille at 6 a.m.—into another battle; we belong to the 19th Army Corps. The roads outside Lille are blocked, we only advance seven kilometres in the whole day, and go into position in a village. We meet hundreds of British prisoners-of-war being evacuated. We belong to the 2nd Battalion, the 77th Field Artillery Regiment. The gun-limbers are standing without cover and are under constant small-arms fire.

21 October: Change of position. We pull forward, get our first glimpse of this battlefield, and have to get used to the terrible scenes and impressions: corpses, corpses and more corpses, rubble, and the remains of villages. The infantry has taken the village of Premesque by assault. The bodies of friend and foe lie tumbled together. Heavy infantry fire drives us out of the position which we had taken up, and this is added to by increasingly heavy British artillery fire. We are now in an area of meadowland, covered with dead cattle and a few surviving, ownerless cows. The ruins of the village taken by assault are still smoking. Trenches hastily dug by the British are full of bodies. We get driven out of this position as well, by infantry and artillery fire. We stand beside the guns with the horses. A dreadful night comes down on us. We have seen too many horrible things all at once, and the smell of the smoking ruins, the lowing of the deserted cattle and the rattle of machine-gun fire make a very strong impression on us, barely twenty years old as we are, but these things also harden us up for what is going to come.

We certainly did not want this war! We are only defending ourselves and our Germany against a world of enemies who have banded together against us.

22 October: British planes fly over our position and report their observations to their artillery, so that we get a thorough 'blessing'. We cook hurriedly behind some ruined houses.

We see our first air battle, the first attack by a fighter aircraft. Our battery receives its first Iron Crosses, and we feel that each individual's decoration has been given to us all.

23 October: With our support the infantry makes an assault on the British positions, but the British have dug themselves in so well that the attack does not succeed.

24 October: Hellish infantry fire, many horses wounded. Enemy fighter aircraft fly over us. Ownerless dogs have found their way to us and give us great pleasure.

Sunday, 25 October: Lovely warm autumn day. Heavy artillery fire began at mid-day. We replied to it, and towards evening fetched ammunition from Lomme. Bringing up the ammunition along roads under continuous fire is very disagreeable; heavy rain and a cold autumn night: we're soaking wet and have to sleep pretty well in the water.

27 October: At 6 a.m. we try another assault, with the infantry, on the British lines: the beggars won't give an inch, and our 109th and 138th sustain heavy casualties. We still get fired on from time to time, the shots coming from ruined houses and farms lying in some cases beyond the front, and on searching them found to our astonishment that the snipers were real heroes: wounded Englishmen.

We kill and pluck any hens still running loose and thus provide our own rations; our trusty gunners prove to be farmers and milk the ownerless cows; they don't get put off by odd shells falling near them. We construct our first crude dug-outs.

28 October: Today we have been in this position for a week. At night we came under heavy small-arms and machine-gun fire. In the meanwhile a field telephone has been laid between the individual command posts. I am a telephone operator. Of course the cable keeps getting shot through and one has to keep on patching it. The job of being a telephone operator is exceptionally interesting, since you are the man who gets first news of all important messages regarding future hostilities. The most difficult job is to keep the cable to the infantry intact. Our position lies 400 metres behind the trenches.

29 October: Fetched ammunition again. British planes drop leaflets saying that we ought to surrender. The other way round would be more sensible!

A Saxon company tries an extremely daring assault entirely on its own, which costs the lives of nearly every man in the company.

There are also quiet hours when we sit in the sun, chat and smoke and play cards.

The red-letter days are always the ones when we get our mail.

We fire on enemy artillery at 2,700 metres: delayed-action

fuses. Our battery has gradually gone under cover, very nicely camouflaged. Artificial trees have been planted so that the enemy airmen can't spot us. The dug-outs are like mediaeval caves.

1 November: Large-scale washing and shaving operation.

We gradually notice that the static war which we have got into is becoming a permanent fixture. Rainy November days follow, all rather alike. Exchanges of fire with enemy artillery are becoming a habit.

We've been in our uniforms for weeks without being able to undress.

At the beginning of November we hear that Turkey has declared war on Russia—all the better for us, thank God!

We get our first newspapers and read about the *Emden* and her heroic exploits. The first replacements for our casualties arrive.

I've been sent a proper sleeping-bag from home. Now I can sleep even in the open when it's raining without getting wet!

8 November is another red-letter day—we are kitted out in field-grey. Up to now we've been wearing our old blue peace-time uniforms.

We have to keep going out to hunt *francs-tireurs*, civilians behind the front who take every opportunity of shooting at us out of hiding-places. People have been saying for some days that America wants to declare war on Japan and Britain—if only it were true!

10 November: Dixmuiden has fallen.

The town in front of us is called Armentières, and another assault is mounted against it on *11 November*. It is pouring with rain, and every inch of Armentières is burning. The battle is raging most fiercely on the right wing. Small-arms and artillery fire are going over our heads continuously. The battle doesn't slack off at night, and a cloudburst of rain and stormy wind help to make a proper Shakespeare night of it all; the limbers are brought somewhat further back, after weeks positioned right behind the guns, with the horses standing day and night with their tack on; the good-natured beasts are to be taken to stables in a little village, one kilometre to the rear. The poor creatures badly need a rest.

So now the limbers are at Perenchy, in a flax-spinning factory. I am here for a few days, and in the evenings drive up to the guns with mail and rations. This is generally a frightful drive through pitch darkness made even more dreadful by the fires in burning Armentières.

I'm just managing to write to my family. It is a relief to be able to report your experiences in detail.

You also get time to think about beautiful things from the past, but you don't have thoughts about the future. My friendship with Kurt Reinhardt fills me with complete happiness. We see less of each other because he has had to stay with the guns.

15 November: The first snow is falling; icy wind and stormy weather.

On *18 November* comes the shattering news that the *Emden* has been sunk in Chinese waters, after very many heroic exploits which have been acknowledged with honour even by our enemies. They say the crew has been saved.

We hear that a great sea battle has been fought off Chile, ending in a victory for the German squadron.

Another 20,000 Russians have been taken prisoner in the East.

The snow is covering the ground now and has turned the plains of Flanders into a winter landscape.

19 November: Mail arrives in the evening, and among other things I get a parcel as a present from my old school. Then we read the newspapers out loud to each other. At the battery meanwhile they have made themselves much more cosy. The dug-outs have tables and stoves and one even has a piano in it.

Now we have been a whole month in this position. We exchange greetings with the British every day in the shape of shells; everything is gradually becoming a habit. Great excitement and interest as we watch air fights between German and British flying men. Now and again we use our guns to attempt to knock down an enemy plane, but each time it remains an attempt. It is still a winter landscape with cloudless days, cold and sunny.

A piece of special praise from my extremely strict sergeant nearly fills me with delusions of grandeur.

I have taken on one of the ownerless dogs. A small mongrel terrier bitch. It is very touching, by the way, how fond all our men are of animals; it indicates a good character. It's very moving to see how our old driver Strobel can never go to sleep without his little dog, and looks for him for hours if he isn't there.

We are preparing more and more for a static campaign. The infantry positions have been surrounded with strong barbed-wire entanglements.

The sea battle which I mentioned on 18 November was the battle of Coronel.

27 November: Report that another 129,000 Russians have been taken prisoner in the East. Bravo Hindenburg!

We keep hearing of more heroic exploits by the *Emden*, which was sunk in such a famous action, and now further stories about the *Karlsruhe*.

Really marvellous food parcels come up in the mail, and the whole battery enjoy them.

1 December: I get leave to spend a day in Lille with two friends. Can you people at home imagine how we felt to get out of the mud of battle into a town actually inhabited by civilians and looking almost like peacetime? Shops, restaurants, cafés, civilians and military in clean clothes. We gorge ourselves at the Café Mert, but at the same time we can't avoid seeing how wretched and impoverished many French civilians look and how grieved they must be feeling. On the way back we also sat in a bar at Lomme, where we met several chaps from the 107th. They sang patriotic songs of home, but also some sentimental ones. Tomorrow they have to go back and lie in a trench: here they forget the situation and also the fact that tomorrow they may be dead.

In the evening we are back in the battery. The next few days passed monotonously, until we got a warning order on *9 December*: rumours that we're going to Russia.

At which I close my first book of war notes.

•   ○   ○   ○   ●

I start my second war diary in the flax-mill in Flanders on *9 December, 1914*. It is very difficult to bring the guns back over this completely flat Flemish country without incurring any casualties, and actually the job ought to go to drivers of long experience, but since I am the only war volunteer, I am entrusted with the responsibility of being No. 1 driver. It is a pitch-black night and foggy as well, a difficult run, but we manage it.

10 December: At 7 a.m. off to Lomme, where our whole Wahnschaffe Detachment assembles; we make our way through Lille and Marcq-en-Baroeuil and move into quarters in a brewery. The other ranks get private billets, we are put up by pleasant people.

11 December: Rest day.

12 December: We march to La Madeleine and entrain there —done very quickly; before that there were another four sacks of mail.

My 'pure-bred' terrier is still with me. We are given our evening rations at Hirson, and sleep in fours with the horses in the waggons.

We aren't clear yet whether we're on our way to Russia or going across to the Champagne country.

13 December: We detrain at 6.30. It's as black as night, we have to saddle and bridle the horses in the dark; then we stop at a main road, we're between Rheims and Verdun. We go into quarters in Pont-Faverger, a pretty little village; the horses have good stables, and we have straw to sleep on beside the horses. We had hardly unpacked when splendid military music drew us out into the market-place, where we were surprised to see a number of senior officers strolling about, listening to the music: they gave us a really good selection, *La Bohème*, then folk-songs and waltzes. Then a new infantry regiment marched past with its band playing. We are just a few kilometres behind the front here, and apparently at the front itself troops are being moved about a lot. We belong to the 6th Silesian Army Corps. We see to our horses and groom them, and watch our airmen flying up to the front to reconnoitre. Pont-Faverger is in a charming position, surrounded by woods and undulating fields, and a little river flows through the centre of the village.

I spend the first evening with Kurt Reinhardt. We turn in beside the No. 1 gun horses, and before we go to sleep we tell each other all the things we have been thinking about. Kurt's father has been given the Iron Cross First Class. Kurt is as pleased about it as if he had had the medal himself. Before turning in we go and have another Bavarian beer at the Uhlans' canteen.

14 December: Duties. Then we have time to go for a walk through the village. The sun is out, really rather like spring, and I sit with Kurt Reinhardt in a garden with the little river flowing past and beside us two beautifully kept graves, belonging to men killed in action at the time when Pont-Faverger was still in the fighting line instead of being behind the front as it is today.

The next few days pass at an even pace, almost peacefully, and we can do with the rest after the strain of our exertions in Flanders in October and November.

17 December: Parade taken by General von Pritzelwitz.

News of further large-scale victories against the Russians.

20 December: It is *Golden Sunday*, the last Sunday before Christmas Eve! God, what memories from peacetime! You feel that peace is something which ceased to exist ages back and that war is mankind's permanent situation. The first Christmas parcels are arriving.

21 December: Warning order—what's going to happen to all the lovely parcels? However, the order gets turned off again, so we are able to enjoy our parcels. Meanwhile, nearly everybody has got hold of a mouth-organ, and we put on a splendid concert without a brass band or anything. The C.O. of the 51st, who are here too, is very jolly with his men, a real charmer.

Some of my mates have got cameras too, and people are busy taking snapshots.

In the evening we organize a serenade* for Reinhardt, as it's his birthday: the music rings out under the bright moonlit sky. Another warning order at 10 p.m. It doesn't look as though we'll be staying here much longer.

The next few days before Christmas bring us more mail and such a lot of food parcels that we can't possibly eat everything. People at home must think we're about to die of starvation.

23 December: We're getting in the mood for Christmas and go and fetch trees out of the woods. We feel well and happy. Our No. 3 and No. 4 guns leave us to become what they call Anti-Balloon Guns.

In the evening we get the shattering news that after many victories at sea, the *Graf Spee* squadron has been out-gunned by the British and sunk off the Falkland Islands: all those cruisers—*Gneisenau, Scharnhorst, Nürnberg* and *Breslau.*

24 December: It's snowing, a proper Christmas atmosphere. We are given inoculations, and at 5 there's a church parade; a big garage has been transformed into a church. On each side of the altar a fine Christmas tree is bright with candles, and 'palms' have been put up all round the walls. The officers sat at the front, with the choir on the left, and the men standing behind. It was all so solemn and uplifting that you had tears in your eyes even before you heard the strains of *Silent Night.* We were all much moved and felt quite melancholy, each of us taken up with his own thoughts of home.

Then our battery celebrated Christmas† in our own back yard, under a splendid tree of our own—it was a Christmas Eve worthy of the name, and very beautiful too.

The Regiment gave me a most splendid Christmas present: I was promoted to the rank of *Gefreiter*, lance-bombardier,

* A German-style serenade, the *Ständchen*, is sometimes put on for a woman admired by one of the performers, but is more often a birthday present for a friend of either sex. The serenaders, usually a group of men, generally sing unaccompanied part-songs. The serenade should be a surprise.—R.T.

† In Germany and other areas such as Scandinavia, the main Christmas celebration takes place on the afternoon or evening of Christmas Eve, round a lighted tree.—R.T.

and it did me good to be picked out like this after so short a time.

25 *December:* Christmas celebrations are over. At 10 o'clock we get a warning order to march off immediately. We entrain and proceed to Challerange under a bright moonlit night, icy cold and sparkling with stars, and on to Montois, where we go into billets.

26 *December:* We move off again, this time through Ardeuil to Ripont. Here we are in the middle of the district whose name you know so well: Champagne! From Ripont we have to go up steep slopes over hard-frozen ground to our new firing position, which we move into at 6 o'clock. And that's our Boxing Day, our 'second Christmas Day'. The limbers stand out in the open, in the icy cold night, and we stand beside the horses, but relieve each other to get warm in the dug-outs belonging to the 16th, to whose 2nd Battalion we now belong (8th Reserve Army Corps). Christmas, 1914, is over.

The horses are withdrawn to Ripont Mill, then to another position; it's thawing now and is cold and wet as well, we are sleeping in holes in the ground and the horses are standing up to their knees in mud. Every scrap of woodland looks like a Red Indian village. Cave after home-made cave, and rough stalls, hastily knocked together, for the horses; the limbers, with the horses beside them, wait quite close to the guns as they fire. It seems even more disagreeable here than it was at Armentières. The weather and the Champagne mud reduce our morale. There are exchanges of artillery fire which do not involve casualties.

29 *December:* I am given orders to ride to St Morel with Lance-Sergeant Debler. I take Lance-Sergeant Lauer's horse and we ride off on the two little Arabs, across fields to Granddeuil. Nothing but mud. Lance-Sergeant Debler had business with the Captain, while I waited outside. We made our way back as night was falling, and it was very hard indeed to find one's way.

In the evening I was on guard duty.

We receive our first mail in this position—that is, we have

to fetch it ourselves from the rear by limber, which is a dreadfully difficult operation, with the vehicle and horses practically sunk in the mud. After these few days we really look like pigs. The fire gets heavier, it's developing into an artillery battle, what they call a 'gunners' duel'.

31 December: So 1914 is winding up today. A year to raise your spirits, but also a year of pain and sorrow, not only for us but for the whole of what is called the civilized world. This terrible war goes on and on, and whereas you thought at the start that it would be over in a few weeks, there is now no end in sight. Your feelings harden, you become increasingly indifferent, you don't think about the next day any more. It's my sister's birthday today: how will she be feeling without her husband?

A wish for us all for 1915: may this new year make up for 1914 and bring us peace.

We drank the New Year in: there was no firing, we felt happy and for a few hours were able to forget the present.

II

1915

THE first days of January were filled with heavy artillery fire in rainy, miserable weather. We are beginning to get a bit more domestic comfort into our dug-out, but we can hardly do anything about the damp. The only pleasure we get is from our mail and our beloved dogs.

9 January: For the first time our position was given quite a heavy dose of fire: salvo after salvo of shells to the right or left of our little wood and some right in the middle of it. The shrapnel sang over our heads, and the dreadful mud was churned up even more. Our little wood is wrapped in clouds. Now and then you have a feeling, here, too, that your last hour has come, since you're quite helpless in artillery fire: there is no defence against it. In the night the limbers were taken to another position. Shortly before we pulled out we had another stiff 'dose', but miraculously not a single man or horse was wounded.

I often go to fetch mail and orders in the evenings, and when I reported to my sergeant today, he poured me out a stiff drink and said, 'What's this—you don't sing any more!' I can't help it: the gay and easy mood has worn off, even for me; in fact, my good old sergeant has noticed it: he used to think of me as the chap with the indestructible good spirits.

Orders to go to Sechoux take me to Army G.H.Q., a most interesting experience. One order after another. I have to go on further, through Cernay, and carry out my instructions;

then I come back to the firing position via Ripont. At home I found my dog surrounded by five puppies that looked like little white mice. Don't know who the father was.

The days are getting quieter, the artillery fire has slackened off.

18 January: My sister's wedding-day, and now she has to spend it as a widow.

It has been snowing, and at odd moments when there is no firing the landscape becomes unbelievably peaceful.

21 January: I receive another special order, pick one of the little Arab horses and ride to the Battery. It's 6 a.m., still pitch dark, and you can only just find your way about. From the Battery I get an order to proceed to the Battalion Staff, lying this side of some high ground only 100 metres behind the front trenches. Since this high ground lies in front of the enemy trenches, I can ride towards the front without being seen by the French; but a hellish burst of fire starts up, and small-arms and artillery fire compete with each other in making things hot for me. I'm as hoarse as a crow and can't speak a word. I get my orders and ride back to the Battery, which is now commanded by Captain Henn, while 2/Lt Reinhardt is what you might call his right-hand man, and acts as a liaison officer with the infantry.

23 January: Once again, dreadful fire on the limber and battery positions, we think it's better to get out of the dug-outs and lie flat in the mud. Several casualties, and two of our trusty horses are dead. It's a good thing you don't get round to thinking much now, but when you do have time to think, you always paint pictures of marching back victorious into your regimental depot at home. We mustn't weaken, mind, we're old soldiers now—but will proper peacetime ever come back again?

27 January: The Kaiser's birthday! Memories of peacetime parades.

28 January: I've been posted to the Battalion Staff as a mounted messenger. Battery Staff is further up, with the infantry; this is actually quite an honour, as Captain Bachmann picked me himself. I have to leave my little dog behind with the Battery. I report to Captain Bachmann, who gives me a highly encouraging reception. Duties are not very arduous, but most interesting; however, during this tour of duty I have an experience which upsets me for some time: one of my mates keeps having terrible attacks, going completely out of his mind: it is very hard indeed to calm him down.

31 January: My mate Hemp and I got the job of travelling back to the rear area, or through the hinterland as far as Metz, to do some shopping for the unit. The path from the gun-pits to the limbers and further back to the nearest railway station is a tiresome journey on foot—your great boots get nearly stuck in the mud all the time. We took the train and went first to Luxembourg via Sedan and Montmédy; we went to a tea-shop, and had a little walk through the streets, although we didn't seem to make a very good impression, in the filthy state we were in—'in Champagne order' as you might say. Got to Metz in the evening. We put up at an hotel and had a bath. That was a luxury, I can tell you! Metz was full of military, including Austrians. We took the liberty of going to a restaurant in the evening and having a proper blow-out. And then the best of all: sleeping in a white, soft bed, just like Paradise.

On *3 February* we did our shopping for what the unit wanted, although with the best will in the world we were hardly able to get hold of any flour at all. At 1 o'clock in the morning we took the train back through Sedan, Mohon, Bazancourt and Pont-Faverger to Ardeuil. Very many wounded at Ardeuil, sad scenes. What had happened was that on 2 and 3 February our chaps had mounted an attack on the famous Hill 191 and inflicted heavy losses on the French. The artillery fire had been directed by captive balloons and aircraft. We were back at the gun positions in the afternoon.

8 February: We celebrated my birthday on a day when not a shot was fired, and I invited my friends and mates. I spent the day with my Battery, on a sort of leave from the Battalion Staff.

On *10 February* my tour of duty with the Battalion was

over and I came back to my beloved Battery. The firing is getting more and more lively.

Even on the quieter days there is firing from both sides, while the infantry never stops having little skirmishes with the French.

On *12 February* I rode with 2/Lt Reinhardt on a tour of inspection, taking in the neighbouring troops and the limbers, and found out a lot of things which interested me; among other subjects of conversation, I asked him whether he thought the war would be over soon. When he said no I began to think, all the more because when you are a soldier you haven't been thinking about this very often. You live day by day in a sort of gipsy existence, but it's quite a good thing not to worry about it too much.

15 February: We are expecting heavy attacks from the French.

16 February: On Shrove Tuesday a fearsome enemy artillery fire, such as we've never had before, is laid on our trenches and gun positions: thundering and boiling and banging away. Our batteries open rapid fire. The small-arms fire is drowned by the noise of bursting shells. The telephone cable is only working occasionally. The French have forced their way into our front trenches. At 6 o'clock comes the order that all limbers are to be brought up at once, to allow the guns to be taken back at any moment: this because the French have captured our main position. There is a good deal of confusion, with the limbers coming up all the time from the rear and taking up positions near individual batteries. Column after column of troops waiting down at Ripont Mill. I rode over at top speed to 2/Lt Reinhardt, who was about the only one to keep completely calm, and was issuing orders as though we were on an exercise. Meanwhile our limbers are waiting only 100 metres back from the guns, and I keep the liaison going between the limbers and Battery.

We hold the position, and quite early on *17 February* the first of many French who have been taken prisoner come past us. Most of them are severely wounded and many cannot hide the pain. Losses must have been very high on both sides. One of our regiments is supposed to have lost nearly a whole infantry battalion. After the French had forced their way into our main position, we counter-attacked and threw the beggars out again. The firing continued unceasingly on the 17th as well. The French certainly don't seem to be suffering from shortage of ammunition. Our infantry who come past are jolly good chaps, not afraid of anything, and though we gunners do get exposed to fire all the time, the infantry have a much worse time of it. The limbers keep near the Battery on the evening of the 17th as well, as the French attacks haven't stopped. There really could be a bit less artillery fire!

18 February: News that the blockade on the British coast is supposed to be starting.

In our own sector the fighting continues; we get new regiments, which are allocated to our 16th Division. French prisoners tell us that General Joffre 'wants' to have broken through our front by 20 February! A new attack by the French begins on the evening of the 18th. We repulse all the attacks; infantry and artillery working perfectly together. We have taken another 800 prisoners. The main danger seems to have been averted.

19 February: This damned shooting begins all over again and nearly always even heavier than before. Our thoughts on the matter last night don't seem to have hit the nail on the head. One of our regiments was thrown back, but another regiment recaptured the position.

I haven't mentioned the minor or less serious casualties in our troop, but today our very popular Lance-Sergeant Bode was killed in action, and also Fabian, our youngest war volunteer (he was seventeen), and other comrades, I'm sorry to say. Many others have been seriously wounded. The French have got every one of our battery positions pin-pointed, and in the last few days they have plastered us so thoroughly with shells of the heaviest calibre that it's a wonder anyone is left alive, and that the guns can still fire. If only some reinforcements would arrive in our sector!

20 February: The firing is slacking off and you're able to

breathe again at last. My duties are some of the most interesting of all. I shuttle to and fro between the limbers and the batteries and the Battalion Staff, and turn back into a gunner as well if that happens to be necessary. The next few days are quiet.

26 February: The French start their attempt at a breakthrough with renewed strength and reinforcements. If any increase in the weight of fire were possible, the fire is stronger still today, and as I reached Battalion at 6 o'clock, I saw 2/Lt Reinhardt with his arm heavily bandaged. It is miraculous, his being only wounded: the observation post which he was in with the infantry received five direct hits, one after the other, and they are nearly all dead. Reinhardt has had his left thumb blown off and he is covered with blood, mud, dirt and powder-smoke. Now I'm afraid our very popular Lieutenant has to go into hospital. The whole Battery is mourning. He says good-bye to everyone individually and then drives back to the rear in a limber.

And we all felt bad about it, as we were very fond of him; he was as imperturbable as he was human. The whole troop was staring after the limber long after it had disappeared behind the woods. We feel that we have been fighting for *him.*

On *27 February* another French artillery attack begins at 4 o'clock. Direct hit on the ammo limber, left-hand wing gun! Our comrade Fischer is dead and two others wounded. Our morale has gone to rock bottom.

28 February: The French attacks are still not letting up, nor is our depressed morale. Our nerves and strength will really soon be exhausted, as these attacks and battles in static warfare seem heavier than they would in mobile warfare. Wherever are the reinforcements? The men are saying that the 1st Guards Infantry Division is on the march.

1 March: The battle is still raging. Why ever are we still alive? In the evening a bit of snow comes down and there is another full moon, which makes us feel quieter and more reconciled to things.

3 March: Thank God: Guards Infantry, Guards Light Infantry and Guards Field Artillery have all arrived.

4 March: The trenches which we lost before have been re-captured by assault.

5 March: Zobel is dead, the popular and tireless war volunteer. We are mourning him just as we mourn all our chaps who are killed in action, but young as we are, our feelings are gradually getting more blunted. At last I see my friend Kurt Reinhardt, Lt Reinhardt's brother, again, and we have an enormous amount to tell each other. We are supposed to be getting some rest and we shall have earned it too. We've fired 17,200 rounds here as against only 3,200 rounds from the position in Flanders in double the time, and some of the time in Flanders it got lively enough! You can only make brief notes, you've no time for long-winded reflections, and you can never give the people who've stayed at home, if you handed them these war diaries to read later on, a real impression of what we are going through, what we are putting up with, and how much determination and fighting spirit has got into every single one of us.

11 March: We get some mail again at last. That reconciles you to a lot of things. The mail includes a letter to me from 2/Lt Reinhardt, with a photo of himself and the dedication:

To Herbert Sulzbach from Lt Reinhardt as a souvenir of February, 1915.

Military Hospital III, Frankfurt-am-Main,
7 March, 1915.

You would really have wanted to weep for all the feelings of mourning, joy, happiness, admiration, longing, but you can't cry any more—you just can't do it.

The Champagne winter battle—that's what they call the battles of these last few weeks—has come to an end. It was the first great battle in the period of static warfare, the enemy's first attempt to break through the positions which we occupied in autumn 1914 and the first time massive artillery fire, what they call barrage, was used. At the same time, however, it was also our first victory in defence against a force many times our superior in numbers, and taught us a large number of lessons useful for defensive actions in the future. The French losses in this battle were 45,000 men, but ours were also, I regret to say, very considerable.

Actually we war volunteers can feel proud of the fact that so far we've been in everything big that's happened in the West since war broke out: we were in on part of the advance, then in the first defence battle in Flanders, and now in the big Champagne winter battle.

On *13 March* we actually get withdrawn, and in the evening Colonel-General von Einem's army order is read out, stating that we, two under-manned divisions, fought a heroic defence action, beating back attempts by six French Army Corps to break through our lines, and that we—and all Germany—could be proud of these few weeks.

So we had been eleven weeks in this area, eleven weeks of uninterrupted fighting, in the biggest battle fought so far —and on 14 March we pulled out. Through Vouziers, and on the way we pass horse-drawn or motorized columns filling up the roads to the rear. On the march someone I know drives past me in an open car; he recognizes me and pulls up. It's my cousin, Lt Lotichius. To the rear of Vouziers the district starts getting prettier and prettier. Through woods and over fields; and what a miracle, the little villages haven't been destroyed. We arrive at Les Petites Armoises. We move into billets and fall into a long, long sleep, on hay in a loft, and there is no firing or banging any more.

15 March: I'm sitting in the garden which goes with our barn in this little village. To my right, a little church in another little garden, and straight ahead, the farmhouse and the broad village street, nice and clean. On my left, some ploughed fields already letting the spring green through, the sun is out and you can hear the wild birds sing. You have to write it all down because it's something you're completely unused to and more beautiful than you can imagine. You suddenly notice once again that you are alive; actually it's more like feeling that you've risen from the dead. You feel a wave of homesickness. You're only reminded that there's a war on by the distant, muffled roll of artillery fire. Hope we'll stay here a few weeks. The farm people are giving us milk and butter. It's all so quiet and peaceful. I chat to the local civilians, and everything these good country people have to say is interesting to me. I go with one of my mates into the church, where a French country priest is just taking a service.

We look after the horses, have a bit of duty and take a real rest as well in the next few days, lovely spring weather. I'm still with my mate Kurt Reinhardt. He and I and two others have a room between the four of us, with some French farm people, and a view over miles of ploughed fields turning green. Our landlady is a widow, and has her daughter Valentine living with her.

In the next few days we exercise the horses and ride through woods and meadows; we find this peaceful area really enchanting.

23 March: 2/Lt Reinhardt has been given the Iron Cross First Class, and our Corps Commander has had the *Pour-le-Mérite*, one of the first to get it. The evenings are pleasant, and we often sit about, eight or ten of us together. We get good rations, we can buy all sorts of things at the canteens, our landlady cooks us anything we like and we give her food she needs in exchange.

We exercise the horses every day, riding in spring weather, it's almost like spring in Germany. The anemones are out, and that reminds me of home and makes me long to be there.

On *22 March,* incidentally, the Kaiser was at Vouziers. Sorry to record that Przemyśl, the fortified town, has fallen, the Russians have moved in, 40,000 Austrians have been taken prisoner. But that won't do them any good!

29 March: Our rest period seems to be over, and after a warning order we pull out at 6.30. Once again through Vouziers, Monthois and Ardeuil. From there to the firing positions near Ripont. Only part of the Battery goes into firing positions, part of it is to go back to rest stations, and I'm pleased to say that the part of the Battery which has to go back to rest stations takes me back with it to Les Petites Armoises. It was a horribly strenuous night ride, over forty kilometres, and freezing as well that night, and they could have saved the men and horses the double effort: why ever did we go to Ripont in the first place? We move back into the old quarters at L.P.A., only this time with Bombardier Schott.

1 April: Centenary of Bismarck's birthday.

I have a terrible itching on my skin and want to get it looked at. Proceed on foot to the Bazancourt-Ferme, from there to Chatillon and on from there, in heavenly spring weather, through ploughed fields and valleys to Bally, where there was a concentration of troops such as I've seldom seen. New regiments with new numbers, in brand-new kit. On from there to Vouziers. Quite a lot going on in V. It's the head-quarters area, plenty of military hospitals there too, and in the road I heard—the first for a very long time—a German girl's voice. Into hospital at Sedan at 6 o'clock. I've got a rash, it comes from not washing, from the dirt we were lying in all those weeks. However, in two days I've been cured.

Easter Sunday, 4 April: Thoughts about the past and the future. I think of Easter 1913, which I spent with Bob* at Lugano, and build castles in the air for other Easters after the war.

On *8 April,* back in Les Petites Armoises. One section from our Battery has gone into firing positions in the Ripont area in the meanwhile, but I stay in L.P.A. and hope for a few more quiet days. During this time I've really made friends with the people I'm billeted with. I talk to them a lot and hope, although of course they're fairly anti-Prussian, to succeed in putting their ideas straight. You have the feeling that every individual can contribute towards getting rid of the seeds of hatred, and that every single chap who comes into contact with French civilians has got a real job to do for his country by behaving decently and in this way providing an antidote to the poison.

I've started to itch again all the time. Captain Bachmann is highly concerned about me and insists on my going off

---

* 'Bob' was my nickname for Friedl Schneider. The Lugano trip was my first unofficial honeymoon.—H.S.

again, this time to a better hospital at Rethel, as he needs me, he says, for further fighting. He was a proper father to me and gave me fifty marks to take with me for emergencies.

The *U.29* has been sunk, and Otto Weddigen has gone down with her. He used to command the *U.9*, and in her he destroyed three British armoured cruisers in one hour. His name and his achievements will remain unforgettable.

10 April: Back in Les Petites Armoises.

The evenings are very pleasant with a few of my mates and the old people, Madame Louise, Appoline and young Valentine. The civilians always give us wine with our meals (every Frenchman's got Bordeaux in his cellar, even the poorest peasant farmers, like people at Frankfurt with their apple wine), and we keep them supplied with food and give them what we can. A few quiet, really charming days.

17 April: It's still itching, no one seems able to do anything for me.

We don't have many duties.

20 April: I visit Major Rückward, my parents' friend whom I mentioned earlier on, and who is commanding a unit near here. It was such a splendid day that I struck off on foot over this enchanting country, past Pont Bar and Le Chesne, where at the request of my landlady at L.P.A. I visited her sister, was received in a most friendly manner and lavishly entertained. Continued on foot through the sunshine and arrived at Major Rückward's unit; I hadn't seen him since July, 1914. We were very pleased indeed to be together. In the evening walked back to L.P.A.

The itching which I've mentioned so often has actually been bothering me without a break since Lille: I wouldn't like to go into a military hospital, I'd rather stay with the unit, but I really can't bear it any more. Meanwhile I hope to get a few days' leave to go home to Frankfurt-am-Main.

1 May: Had to go to Rethel to buy medicines, got a ride there via Vouziers and was back at V. about 11 o'clock. No further chance of any kind of lift back to L.P.A., but

I didn't want to spend the night in V., and felt so fresh that I struck off on foot.

I'll never forget that night trek. A brilliant starlit May night, the meadows and ploughed fields were fragrant with spring smells, and the large number of nightingales which they have in this area were singing away, so that you could have walked on for ever, only hoping that a night like this would never come to an end. Didn't meet a soul. It really did look as though there wasn't a war on, and it was like a fairy-tale, tramping on through the little French villages, all sound asleep. The moon, which was on the wane, rose at midnight and lit up this lovely district: it was almost as bright as day. I got to L.P.A. at three in the morning.

We hear about a victorious action fought by our troops near Ypres; and about a Turkish victory on the Dardanelles; and a very large victory in the Carpathians (near Gorlice).

7 May: Papa's birthday. What a lot of memories!

There's talk of diplomatic relations being broken off between Italy and Austria, that means with us as well. Large bodies of German and Austrian troops are supposed to be concentrated down there already.

We shell Dunkirk with our new 38-centimetre guns.

9 May: Can't believe it: I get a few days' leave to go home to Frankfurt. I confess I found it very hard to say good-bye to the Vesserons. I go off in charge of a convoy, make for Frankfurt via Sedan and Metz, and at mid-day on *10 May* there I am in Frankfurt. I came as a complete surprise to my parents and friends. You just can't describe how it feels to get out of the war and come back on leave to your home town, after everything that's happened to you in the first nine months of the campaign. I get well spoilt and visit old acquaintances, as far as they are still here. I've brought my little terrier back with me, and want to leave her at home, so that she'll be in one piece when I come back and see her again after the war.

Those were two splendid days on leave at home, and on *12 May*, in the evening, I set off once more. Actually you had thought it would be different, starting off again like that, back into the war, and this is another thing which shows how unfeeling you become: you don't feel that it was anything worth mentioning at all, you don't think, or feel, that you won't come back—you just go off as though you were back at school and leaving for the summer holidays. Actually of course saying good-bye on these occasions is much worse for our people who have to stay at home.

13 May: In the morning got to Charleville, where the main H.Q. is. The Kaiser is on the Eastern Front at the moment, however. In the train I met our new Adjutant, and when we came to Charleville he invited me to go for a walk with him, and we had a meal together; I was just the small Lance-Bombardier Sulzbach, but he made a lot of me.

Only a few days left at dear old L.P.A. once I'm back, and it's very hard for me to think of saying good-bye to the place. I know nearly all the civilians here and feel that I've made friends with them. Especially old Bertholet the mayor—what a charming person! Still, I was in this place, which is particularly charming anyway, to enjoy the coming of spring, and enjoy it I did, a thousand times, after the deadly months before.

On *18 May* I bade farewell to my French friends and Valentine. I'll never forget these good people.

On *19 May*, at the gun-position near Ripont, in this miserable district, all shot to pieces, I felt homesick, and I feel depressed. On the same day I get news more sad than I can express: my friend Kurt Reinhardt is being posted; he's going to a regular regiment, the 63rd. What friends we had become! I just can't imagine what it means: now we two are going to spend the war in different units. We've been through every kind of good and bad together; I loved his quiet style, and he was witty, often a bit of a fatalist. And how kind he was, what a strangely soft heart he had! He was always afraid he might say something to hurt someone. I went a bit of the way with Kurt, but we really couldn't say much more to each other, and just said good-bye.

They've made themselves quite snug, meanwhile, at the limber position. The horses have good stalls, and it's more domesticated at the gun-position too, and if there's no firing you sit about in the open. Actually the whole front is fairly quiet anyway.

On 22 *May* I was on duty on Hill 196. It was a fine, warm May morning, but the countryside was bare and torn with shellfire, the tracks all churned up, dug-outs and narrow-gauge tracks everywhere—the whole landscape had turned into war; but the cuckoos and turtle-doves don't mind, they say 'pooh' to everything and carry on billing and cooing as though the war were none of their damned business. At 5 in the morning a senior Staff party come up on horseback to inspect the foremost position: the Crown Prince of Saxony. It stirs up childhood memories, when I was at Zandvoort in Holland, building sand-castles, and there were two little boys just next to us— those were the Saxon princes.

Whitsun 1915: A peaceful day, hardly a shot fired, no clouds, birds twittering, and once again all you can do is to grope about among your memories.

In the evening we sit outside our dug-outs and sing.

On Whit Sunday, 23 *May,* we get news in the evening that Italy has declared war, as expected: so that's one more! There are cheers in the trenches and round our gun-positions as the news arrives, and there's a terrific feeling of anger against these traitors. The French reply to our cheering with a burst of heavy, angry fire, as though they meant that *we* oughtn't to be allowed to cheer this news and that they were the only people entitled to be pleased about it!

I've got an inflammation on my leg and on 27 *May* I go into the military hospital at Vouziers. No medical cases in my ward, nothing but wounded, and you take in all the awful things that go on in a military hospital. Wounded men groaning, and doctors, medical N.C.O.'s, medical orderlies and nurses all buzzing about. I've got an inflammation of the cellular tissue, and feel so very unimportant compared with all these poor wounded chaps. We get good food and plenty of it, and the doctors give us excellent medical treatment.

The battle at Gorlice under Mackensen's command, which I've already mentioned, lasted from 2 May until the 20th; the

Allied armies have broken through the Russian front and taken nearly 200,000 prisoners.

Here at the military hospital you have time and peace and quiet to do some reading again.

We hear of more heroic things done by our U-boats.

The badly wounded men are lying in their beds with serious faces, and the convalescents are sitting about in the garden, playing games.

3 June: Przemyśl is in our hands again, we went in and took it back.

What we captured in May in the East was 300,000 prisoners, 1,000 officers, 200 guns and 450 machine-guns.

The survivors of the crew of the *Emden* have arrived at Constantinople after incredible hardships.

On *7 June* I get news that I'm going home on a hospital train.

At the military hospital we've been making friends with people who do strange things for a living. In this kind of hospital you are all put together, and it is a good thing that there are no class distinctions. For instance, over there a circus performer is lying in a bed next to a famous sculptor, and they are good friends.

So on *8 June* off I go in the hospital train with well-lit carriages all beautifully fitted up.

On *9 June* Kaiserslautern: you breathe in as much as you can, looking at our beloved Germany, you feel all enthusiastic and very happy. We travel on through Ludwigshafen, Mannheim and Heidelberg, Würzburg and Schweinfurt, and then night falls.

On the morning of *10 June* we reach Hof, and at 10 o'clock we detrain at Zwickau. There I am put into the Reserve Military Hospital, and since I am not all that ill I hope I shall soon be able to get to Frankfurt. We are well looked after, we get good food; and we're bored.

On *16 June* I was strongly impressed by the words of a Roman Catholic chaplain, who urged us to have faith and to put our trust in God in the plainest way, without any dramatic effects.

22 June: The bells are ringing out: Lemberg has fallen, and the remainder of the Russian armies on this front have been put to flight. But for many, many people it is another bell, tolling once again over the churchyard.

My ward at our hospital is just opposite a factory which is absolutely swarming with girls. What a very unusual sight!

26 June: I'm well again, and get my uniform back and my discharge and travel via Leipzig to Frankfurt-am-Main, arriving on the morning of the *27th.* I arrive home, and see my family again in a glow of happiness. Goodness, the feel of being able to go out and waste my time in the evening! I report at once to the reserve Artillery Battalion at the barracks and get put into No. 3 Battery, and what do I find out there? 2/Lt Reinhardt, who has been restored to health in the meanwhile, is just about to pull out with No. 4 Replacement Battery. I succeed straight away in getting into his battery and I've got two reasons for being happy—getting out of the depot again quickly, and with him as well. I'm given a few more days' convalescent leave, go cycling in the forest with my old-time sweetheart, and feel just as though it were peacetime. One day I drove into the Taunus, up to the Jagdhaus, with my parents and friends, and sat up there in the wonderful air, surrounded by perfect peace. You could hear the bees humming and you just couldn't realize that only a few hours away by fast train the most dreadful war ever known is raging. I feel very well and won't be able to stand it here much longer, even if 2/Lt Reinhardt doesn't take his battery away soon. It just won't do, you can't hang about at home, you have to fight and do your bit to win this war for us and get it finished!

I hear that my little terrier bitch from Flanders has run away.

A few more quiet days follow with barrack duties and a few hours of time off now and then.

Superficially, town life here has not changed much yet. You still go out to restaurants and go dancing, only there aren't many civilians left. People don't seem to be going short yet, though.

My job in the new battery is mounted lance-bombardier and

telephone operator. In a few days we are going to Gonsenheim, near Mainz, to entrain there.

At Gonsenheim we have a few more quiet days with duties and opportunities for exchanges between individuals; our Lt Becker, a very jolly chap, is as pleased as Punch to spend his time with us on the few evenings left before we pull out again. You gradually get friendly with your new mates, they're partly new war volunteers, partly chaps who've been wounded and are pulling out again, partly older men who have just been called up.

I've got myself a little Goerz pocket camera, always carry it with me, and take my first pictures.

29 July: Ready to move.

30 July: Entrain for the Western Front. Our Battery Commander is 2/Lt Reinhardt, and our Battery officers are 2/Lt Becker, whom I've mentioned before, and 2/Lt Bremshey. Our guns are decorated with the German, Austrian and Turkish flags. We travel the same way we went on 2 September, 1914, along the Rhine, and the 'Rhine maidens' bring us food at the stopping-places.

31 July: Liège; then we go past my dear old Namur, and also pass Maubeuge, where I see the first permanent Zeppelin hangar built on enemy territory. We detrain at Baboeuf.

1 August: A whole year of war! Whoever would have thought that, a year ago! We spend the day at our billets, which remind me of Les Petites Armoises. Towards evening 2/Lt Reinhardt, a bombardier, another lance-bombardier and I ride past Noyon to our new gun-position near Evricourt. I've never seen such a peaceful gun-position before. After inspecting it we ride back to the Battery, still very peaceful.

2 August: We ride to Evricourt again, through quite idyllic country, hills and valleys, little woods and meadows—it is Picardy. We ride further than yesterday, then leave the horses and walk to inspect our new observation post in the infantry lines. It is really remarkable in this battle area that the pretty little villages, which have only been partly damaged by shellfire, are still completely inhabited by civilians. People just haven't left their villages when they're not even 200 metres behind the trenches! The civilians are great friends with the infantry. The trenches along the front are a model of how trenches should be built, and the dug-outs are comfortable to live in and very deep. Our observation post is on a tall fir-tree, and in the French trenches you can see the Turkos walking about in their white burnouses. Our dug-out by the observation post is very snug. In the evening back to the gun-pits near Evricourt. Our guns are standing on a meadow which slopes diagonally downwards, not fifty metres from this pretty village, and part of the gun-teams can even live in Evricourt. It seems to be turning into a peaceful war!

I get posted with 2/Lt Becker to the infantry to man the observation post, and we practise shooting at our new targets. The infantry officers and infantrymen have a look at their new gunners, and several friendships spring up between the two branches of the service. In the next few days the officers of my battery relieve each other at the observation post, and I stay up there. You get to be more of an infantryman than a gunner. We keep in touch with individual company commanders, and from our O.P. we direct fire from our battery by telephone on to one target or another—occasionally worth it. The enemy hardly reply to our fire.

Incidentally, there have been more big successes in the East; Warsaw has been in our hands for some time.

On 9 *August* the French suddenly fire at our place, Evricourt, but nothing much happens.

13 August: 2/Lt Reinhardt took me on a ride along behind the front to visit his brother, my friend Kurt, whose regiment is stationed a few sectors away to the north. We gave him a surprise, and how marvellous it was to see him—for me, it was one of the finest days in the last twelve months. We rode back towards dusk, having done quite seventy kilometres in the saddle.

At a cross-roads on the main road from Noyon to Roye stands a war memorial built of nothing but empty shell-cases (what we call *Ausbläser*, 'blow-outs'). It is dedicated to the heroes of the X Regiment who fell in fierce fighting near Roye during the 1914 advance, and bears the words:

Aux braves soldats français
Tombés pour leur patrie
Dans les graves combats
Près de Roye
Au Septembre 1914.

We pulled up our horses in front of this monument put up by the Germans to their enemies killed in action: sunk in thought and much moved by this deep sign of honour and recognition of the enemy dead.

I spend the next few days in the trench at the O.P., and there is only a little bit of artillery skirmishing now and then.

The infantry regiment whose sector we're stationed in mainly consists of older men, while the light infantry battalion next to them is made up of quite young fellows.

One of the next starlit summer nights, a decent Landwehr chap came up suddenly and said to 2/Lt Reinhardt, 'Sir, it's that Frenchie over there singing again so wonderful.' We stepped out of the dug-out into the trench, and quite incredibly, there was a marvellous tenor voice ringing out through the night with an aria from *Rigoletto*. The whole company were standing in the trench listening to the 'enemy', and when he had finished, applauding so loud that the good Frenchman must certainly have heard it and is sure to have been moved by it in some way or other as much as we were by his wonderful singing. What an extraordinary contrast! You fire on each other, you kill each other, and then all of a sudden a Frenchman starts to sing, and the music makes us forget the whole war: music seems to overcome every kind of difference. Anyway, that was an experience much more splendid than anything you can express in words.

We use horses here on duty, and when we want to go to a neighbouring regiment, we cut along close behind the front, through the villages. Now and then you sometimes receive what we call a 'blessing' of shellfire, and being fired on when you are riding through the villages is extremely disagreeable.

19 August: From the East: Kovno has fallen.

20 August: Novo-Georgievsk has fallen.

On one of the following afternoons, the whole battery unit rode over to our new observation post south of Loermont. We dismounted by the most splendid—and the largest—natural caves you could possibly imagine; they extend for kilometres under the high ground, splitting into a maze of passages which in many cases come out on the other side, in the French lines. These exits have of course been walled up and guarded by particularly strong machine-gun nests. The caves have been converted into a regular town, with ambulances standing ready, and horses, kitchens, and whole reserve infantry battalions, all quartered in there. It's terribly hard to find your way about inside. Our O.P. is opposite Uttèche-Ferme, a completely shelled-out farm building strongly fortified by the French; you can see them building trenches.

One of the following days I was sent on duty to Noyon, a whole day in the rear area. Noyon is a very handsome town, full of servicemen and a lot of civilian women and girls.

The telephone lines from Battery to the O.P. get cut by shellfire fairly seldom, but they aren't used very often either, since we aren't shooting very much. I do a lot of photography and have already taken actual pictures of the French lines from the infantry listening-post. We now frequently score direct hits on the Uttèche-Ferme.

One evening a little later I went off with my mate Graffunder and a few infantrymen on a patrol which included going back behind the German lines, because there was supposed to be a French spy about.

Now and again we spend some cheerful evenings drinking.

I do a bit of telephone cable repair duty; that's a miserable job.

2 September: Now I've been a whole year in the field. When you consider what the German troops have done, you can hardly believe we have succeeded in facing a world of enemies victoriously for so long.

Meanwhile I've been put in charge of a gun and so have to stay more in the battery instead of being with the infantry where it was substantially more interesting. The autumn is coming on, and some days not a shot is fired.

A few days later we had an incredible stroke of luck: I moved with my gun to another position to do some ranging shots for a new battery. We had hardly started back for our old position when the French put down fifty rounds of the largest calibre they had exactly on the spot where we'd been. My telephone operator had gone for cover with three infantrymen when their cover took a direct hit and all three infantrymen were seriously wounded, while by some miracle nothing at all happened to my operator. Incidentally I am the only lance-bombardier to be in charge of a gun.

The famous French loop-the-loop airman Pégoud has been killed in action, and the German who shot him down dropped a wreath next day bearing the inscription:

A Pégoud mort, un héros, son adversaire

Up there in the sky there is still a fine spirit of chivalry.

9 September: I've gone up to bombardier and been made an officer cadet at the same time.

We are now trying to do ranging shots with an airborne observation post.

14 September: Kurt Reinhardt returns my visit and stays for two wonderful days. I took Kurt round the infantry lines and showed him our interesting caves, and we chatted about all the things that we'd done and seen.

Vilna has fallen.

We are given talks by medical officers about bits of equipment which are supposed to stop you inhaling poison gas.

25 September: Bulgaria declares war on Serbia.

Evricourt under artillery fire: five horses killed in a stable.

Heavy fighting has broken out again in the Champagne country where we were stationed in January and February. In spite of the static warfare, the French are supposed to have thrown huge masses of cavalry against our trenches, but they were only partially successful—quite small gains.

Up there in Flanders, too, it seems to be really starting again. The British are trying to break through our lines at

Loos and down in the Champagne country the French are trying the same with twenty-two divisions. The losses must be very heavy on both sides. But our wall is still standing!

French airmen seem to have left our captive balloons alone so far, but our anti-aircraft guns often intercept successfully. It's very lively in the air anyway.

Here we belong to the Corps of Guards.

Meanwhile, Belgrade has been taken by Mackensen and Gallwitz. The Entente Powers are giving up their campaign in the Dardanelles and admit that the offensive on the Western Front is failing.

Our advance in Serbia is proceeding.

On *13 October*, the anniversary of our capture of Lille, Kurt Reinhardt comes over on a bike and visits me for the day.

The Generals, whom we call Their Excellencies, often come on tours of inspection.

A large number of troop movements taking place in our sector at the moment. The 9th Army Corps is being pulled out too and in the morning, before the infantry were relieved, the French had put up a notice-board in front of the barbed wire with huge letters on it saying

ADIEU, 9TH CORPS!

It was really quite nice of them, but their espionage seems to be working brilliantly.

The general war situation is very good: the Western Front is standing firm, and in the East it's victory after victory. In the Balkans the united German, Austro-Hungarian and Bulgarian armies are storming ahead. Mackensen and Gallwitz are sharing the successes with Koevess, the Austrian general. The U-Boats and Zeppelins are doing splendid work.

Jolly old 2/Lt Becker goes on being the friend of all the war volunteers, and once he invited me to Noyon. The French girls there are nice and pro-German, in every way.

3 November: I ride with 2/Lt Reinhardt through Chiry to Pimprez, along the canal, which has one bank shielded from enemy observation by screens which we've put up. It is too strange: you ride right into Pimprez, in spite of the French trenches running up to the other end of the village. The artillery O.P. is inside the village in a house with French people still living in it. I can't understand such carelessness.

We visit our No. 6 Battery, 15th Field Artillery Regiment, commanded by Lt Freiherr von Marschall, with whom we discuss various points for a piece of joint action.

6 November: Nish has been stormed by the Bulgars.

8 November: I go with 2/Lt Reinhardt for two days' leave at St Quentin. It's a lovely feeling to be sitting in a fast train again, and even the journey was pleasant—we were with a jolly crowd of infantry going on home leave. St Quentin, which the Guards gentlemen pronounce 'Seng-Kang-Teng', is a very handsome city, lying in the rear area and still completely undamaged. It's swarming with high-ranking officers, and as I sauntered round the town I met a string of people I knew straight away, as there are great masses of troops stationed here in reserve. There's a German front-line theatre company here too, and some of the actors in it come from the Frankfurt Summer Theatre. We get allocated a billet by the Town Commandant's office. My room is opposite 2/Lt Reinhardt's and I've got a splendid bed—it's the essence of every kind of happiness. Then we walked on through the town and ate together —actually, we had thought we were going to have a bit more of an evening. Incidentally, 2/Lt Reinhardt has asked his brother Kurt to come to St Quentin tomorrow too.

Marvellous night in a soft bed. Next morning I acted the part of 2/Lt Reinhardt's batman and got a fine breakfast ready for him. Then Kurt arrived, in a little two-wheeled cart, and to our astonishment there was a charming little demoiselle sitting beside him.

Those were two peaceful days that we spent in St Quentin, even if life in a rear area wouldn't suit me in the long run. They mount guard at St Quentin every day at noon, and everything else is barracks-style too.

In general the civilians are highly reserved.

On *11 November* back to the battery. It's still quiet on this front. 2/Lt Reinhardt sometimes invites guests to his officers' dug-out, sometimes even the C.O. of the regiment, and some of us war volunteers also attend these evenings. War Volunteer Wollweber always gives us a treat on the piano. It's a real matey atmosphere from the Colonel of the regiment down to the war volunteer.

Winter is coming on. Except for a few bursts of fire from the French, nothing happens of any importance. Nothing for the next few weeks either. Just the iron spirit of wartime duty: stick it out, firm as a rock!

Meanwhile I've been put in charge of No. 4 gun. This advanced gun is not stationed in the battery area, but two kilometres further on, right behind the infantry. We get particularly friendly treatment from the kindly infantrymen because we're stationed in their lines. Straight in front of us lies what they call the 'Sparrow's Post', an isolated front-line post in a V-shaped trench which stretches across to the French lines like a peninsula, and straight in front of our trench stands a little shelled-out chapel. However, when dusk is falling you can walk about in the ruins. There's something solemn about this chapel, and when you stand in front of it and the French aren't even 100 metres away, you get back into a mood that someone who's stayed at home just can't understand. Just next to it is what is known as the Painter's Castle, also quite shelled out, sticking out in front of our trench. There's a group of infantrymen lying in the cellar of these ruins. And once we went with some of them through the German barbed wire and beyond it up to just short of the French positions—but it was a bit uncanny, that little walk was. And since the mist had meanwhile withdrawn itself, we had to crawl back on our bellies.

People often talk drivel about Staff officers not daring to come up to the front. For one thing, as I see it, it's their duty not to expose themselves to danger, but on the other hand, we have quite a number of inspecting generals up at the front. Today we had General von Plettenberg, the General Officer commanding the Corps of Guards, up at the front gun.

One day our gun was brought back into the battery because that evening several batteries were to direct combined fire on the Carmoy-Ferme. That night at 11 p.m. we fired off some rapid shellfire, quite unusual in this area. That was proper banging again all right. Next day my gun was brought forward again behind the infantry lines. Life in a 'proper' gun-position is much more pleasant than it is in quieter positions, because the greater the danger gets, the more comradeship there is and the more unselfish the men become.

I'm really very happy up here with my No. 4 gun-team mates and my infantry friends. When the chaps have a little to drink as well, they all get so gay and good-tempered that you know they have a genuinely good character, since the drink brings it out.

We'd be sitting deep in our dug-outs of an evening, when one of the infantry chaps would come clattering over and call. Come along, he'd say, they had something nice for us, we were to come and get it. If they ever have any delicacies to spare, they make us a present of them, partly of course because they feel that we are protecting them. And then some quiet evening the telephone rings and someone speaks up from one of the batteries or companies, and tells us that he's now going to make a bit of music with a concertina or some other instrument, and then everyone hangs on what we call the *Quasselstrippe*—the 'chatter-strip'—and listens to the nice little concert. Those are really enchanting moments.

On our daytime programme we have little bursts of shellfire and up above, dog-fights between aircraft, which are sometimes quite interesting.

Today a French aircraft was trying once again to knock down a German captive balloon, when a German fighter plane which was guarding the balloon swooped down like a bird of prey; then you heard the usual tack-tack-tack, tack-tack-tack—and down went the French plane. It was the first successful air-battle I'd ever seen.

The little village of Thiescourt lies right near us, and French civilians are still living there, in spite of the French troops shelling it every day.

You keep noticing the inexpressibly sorrowful expression worn by French girls and women. Any soldier who has a bit of feeling and tact will recognize this so quickly that cases of Frenchwomen being pestered seldom arise; but you very often see friendships between Frenchwomen and our chaps. There's a young woman in Thiescourt who was staying in the village to visit relatives; the Germans came and she couldn't get back, and now she'll soon have been sitting there in Thiescourt for eighteen months (and how much longer will she have to?), and hasn't heard a thing from her family since August, 1914. And it's the same for hundreds of thousands of others.—I find I have to keep emphasizing that the French civilians are enduring their unenviable fate with as much courage, dignity and pride as any human beings could possibly muster.

One afternoon I get a visit from 2/Lt Becker, who has been on leave in Hanover and tells me his experiences. He's such a kind, cheerful person, and also a chap who doesn't know the meaning of danger.

We have musical evenings quite often now. When we hear a particular signal on the buzzer, we know that a concert is beginning!

The Reichstag is in session in Berlin at the moment. Many fine speeches have been made, on the left and on the right— the unity which binds us together as we soldier at the front seems to have transferred itself even to the Reichstag.

One day I had a 24-hour tour of duty at Noyon as guard commander of the main guard.

Shortly before Christmas our fine No. 4 gun is withdrawn to the Battery.

On 21 December we celebrated 2/Lt Reinhardt's birthday. As early as 6 in the morning we sang him a serenade that was really a surprise for him, and a very pleasant one at that. He also got presents, so far as we were able to make them out here, and the infantry lent us a few of their musicians so that we could give him another musical treat in the afternoon. The French showed their consideration that day by doing no shelling at all.

24 December: The second Christmas Eve in the field. Today I was on duty again in Noyon and only got back to the battery in the evening. Lovely parcels and letters from my parents and friends at home. For the second time candles were burning on the Christmas tree for us at Frankfurt. 2/Lt

Reinhardt said a few words to us, but we were all in a some-what doleful mood. At 11 in the evening the Colonel of the regiment visited our gun-positions, and we thought a great deal of him for doing so, as he didn't stay to enjoy the party himself but took the trouble to go round all his batteries to wish them a merry Christmas.

We celebrated New Year's Eve 1915–16 too (and there wasn't much shelling then either) with infantrymen and infantry officers whom we'd made friends with, and since 2/Lt Becker had been on duty for some time at another command post, I visited him at night, so that he wouldn't be so lonely, and took along something to drink into the bargain.

III

1916

1916 has begun and we hope that at least this year we'll have a victorious peace.

At the beginning of January I was given leave to go with 2/Lt Becker to St Quentin. He wanted to see a doctor and asked for me to accompany him.

On *6 January* we were back at the gun-positions. Evricourt is getting shelled fairly often now.

13 January: 2/Lt Becker has been posted away for flying duties, at his own request, and is giving a farewell party.

18 January: On the anniversary of the foundation of the German Reich, Montenegro surrenders unconditionally and lays down her arms.

We are doing more firing again now and shell any worthwhile enemy targets we can find.

At the end of January we hear about the amazing long-distance flights made by our Zeppelins to Paris, Salonica and London.

In the night of *1 February* London was bombed by an air group consisting of several Zeppelins.

I must mention a wonderful piece of work done by an Austrian naval plane: Austrian fleet air arm pilots were bombing the Albanian port of Valona. They were fired on, and one aircraft was forced down on the sea. The enemy coastal batteries shelled it, and two enemy destroyers set off to hunt it down. Then, in a choppy sea, a second Austrian plane landed on the water beside the damaged aircraft, rapidly took the shipwrecked crew on board, destroyed the other plane since it could no longer fly, and flew back with a double load, all safe and sound.

8 *February*: My second birthday in the field.

I was on duty at the gun-pit and therefore arrived late for the meal which we took all together. As I was sitting 'at table' with my friends and the officers, I couldn't believe my ears when suddenly a sound of singing began outside the door; 2/Lt Reinhardt had organized a serenade for me, and being just a young bombardier, I was so moved that I almost had tears in my eyes. The whole battery, as far as they could be spared, had gathered round the choir. My dear, kind 2/Lt Reinhardt was almost as pleased as I was at the success of this pleasant surprise.

One day our battery received orders to change position for one day, using another site to attack a particular enemy battery—this would have been impossible from our site at Evricourt. We pulled out as though we were going into mobile warfare. The change of position was carried out at night to avoid enemy observation. There was snow on the ground, and the moon lit up the hilly, almost peaceful-looking country. We pulled past Plémont on the main road and went into firing positions in a hollow, and this little detour made a change in the increasing monotony of static warfare. We fired for half an hour and must have done the job straight away, as the French battery was silent after that.

On 23 *February* a huge noise of gunfire started up far away to the south of us. This was the barrage at the beginning of our offensive at Verdun.

On 25 *February* the wireless reported that several villages near Verdun had been taken by assault, countless quantities of equipment captured, and a general advance begun.

Meanwhile there's the interesting news that airships are being built in continuous production at the Zeppelin yards in Friedrichshafen and that over 100 of them are in service. News from the Verdun battle area continues to be favourable. One fort has been taken by assault and the Woëvre Line has been broken.

27 February: I get promoted to lance-sergeant.

Down near Verdun the banging and rumbling never let up. There is still a bit of snow on the ground, but in spite of that it already feels like spring.

We hear about a marvellous new solo performance by the S.M.S. *Möwe.* She is back at her home port after a cruise of several months on which she captured and sank 15 ships and took 114 prisoners on board. On top of all that she had laid mines along the English coast.

At Noyon they put on a concert from time to time for troops in quiet sectors, and we go to one of them. It is touching to see how completely these nice fellows surrender to the unusual pleasure as they listen to the music.

10 March: State of war with Portugal.

I often go back to duty as an observer in the trenches, and I'm fond of life with the infantry. Our O.P. is now opposite Uttèche-Ferme again, among some rocks. Spring has come, and out there the birds are singing and still aren't bothering about the shot and shell. We have to live in our stuffy holes underground while it's getting green outside, and enjoy the peace and quiet as much as we can in spite of it all.

Portugal's declaration of war brings us to the 32nd declaration of war which this World War has so far produced.

Aerial dog-fights continue to take place, and several of them end sadly for us. The French try diversion tactics to take the pressure off Verdun. We are kept standing to continuously. Red flares go up in the air, whereupon we lay down a devilish curtain barrage.

The telephone lines to the batteries have all been shot through. When it gets quieter at 2 a.m. we go out on telephone patrol, mending lines. The respite from this heavy fire, however, only lasts a few days. Our duties out at the front also take us into the neighbouring sectors, as far as Dreslincourt, where the trenches run through houses and cellars. We make our number with the neighbouring infantry sectors, so as to find out what they want.

General Sack came and inspected the trenches and our O.P.

as well—he was particularly pleased with that and asked me all kinds of questions. He knew that Reinhardt was my Battery Commander, and asked me whether I had been in the 1914–15 fighting under Reinhardt—this interested him particularly since he knew about Reinhardt's experiences, from a short series of books which R. had published. After this conversation I was understandably in the best of spirits.

The French are getting cheeky. One day a whole staff of them appeared on a wall in the Uttèche-Ferme, and I shooed them away with a well-aimed salvo. And in the French trenches they don't hesitate to go digging, between five and twenty men at a time, in broad daylight. There seems to be a new regiment there which hasn't a notion what a war is all about.

Meanwhile it has been raining hard, and walking along the trenches means sinking nearly up to our knees in the mud. Weather like this is not exactly pleasant for the infantry or ourselves up at the front.

On 27 *March* we execute another little change of position, in order to achieve the same effect as we did a little while back—to shell a target which we couldn't reach from the gun-sites at Evricourt. We go into position in a gully near Dreslincourt and knock down a chimney, belonging to a brick-works, which an enemy O.P. has been nesting in.

In the course of time our chaps have given nicknames to particular positions or ruins, and now the names have stuck fast. They're quite pretty; I've mentioned the *Malerschlösschen*, the 'Painter's Castle', already. One hill is called *der Kapellen-berg*, 'Chapel Hill'. Sometimes they are names of infantry C.O.'s whose units used to be stationed at the place in question.

For some time now a new anti-balloon gun, mounted on a lorry, has been in position near our gun-sites. We are much interested in this new gadget.

I often have to move from my duties on the O.P., because other chaps have to do the job as well, and in the battery it's a much duller life.

The fruit-trees are starting to blossom, it's a fabulous spring in this gentle district, which reminds me of my beloved *Bergstrasse*.°

Early in April attacks by Zeppelins on Great Britain were repeated on four successive nights. In the course of one attack, L.15 was shot down over London.

I'm at the front again on observation. One night a German patrol brought in the body of a Zouave from the 3rd Zouave Regiment. He had marvellous equipment, and among his papers was a letter with this in it:

> *Pour abattre ces Boches, qui nous font tant de misère.* (To knock out the Boches who are giving us such a wretched time.)

My brother, who has also been stationed on the Western Front so far, is suffering from shock and is in a military hospital at Halle.

Very heavy fighting continues outside Verdun, and there seem to be numerous casualties on both sides.

So far as the infantry is concerned, our battery enjoys the greatest popularity you could imagine, because our outfit takes liaison and contact with our brother arm of the service more seriously than was the case with any of our predecessors: we are always there when we're wanted, every request made by the infantry is carried out, and they feel we are protecting them. That is the highest objective we can possibly have.

16 April: I've got some home leave. If you only knew what the word home leave means! Well, what does it imply? It's the fulfilment of an unbelievable longing; it means feeling as excited as though you were about to go to Heaven. I walked down from the O.P. to Battery and then drove along past the beautiful *Bois*, the stretch of woodland, on a splendid morning, with the turtle-doves cooing and the cuckoos calling, and it smelt of spring, and it all made you more homesick than ever. At Noyon I got into the train, which took me through Quentin and Aachen and on to Cologne. The night journey seemed as if it would never end. After waiting two hours at Cologne, on to Frankfurt-am-Main, past all those

° The *Bergstrasse* is the range of hills and low-lying country between Darmstadt and Heidelberg.—R.T.

villages and little towns along the Rhine. You could hardly believe it was all true.

Getting home was more marvellous than I can say; I gave all my relatives a surprise. 2/Lt Reinhardt happened to have got leave at the same time, and I went to see him straight away. For the next few days I called on my friends and sat about in cafés; and in the evenings one could actually go out dancing! This might seem at first to be flying in the face of reason, people having a good time at home while abroad the battle is raging, and every second some of my mates are getting killed in action. But you'll have to understand that we want to run a bit wild on leave, breathing as much life into our lungs as we can, for who knows whether after this leave one is ever coming back again?

I received the very sad news that Berthold, who had been our faithful manservant at Frankfurt for years, has been killed in action outside Verdun. His last letter to me gave a completely clear impression that he did not believe he would survive.

So I spent Easter 1916 at home, and much as I enjoyed being back for these days of leave, I did have a certain longing for the front and an uneasy feeling that I ought to be back with my Battery. Memories at home of what used to be called peacetime sound a bit sentimental, and one doesn't want that sort of thing. After a last excursion to Wiesbaden, absolutely swarming with wounded officers and soldiers—Germans, Austrians, Bulgarians and Turks—I took the train back to my regiment on *29 April*. And once again, saying good-bye was not an easy business.

The train journey went via Mainz, where a large number of officers and men got aboard, some of them returning from leave and others going to the front for the first time. I saw a farewell scene there, very moving: a second lieutenant from the 24th Dragoons was saying good-bye to his wife and two daughters, and his wife was weeping enough to break your heart. And when it's like that you almost take it for granted that these two are not going to see each other again. And then off we went again, along the beautiful Rhine, in a wonderful evening atmosphere. I spent the night in Cologne.

On *30 April* we travelled on through Aachen and Düren

across the Belgian border to Tergnier. And from there on to Noyon and then to Evricourt, where they gave me a splendid welcome.

I spend my next tour of duty, eight days of it, in what they call the *Bois de la Réserve*, where I have to keep the Divisional telephone exchange informed of everything that happens. I'm quite alone up here; it's enchanting to be on one's own, surrounded by young forest trees all decked out in fresh green, and it seems to be a paradise for wild birds. Flowers of every colour are blooming in the forest, and there are lizards, which I've loved since I was a child, taking the sun, and I don't suppose I'll ever be sitting like this again, out in the midst of Nature for several days. You have an untroubled mind and can devote yourself to all your thoughts. What a contrast, being able to enjoy these splendid natural surroundings in this wonderful month of May—and Death, a million Deaths, sitting as it were just next door. My duties are not arduous, there isn't even any firing, and I'm able to spend my off-duty hours sitting reading in the forest outside the dug-out. Of course my thoughts also wander back to past times which had a carefree quality unlikely to come back again. These peaceful days were only interrupted by a little patrolling job which we organized, with preliminary artillery work and mortar-fire. It went according to plan and brought us in five prisoners, with whose assistance we were able to ascertain a number of important facts. The district and the whole sector were so quiet that Sister Agnes Braunfels, who is a singer in Frankfurt, performed a troop concert at our unit, and since she knew I was in this regiment, she got Regimental H.Q. to put her through to me on the line. It was a pleasant, quite unusual surprise. Another time we achieved a little variety by changing position again, this time to attack two enemy batteries, and it was fine getting another chance to put down 515 rounds one after the other.

One day I went with my friend Kirsten to visit his cousin Lt Kirsten, who has a unit near Noyon. I mention this little outing because it took me into a district which to my mind was just like a fairy-tale, and into a fairy-tale billet as well: a little French château, with a park on the right and a pool at the front, sheltered by a semi-circle of ancient trees. A gap had been cut in the trees through which you got an enchanting view into a great, broad meadow, dressed in the most sumptuous green, and an avenue of old trees in the background, along the Oise Canal; horses and cows were moving about in the meadow, and an Italian-style blue sky above them was shining away as though there were nothing on earth but peace, perfect peace.

Towards evening we went back again via Mont St Siméon: an observation post there gives you a view far into the enemy hinterland. Our sector here near Noyon, and the one at Plémont, are the most advanced positions held by the German Army—and so the positions nearest to Paris too. And if I now say that I looked through the stereotelescope and saw the Eiffel Tower, you people will perhaps—or perhaps not—be able to understand how I felt as I stared: Paris in sight! And still almost too far to reach, even though our troops got to within a mere ten kilometres of the Paris forts at the beginning of September, 1914!

A battle has been raging since 15 May on the Italian–Austrian front, and the Imperial and Royal troops have broken through the Italian line, taken 25,000 prisoners and captured 251 guns.

On 2 *June* news reaches us that the largest naval action ever fought between the German and British fleets has taken place off Hornshorn on the Skagerrak.* The action concluded with an unquestionable win for our fleet, which has thus been able to try conclusions with its principal adversary—Great Britain, the ruler of the seas—for the very first time since it was brought up to its present strength by the Kaiser and Tirpitz. Several British battleships have been destroyed, and no fewer than 150 naval vessels were drawn up in battle array. Even our Zeppelins played their part.

7 *June:* Lord Kitchener has gone down with the cruiser *Hampshire* after she was torpedoed on her way to Russia by one of our U-Boats.

* The Battle of Jutland is usually known in Germany as *die Schlacht am Skagerrak.*—R.T.

In the East the Russians have started a huge offensive as well, along a 350-kilometre front.

I go over on horseback to visit Kurt Reinhardt again: he's at Filain near Laon with his regiment. Seeing this good-hearted chap again, and having a talk with him, was particularly rewarding. Kurt's battery has firing positions on what they call the Chemin des Dames. We swapped a lot of experiences, of course—thinking of Namur, Lille, Belgium, Flanders and so into the Champagne country.

In the naval battle off the Skagerrak we lost the *Bremen*, the *Elbing*, the *Wiesbaden*, the *Frauenlob*, the *Lützow* and the *Rostock*.

I've read in a Swiss paper that a new giant Zeppelin is under construction in the Zeppelin yards at Friedrichshafen.

Whitsun, 1916: They're suddenly firing away again like fury; it is actually somewhat unusual to hear proper gunfire in our area, but neither side puts on a serious attack.

Fort Vaux, outside Verdun, has fallen.

In the course of time I have become really quite friendly with my mate Kirsten, the war volunteer who is a lance-sergeant. In the meanwhile, a few of the battery officers and lance-sergeants have been posted away or sent on leave, and I'm alone with 2/Lt Bremshey. One morning 2/Lt Bremshey was on duty with the infantry, and while he was away I was battery commander for the first time, even if only for a few hours. A report had just come in from the infantry that there had been a lot of trench-digging in front of one sector in the French lines, and that a small clash had developed between patrols, whereupon I plotted the position in question on the map and got in sixty rounds. That was my first piece of personal action.

Once again I was sent on a few hours of duty in Noyon and rode back to the battery at night. One of those fabulous night rides such as I have often described: full moon, a clear, warm summer's-night sky, and as you sat on your horse you could let your thoughts run on so splendidly, not at all disturbed by the dull growl of gunfire.

Back at the battery I hear that the French have been giving

us a good dose of shellfire, shooting into the village and the battery itself. We have had some men wounded again, the first for a long time, but luckily no one killed.

Other theatres: the Russian offensive which I've already mentioned continues, and unfortunately it is producing some localized gains.

Salandra* has resigned.

This area, which I've described often enough, has become very dear to me, and I'm beginning to think of Evricourt and its surroundings as a second home. The summer is coming on, they're beginning to make the hay, you can smell the scent of hay past the deadly cannon, and at night the nightingales sing; they seem to be very strongly represented here.

General Linsingen is attacking on the River Styr, Hindenburg at Dünaburg, and the Russians on the River Sereth; and at Verdun the gigantic battle of heavy weapons rages on, without our being able to take Verdun itself.

Certain small attacking operations which we put on are now being given code names, so that the French can't listen in to the telephone messages, or at least can't understand them. A little one like this, called *Veilchenfest* or 'Feast of violets', was mounted on 22 *June* as a combined operation with the Guards on our right flank. The French counter-attacked, but once again we took quite a few prisoners, who supplied under interrogation the information we were looking for.

Outside Verdun, meanwhile, Fort Thiaumont has fallen, and Fleury has been taken.

General Linsingen is pursuing the Russians in their headlong retreat.

One day when we were in position we received an inspection visit from the Chief of Staff of the Corps of Guards.

Our first airman to receive the *Pour-le-Mérite*, 2/Lt Immelmann, has been killed in action.

Up at the front in the O.P. one is becoming unpleasantly aware of enemy trench-mortar fire. The things come humming

* Antonio Salandra, Italy's First Minister, took the lead in keeping Italy neutral in August, 1914, in spite of the Triple Alliance. He brought Italy into the war in May, 1915, on the side of the Allies, but had to resign in June, 1916, after the successful Austro-Hungarian offensive in the Trentino.—R.T.

across, at a very steep angle and a comparatively slow speed, and if you look for them very accurately, you can actually see them coming at you out of the air, without of course being able to do anything to save yourself if they go off near you. These damned things have terrific penetrating power, and make a hash of the deepest dug-out.

Our front is gradually getting much more lively; in our own sector, and on our right and left flanks, it's beginning to rumble and bubble; while far over to the right, on the Somme, a strong British offensive has started. It is not yet clear whether the British offensive will spread over to our sector, or whether the livelier enemy fire in our sector is just a diversion put on to prevent us sending any reinforcements away to the Somme. Consequently we put on patrol operations nearly every night, accompanied by strong small-arms, machine-gun and artillery fire.

On 3 *July* the French fire over 1,000 rounds into our 'C' trenches, in the course of which our stereotelescope in the O.P. is shot to pieces. The shells land to right and left of us, in front of us and behind us, and for the first time you're re-minded of a large-scale day's fighting in Flanders or the Champagne country. It appears that the French have serious intentions in our sector as well. The enemy trenches are heavily manned, and you see the French infantry with bayonets fixed, apparently ready for the '*Sprung auf, marsch, marsch*'—'Over the top, lads!' Our artillery is quiet and for the moment is not firing a single shot. For the next few nights we obviously don't get any sleep, and our division is screwed up to the highest state of preparedness. These difficult days I spend alone, up at the front in the O.P.

Meanwhile the battle for Verdun is still raging, and the British offensive on the Somme is designed to make us with-draw troops from the Verdun area.

In the East, Linsingen's army and Bothmer's are pushing ahead, and the Russian counter-attacks have been thrown back.

On the remainder of the Western Front, the line is static—bomb-proof, in fact—and prepared to repulse any Entente offensive successfully. The general situation is better than ever, and the enemy Alliance is using everything it's got in its attempt to crush us; although very likely they will scarcely be able to suppress a silent admiration for our enormous powers of resistance. The very strong fire directed on our battery for the last few days has prompted our regiment to order us to a new position.

On 3 *July* we leave our position: we have owned it for eleven months and learned to love it well. It looks nasty there now. Direct hits everywhere in the gun-sites, on the grass and along the road. Evricourt village has suffered a great deal as well. This is how the most peaceful villages along this great stretch of front, even though they were completely spared till now, are being gradually reduced to ruins. Bombing by enemy planes, too, is getting more and more unpleasant in villages along the front and just behind it.

The heavy firing in our sector has slackened off. Our new battery position at Le Loermont is not very nice, the pits are not quite finished, with dug-outs as cramped as a ship's fo'c'sle.

I hear that a German merchant U-Boat has arrived in America. That's a fantastic achievement: a U-Boat just walks through the British blockade and gets to America as though there weren't any war at sea at all!

The *U.35* has pulled off another master-stroke and reached Cartagena, bringing the King of Spain a whole ship-load of pharmaceutical products accompanied by a personal letter in our Kaiser's hand.

There's now been a dreadful barrage on the Somme for a good fortnight, but thank God, the British haven't managed to break through. At one small place they attacked with 17 divisions—that is, some 250,000 men—and our few battle-weary regiments have stood like heroes against this over-whelming numerical superiority. I believe that General von Gallwitz is the Army Commander over there.

I still like it best being on observation duty with the infantry. When there isn't actually any heavy firing, you spend rewarding hours with the company commanders and the men. With time I've really found my feet in the infantry world and become fairly independent as well, and I often get together with the infantry leaders to discuss the artillery preparations required for a patrol operation. And afterwards I accompany these friends of mine on their night walks through the trenches, when they are inspecting their sentries, and can't help thinking of the song, *'Steh' ich in finstrer Mitternacht'*. The way these good-hearted infantrymen, some of them ex-Landwehr, stick to their work and do their duty, each man among them really standing at his post like a *rocher de bronze**, is the highest personal fulfilment of one's task in life, faith incarnate in the justice of our victorious cause!

Meanwhile the second anniversary of the outbreak of war has passed, but you don't really think any more about our entering the third year of war, and still less about whether, and if so when, there is going to be peace again.

It would seem that the fighting on the Somme is attempting to decide the outcome of the war. Gallwitz has given his Army Group an order that not a single metre of ground may be lost. I assume that we too shall soon be involved in this, the greatest battle in the history of the world, and that it will be still worse than the Champagne fighting eighteen months ago, because for one thing the enemy have increased their numerical superiority and for another, they have achieved a substantially greater superiority with an incalculable quantity of equipment, guns, ammunition, airmen and so on.

4 August: We hear that Hindenburg has taken over the Supreme Command of the entire Eastern Front, including Austrian troops.

8 August: I move house to the Loermont site already mentioned, a hillside position which is given the official title 'Christian'; this position is, if anything, even more idyllic than the one down below on the edge of Evricourt village—it is in a meadow at the edge of a wood; there is still a huge amount to be done, what with reinforcing dug-outs and completing the concrete gun-pits. It's beautiful up here at this position, lonely as it is; the late summer days pass, full of atmosphere. In the evenings we sit at the guns and entertain each other; and in addition we get entertained by our Very light look-

* The author recalls Frederick the Great's phrase about himself as a 'rock of bronze'.—R.T.

out, who sits up a tree on observation duty and sings songs at the same time. This sentry is up there to keep track of the various coloured lights which the infantry fire off from time to time, since each colour has a different meaning for us, the field artillery. The colour codes are often changed, of course, so that the French don't find out what each colour means.

We hear from the Italian front that the town of Görz has been occupied by the Italians.

I still have duties in Noyon now and then, and these 'outings' make a nice change—you can actually go to a military club, what they call a *Kasino*, and have a meal at a table with a cloth on it, as though it were peacetime.

Our merchant U-Boat, the *Deutschland*, is supposed to be back already from her astonishing trip to America.

At the end of August, thank goodness, I was given another tour of duty with my infantry friends, occupying our O.P. and sharing quarters with Sergeant R. of 315 Trench Mortar Section. At the same time the French began to give us another good going-over with trench-mortar shells, and we had a fair number of casualties. We returned the fire, lobbing 250 heavy-calibre jobs with our trench mortars.

We hear in the meanwhile that the Bulgarian offensive in Macedonia is making progress, and that the Russian offensive has come to a halt.

Whereas Italy joined the Entente purely with a declaration of war against Austria, she has now sent an official declaration of war to us as well. And Roumania has sent one to Austria; and Germany one to Roumania. So Roumania, which had in fact been in alliance with us, just like Italy, has gone over to the enemy too. But these new 'Allies' will hardly be much use to the Entente, even though many of our troops will have to be taken from the East and West and thrown into action along the new fronts.

My friend Kirsten has been commissioned in the meanwhile and gazetted a second lieutenant, and it is sad that we have to be separated; he is being posted away to another battery.

31 August: Field-Marshal von Hindenburg has become Chief of the General Staff and is thus Supreme Commander of all troops and armies, and General Ludendorff has been made Quartermaster-General. It is a fair promise of success that these two supremely gifted military leaders should now be, as it were, *one* team. As far as the number of our enemies goes, the war seems to be approaching its maximum intensity —it just *must* bring us victory on all fronts!

Now we're into early September, and the gigantic battle of the Somme goes raging on with so far unheard-of violence and a huge expenditure of men and ammunition. It seems to be a combined operation by the Entente: here, over to our right, on the Somme; and over in the East the Russians attacking with a fresh assault in the Bukowina, and Roumania attempting to push into Transylvania—but they've all been brilliantly repulsed, on all fronts. Resistance on the Somme was particularly successful, where only Guillemont was lost; the barrage, which was quite near, has never been so dreadful as in these last few days. We read the army communiqués, which of course only give summaries of the brilliant exploits achieved by our troops, and perhaps we are the only people who can see and recognize the heroic deeds of hundreds of thousands of individual soldiers.

Meanwhile our Zeppelins have bombed London again, and Bucharest as well.

German and Bulgarian troops are advancing together in the Dobruja.

Over here, in the West, Captain Boelcke has shot down his 20th opponent.

On 5 *September* we had another little celebration in the Battery, the occasion being the successes on all fronts; it was very jolly, as always; the good-hearted chaps, once they have a bit of drink in them, start singing a mixture of folk-songs and military ditties, some gay and some sad; this time our accompaniment was a mouth-organ.

Meanwhile the Entente has managed to pull even Greece, which used to have friendly feelings for us, over to their side.

8 *September:* Big Bulgarian victory against the Roumanians at Tutrakan.

A highly unusual episode took place on the *11th:* a small

German fighter plane made a number of circular flights round our position, and then landed in a highly unorthodox manner on the meadow beside our battery. The pilot was 2/Lt von Mellenthin, using this method to come 'on a visit' to his father, the C.O. of the infantry regiment stationed in front of us. It sounds so simple, but it was such a daring and original thing to do, and we all felt highly enthusiastic when the young pilot flew off again. It was all the more shattering when we heard a day later that Mellenthin had been shot down on the Somme—as though it were a premonition of his death which had moved him to visit his father once more.

The French and British attack on the Somme goes on continuously; they lose 1,000 killed in action and replace them with 2,000 fresh troops. At first it was thought that a battle of this kind would have to be over in a few days, but now it's been going for weeks, and it may even last for months.

News from the Balkan theatre gets better and better: under Mackensen's command, troops of the Central Powers are pursuing the routed Russian-Roumanian army.

So my friend 2/Lt Kirsten has been posted away to another battery, but I see him now and again. If it doesn't get any livelier in our sector, I'll be able to go with 2/Lt Schellenberg and take a few days' leave in Brussels.

Now the autumn has come, and since everything somehow recalls memories of former times, these warm sunny autumn days remind one now of autumn holidays in one's childhood, or cycling tours with Professor Wünnenberg, the highly respected master at my old school, through the Rhineland and German Alsace-Lorraine. You catch hold of memories as though you could use them to bring old times back again.

An extraordinary thing has happened in the Balkans: the entire 4th Greek Army Corps has come over to our side.

On one of my short leaves in St Quentin I met, among other acquaintances, my former schoolfellow 2/Lt Prince Friedrich Wilhelm of Hesse, and now I hear that he has been killed in action during our victorious advance in Roumania; his twin brother, Prince Max of Hesse, whom I also went to school with, was a Darmstadt Dragoon and fell in Flanders as long ago as 1914. How many of my schoolfellows can still be alive?

20 September: Short leave to Brussels granted to Lt Schellenberg and myself. We travel via St Quentin. In the two hours we had to wait there, a very large number of troops, some in column of route, moved through the town, coming from the battle of the Somme, on their way to rest stations: they were ragged and filthy, with blunted nerves and indifferent expressions; while other troops, all fresh, clean and without a notion of what it was like, were pushing the other way, towards the Somme, to be sent straight into action.

We travelled on via Mons and Braine-le-Comte (memories of September, 1914) to Brussels, arriving in the evening. We were billeted in an elegant hotel. I have to describe this short trip in a bit more detail, because these days make such a weird contrast with front-line existence; because back here it is life, as opposed to being in the front line, continually stalked by death. My room, with a white, soft bed, is the most sumptuous place you could imagine, compared with my dirty dugout. And then we sit downstairs in the restaurant, with music playing and a good meal in front of us, and all round us, swarms of female creatures—what they call women! In the evening we go on a tour of the dance-places, and find this life very agreeable; people shouldn't mind us doing this, just as I don't mind there still being ways of amusing yourself at home—for who knows whether we're going to come back to enjoy it again? In one establishment a young second lieutenant was sitting next to me wearing the highest decoration, the *Pour-le-Mérite*: I recognized him at once, it was Lt Frankl, the celebrated fighter pilot.

Next day we strolled through the city, bought some things for our mates and ourselves, and had ourselves beautified at the barber's. What incredible contrasts, here and out there! The shops are bursting with surplus goods and luxury articles, as Belgium is being supplied by America. The city itself, which I only drove through briefly once in peacetime, in 1912, I find particularly pleasing; the Town Hall, the Saint-Gudule Cathedral and the Bourse are splendid. I meet a lot of people

I know, all on short-leave passes—what they call Front Leave. It's fun to meet again like this! In the evening there I am sitting in a restaurant with a nice little Belgian lady. What strange feelings you get, chatting once again with a not unintelligent female: what a long time one has missed such a thing!

Saying good-bye to Brussels was especially hard on account of this person; Berthe was her name. There are some people you can make friends with in a few hours and whom you feel you know as intimately as if you had known them for years. However, in general, Belgian civilians treat us Germans with very strong reserve indeed—it's nearly the same as hating us. If you talk to any Belgian, the conversation nearly always gets on to the subject of our Kaiser: they try to push the guilt for war on to him, although no one is more innocent of it than he, and no one tried to do more in the cause of peace, even at the last minute, than he did—but the seed of hate-propaganda has been coming up, and here is its fruit.

On the way back from Brussels we had an hour's halt at Namur, and I walked through the town and looked at all the places where we were billeted in September, 1914.

On the way up to the front the railway line was blocked with troop transports—large-scale movements of men from and to the Somme, and more disturbing sights: exhausted batteries and companies, worn out with fighting and incredibly dirty.

Back to the Battery in the evening; very soon you feel really well, fighting fit, a soldier at the front again.

25 *September* is another red-letter day, as Kurt comes to see me.

Now it's *October*. One day I learn that I've been 'put up', which means that I'll be commissioned any moment now. I'm endlessly pleased about it; it's happening very much thanks to that meeting a short time ago with our G.O.C., General Sack, who at the time, they say, was 'agreeably impressed' with me.

Captain Boelcke, our air hero, has been seriously wounded. The flying men, of whom many have already won the *Pour-le-Mérite*, are all going the same way as Immelmann, our first air hero: more's the pity.

3 October: Reinhardt, my Battery C.O., has been posted away to the Turkish Army, and my sorrow at the news is beyond description. His going away makes everything different; it seems that I've got to start a new life without him. It was only because of him that our No. 7 Battery had become almost a celebrity in our sector, for his keenness, bearing, confidence and skill had marked him as a personality from one end of the Division's lines to the other—just the same as he was in the Champagne in February, 1915. As he now made use of the opportunity at roll-call of taking his leave, and said good-bye, every single man of us had tears in his eyes, although getting soft was God knows something we had had ample time to forget these last two years. His successor is to be Lt Lindstedt, who for the moment however is on leave; 2/Lt Bremshey is acting C.O. in his absence.

Our defence on the Somme is still successful, and over in Transylvania we have had unparalleled victories.

Captain Boelcke has recovered from his wounds and shot down his 30th opponent.

Brilliant performance by the *U.53:* she broke through the blockade to America, where she got hold of a list of the out-going and homecoming ships, and at once proceeded with her torpedo programme.

In the Balkan theatre, Constanza has fallen, and the communiqué reads: 'The Russian-Roumanian enemy, who have been completely routed, are being pursued by our cavalry.'

Boelcke has shot down his 38th.

General von Falkenhayn has broken the last Russian resistance in Transylvania.

23 October: One radio message reads: 'Lance-Sergeant Sulzbach (that's me) is posted to No. 3 Group as Telephone Officer'.

I'm pleased with this interesting new posting with Captain Diebhold. The Group is a pool of infantry and artillery telephone officers. We not only have to improve the telephone network but also to develop the more recently introduced light signalling system. Captain Diebhold and 2/Lt Burchardi, the Adjutant, are particularly pleasant people. On this posting

I have a huge amount to do: we're always rushing about in the trenches and continually having conferences, some of them even with the Divisional Chief of Staff.

30 October: Boelcke has been killed in action after winning forty air battles. His name and Immelmann's can never be forgotten—they were heroes all through, fighters, knights of the air, human beings; we are all very much shaken by the news.

11 November: I've been commissioned, and gazetted a second lieutenant with effect from 3 November, 1916. It is really an inspiring moment and I am very pleased about it.

On the Somme the battle is still raging, and we get our marching orders—to the Somme. I have indeed predicted that we should not be spared this. After all these quiet months, off we go to the greatest battle ever known. We have actually been in all the major actions in the West, except Verdun, in spite of the quiet months at Evricourt. And so we are withdrawn from our Division, and on the march, at Noyon, our Divisional Commander, General Sack, solemnly takes leave of us. For the first time, on this occasion, I take my appointed place and salute in front of the front rank. It is a special honour for us to be pulled out of the Division and thrown into action on the Somme. On *18 November* we reach the village of Y. It is just not possible to describe what vast masses of troops are quartered in this tiny place—and all of them troops who are being thrown into action in this great, decisive battle. On top of this it is autumn, rain is falling, and the roads have been rutted and softened by the columns of lorries and troops on foot. As early as the evening of the *18th* our first section goes into position, and the rest of us follow. On Repentance Day, *Buss- und Bettag,* 1916, we go into firing positions at Pertain. For conditions on the Somme it seems to be a 'quiet' day. Nevertheless, our first impression is one of devastation, destruction and unspeakable horror. Pertain! Whatever does the place look like! The dismembered houses lie higgledy-piggledy all over the road, all equally dead, and what ought to be a village street is nothing but a boggy field, full of shell-holes; you can hardly walk along it, you keep stumbling. Then it starts humming and quaking. The heaviest calibre stuff is coming over; you do more lying than walking. Our battery is stationed on the outskirts of Pertain, among ruins and more shell-holes than you can count. German batteries of every calibre are standing as close as bits of bacon on a larded joint. The winter battle in the Champagne, which was bad enough in all conscience, was child's play compared with what is going on here. In a single day you get filthy enough to have been here weeks. We have a deep dug-out, with officers, N.C.O.'s and men lying jumbled together. Straight away, on the following day, I get ordered off to O.P. duties with the most advanced infantry position—that's at Ablaincourt, a place that has already made its name for heavy fighting, which often gets a mention in the communiqués. Vermandovillers and Soycourt lie behind me. Up at the front here there isn't a square metre of earth that hasn't been ploughed up: all that's left of the ground surface is shell-holes. There are observers from other batteries in our dug-out still, including some from the 3rd Guards Field Artillery Regiment. We sleep four together in a tiny recess; we have our telephone operators with us, but a telephone line is certainly never going to stay intact for long here. I take over, and receive my demarcation lines for barrage operations, and my targets: basically the cemetery near Ablaincourt. The following day the French and British plaster our battery with an endless barrage of shells. I get my battery's eye in with ranging shots at a few enemy targets; we're in luck, since for a short while the telephone cable stays intact. Looking through the stereo-telescope at the French sector, I spot on the Vermandovillers–Soycourt road column after column after column of motor transport, some of it ammunition, some of it infantry being taken to the front—driving past the whole day long. But we're not allowed to fire at this target, worthwhile as it is; we have to save ammunition in order to have some over when the beggars fall in to rush us. There is quite an exceptional amount of air activity, and with that we're beginning to get some fine weather. You often see dozens of enemy planes close together, and among them great big observation aircraft just drinking it all in from above without any sense of shame, faithfully watched in their turn by Newport fighter planes looping the loop as though every pilot were Pégoud himself. The enemy captive balloons can be seen in the background, quite close together, gloating across at us; it gives you a pretty uneasy feeling.

We manage to get in an average of 1,000 rounds a day without the enemy indulging in any large-scale attacks, for the moment anyway, but they're shelling us with heavy stuff all the time. The numbers of troops being brought up—I've mentioned them above—give cause, however, to conclude that a new attack is imminent. Pertain is under heavy fire, so that we aren't getting any rations, and all the cables are shot through. Over 3,000 rounds fell on Pertain in one afternoon, including heavy 22 and 28 centimetre shells. The regiment from my home town is supposed to have arrived at the village of Y, so Kurt Reinhardt will be there too.

24 November: The Emperor Francis Joseph of Austria has died.

In the Balkans Falkenhayn is pushing further on towards Bucharest.

26 November: We've had our first dead and wounded in the battery. The first few days, without producing a very large attack, were what one had imagined the Somme to be like— back-breaking. On the *29th* who should actually visit me here but my old and true friend Kurt. There is hardly any part of the French front left where we haven't met.

At home Hindenburg has introduced compulsory service for civilians, and the production of ammunition is being increased several times.

Meanwhile we receive marching orders to change position and go to the Péronne area. On the *30th* we march through Péronne, no, through the rubble that used to be Péronne; what a lovely place it must have been once! In the very early dawn we then go into position south of Bouchavesnes—an even more dismal area, believe it or not! Lt Lindstedt is commanding the battery, as I said. Next day I move into the O.P. in what they call the Pacquet Wood to operate as observer for our own regiment and the neighbouring regiment at the same time.

On 6 December the splendid news arrives that the 1st Bavarian Reserve Division has taken Bucharest. The supplies captured at Bucharest are very large, and the petroleum for our U-Boats is also worth mentioning.

When you are on O.P. duty in the Pacquet Wood you sometimes even have a quiet moment or two and can think things over. We war volunteers, really a very jolly lot, who were together in one battery at Evricourt in 1915–16 and went through everything nice and nasty together, have now nearly all gone up to second lieutenant, each of us in a different place—so these times too are finished and done with.

Now we've been three weeks on the Somme, and the Battle of the Somme has already been going for months; the aggressive spirit of the French and British still hasn't diminished, even though temporary lulls in the fighting occur, for these serve to enable battle-weary units to be restored to strength and ammunition to be brought forward, and of course, to enable fresh plans of attack to be prepared. It is clear winter weather, and German and enemy planes romp about overhead to their heart's content. This is what they call 'flying weather', and very disagreeable it is for us down below.

On 12 December we receive an Army Order by wireless for immediate announcement to all troops:

> Soldiers! Conscious of the victory which you have fought for and won by your courage, I and the Allied rulers have made an offer of peace. Whether the associated objective is achieved by this, remains undecided. Your duty continues to be this: with God's help, to stand firm!
>
> General Headquarters, 12 December, 1916.
>
> William I.R.

Any comment is superfluous, and we hope, hope and hope again!

20 December: Fighting has increased once more, large numbers of enemy captive balloons are strung along the horizon, pilots are humming about above us, and suddenly the enemy start up a barrage, which is liveliest near Barleux. They are shooting a lot of gas into our rear areas. We are laying down a continuous barrage. Once again, the enemy achieves nothing. It

is just not possible to say any more about these hostilities or to give any details.

24 December: Meanwhile I'm back in the battery on the gun-site, in the mud and dirt. Christmas Eve, the third I've spent in the field. This time the French show no regard for this, the highest and most beautiful of all holidays, and at 7 o'clock in the evening I am still having to lay down a continuous barrage. Everyone is very much on edge, and even if it doesn't come to a large-scale attack, it does go on bubbling and banging away along the whole Somme front. Then, late in the evening, I go round the individual guns and we pay a visit to our good lads in the deep dug-outs, where they snap their fingers at the Somme and sing away at *Silent Night.* All the Christmases so far have indeed aroused our deep, partly religious feelings, but this time, embroiled in this great battle, we are quite particularly moved. Everything round us has been shot to pieces; where trees, and avenues of trees, used to stand there now remain a handful of stumps a few inches high, and in spite of that our men have put up Christmas decorations in their dug-outs—a soldier can always get hold of something. Since mail arrived last night, every man has some little present from home lying in front of him. Today, too, reinforcements have just come up, straight from the regimental depot, to make up for our recent casualties; these new chaps are getting a proper idea of war, and a Christmas in the field as well! For once, not all the telephone cables have been shot through, and as far as possible we are saying Merry Christmas to each other along the line from battery to battery or company.

26 December: I have to go out with a telephone operator to take bearings, and the first place I walk across is the church-yard at Péronne. Whatever does it look like! Our guns stand among the shelled-out graves, and every day this churchyard, and a thousand others as well, are shot to rags by the French themselves—nothing is sacred, nothing survives the devastation of war. We went on through Biaches, which lies right on the Somme itself. Biaches village just doesn't exist any more. Our front-line trenches run through the ruined houses and cellars!

We take our bearings and get back safely. You keep having the impression that the very front line is the safest place, and that the worst parts are these walks from Battery to the infantry lines, because the ground between is permanently under fire, and irregular fire at that; whereas when you're an old front-liner, which we have gradually managed to become, you do know your well-beloved enemy's shooting pattern, when it is a pattern. Back through Péronne, that is, through the rubble that used to be that handsome town. Every day the ruins and the rubble get shot into smaller fragments, over and over again. The roads are full of enormous craters.

Meanwhile America has been trying to negotiate, and through Wilson at that, but even this attempt seems to be failing.

One day a little later I'm in Biaches once again, checking my barrage fire, then visit other battery commanders who are up at the front on O.P. duty, and the company commanders who belong with us.

On the way back, near Bussu, I was jolly nearly finished off: once again, the French were shooting into the gully like lunatics, as though they really meant to get me, and I had to chuck myself from one shell-hole into another, right in all the sludge and filth.

Lt Reinhardt has, I hear, been awarded the Prussian Life-Saving Medal.

31 December: So there's another year of war reaching the end of the calendar. Even if the last few weeks on the Somme have been rough for us personally, the Western Front has lost none of its firmness, and in all other theatres of war we are winning victory after victory. Our hopes that the New Year will bring us peace are really justifiable.

Our New Year's Eve party on the Somme, with a few drinks all round, was really quite cheerful, all things considered. The different units got on the telephone to wish each other a happy new year.

The peace offer which I've already mentioned, made by His Majesty, seems to have been rejected by the Entente powers.

IV

1917

THE first days of January are passing with the usual medium-calibre shelling. Every few days, fortunately, we get our mail. On 5 *January* I am ordered to proceed to the rear, duties in St Quentin again, and as always, I meet people in the town whom I know, one after the other, including a man with whom I was in the Lille fighting in October, 1914. Half-way through the joys of seeing him again, up came Lt Becker to speak to me too. Our joy and astonishment were just indescribable! He left us a year ago, became an airman, had a crash, and now he's a gunner again in the field artillery. We had so much to tell each other that we sent messages to our C.O.'s by wireless, asking for twelve hours' leave: we got it too. I won't need to relate *how* we celebrated our meeting. To make sure we didn't forget the Battle of the Somme, damn it, French planes came over in the night and dropped some very large stuff indeed. Next morning I also paid a visit to a French couple whom 2/Lt Reinhardt used to stay with, and they were very pleased to see me. Once more, however, I found it shattering to see the poor, wretched life which the civilian French are leading; they are having to put up with much more now, because the town is getting shelled, and bombed from the air as well; it doesn't belong completely to the rear area any more. But then I always tell myself 'Why feel pity?'—they are our arch-enemies, who after all only want the worst to happen to us—but still: they only hate us out of love for their own country, France!

So the enemy Allies really have rejected our peace offer.

God grant that one day they'll have to come whining for it themselves!

On one of the next quiet days I rode over to Vaux, where Kurt was stationed. We spent a lovely day, and also visited a fighter squadron stationed at Vaux, consisting of fourteen Albatross single-seaters. They're up and about all day in the beautiful flying weather, going on air patrol in threes; they loop the loop, come whanging down in power dives and climb to 3,000 metres in a few minutes. How perfect flying has become!

A few days later I get posted back to the infantry for several days of O.P. duty; I'm stationed below Radegonde Church with the company commander, 2/Lt Willweber of No. 12 Company, 2nd Foot Guards Regiment, and in these few days we very naturally become good companions. We have our residence deep down below in the company of vaults and tombs, and in normal circumstances being down here would give you the cold shivers, but we get used to anything; our feelings have been more than adequately blunted. Even if these Guards Regiments of ours haven't got their peacetime cadre any more—those men must all be lying in their graves by now, in France or Russia—the present Guardsmen are still an elite; it's marvellous to talk to these splendid men. I do a check inspection on our anti-tank gun, because it's just here that these dreadful tanks have been used as assault weapons by the enemy, and we found out at once how to allow for them: in each sector we have one anti-tank gun, which only fires when tanks are sighted. I report this gun to the C.O. of the 2nd Foot Guards Regiment; he is also doing check inspections at the moment. His unit, the battalion stationed here, is relieved on *12 January*. I say good-bye to 2/Lt Willweber. One more of all those good-byes when you wish each other 'all the best'. You separate, and who knows whether you'll ever see each other again!

I've spent six days up here at the front without there being any particular hostilities, even if there is a bit of isolated fighting every day; it is defence all right, it is doing your duty, even if you haven't anything more, special or otherwise, to put in your notebook. On *15 January* it is officially stated that the Battle of the Somme ended on 26 November, 1916.

What we've been having since, up to the present, was just after-effects, but these seven weeks were nevertheless filled with heavy fighting and single actions. We were therefore still able to join in nine days of the greatest defence battle so far recorded in history. Officially, hostilities since 26 November up to the present are called 'Static hostilities on the Somme'.

Our troops are gradually being equipped with steel helmets.

Mackensen has been awarded the Grand Cross of the Order of the Iron Cross.

It is the end of January and 15 degrees C. below zero. For one day I take over the job of steering our No. 8 Battery; their O.P. is in Péronne itself, and I spend twenty-four hours there. I didn't know these gun-crews before I went there. We make preparations for an operation which bears the beautiful name *Giftpille*—'Poison Pill'. This job provides a lot for me to do; I have to go on a long walk to the 2nd Guards Regimental Staff H.Q. and then along the trenches near Barleux. There's a great deal going on there: the Battery Commanders from the field-gun, howitzer and mortar batteries all want to do their range-firing, and it has to be done inconspicuously so that the French don't notice anything. The dug-outs up at the front were icy cold, and you felt frozen and hungry. I spent the night up at the front, because during the day in question I didn't get round to range-firing with my own battery. Next day there was a terrible crush round the only telephone, as every commander wanted his own battery's range-firing to be done quickly. A little operation like this, the kind we did plenty of back at Le Plémont, needs very careful preparation, in this sector particularly. There are all kinds of officers together up at the front now, they don't know each other and have never seen each other before, but goodness, what a marvellous comradeship dominates us all from the very first moment! Everyone is helping someone else, obliging someone else, giving someone else something to eat. Yes, there are an endless number of little details and attitudes, so many that you can't write them all down, but they culminate in one very fine word: comradeship.

They say that the stepped-up U-Boat campaign is supposed to be starting.

On *3 February* I go up to the front again near Baleux and get back dead tired to the battery in the evening.

Then on *4 February* the balloon goes up for 'Poison Pill', and it goes off like a military exercise: artillery preparation, a small infantry assault, and we take thirty prisoners, ten British and twenty French. We laid down a barrage for half an hour, and unluckily had a few wounded on our side as well.

There is a threat that diplomatic relations with America are going to be broken off.

8 February: My third birthday in the field. I've fallen sick with a septic throat and have to go to hospital, via St Quentin and then on to Le Cateau and Sains du Nord; all the military hospitals there are broken up into small departments, and I have a room in a converted villa. I feel really dreadful and am being very well looked after.

At first the days in hospital are very boring because I have to stay in bed. At the end of February I'm allowed to get up for the first time. Meanwhile I've made friends with two fellow-patients in the same ward, a wounded second lieutenant from a mortar battalion and another second lieutenant, a sapper. Little by little we are allowed to go out and find a bit of variety in one canteen or another, or in what they call the Rear Area Cinema. You manage to get a lot of time for reading and give your nerves a thorough rest.

8 March: Count Zeppelin, the inventor of the Zeppelin airship, has died. What a crowd of memories his name brings back to me! I've been an enthusiastic Zeppelin fan since 1905! Nearly all the Zeppelins used to make their first run to Frankfurt-am-Main when completing their trials over Germany, and I never missed a single occasion when one of them arrived. At home I've got the most splendid photos, which I took myself, of nearly all the Zeppelin airships.

Incidentally, while I was in hospital I received the Iron Cross Second Class, for which I had been recommended first by 2/Lt Reinhardt in December, 1914.

On *10 March* I went out for the day to meet Kurt. Took the train to Aulnoye, then on with a goods train. The engine-driver was obliging enough to take the train through Haumont so slowly that I was able to jump off. From there I travelled on to Maubeuge, and there we duly met. It was one of our most rewarding meetings, as we had a great deal to tell each other. We had a meal together and then got a lift to Pissotieux, near St Vaast, where Kurt's battery is at rest station, not far from Valenciennes. Enchanting country and not a trace of war. I passed an amusing evening with Kurt and the other battery officers and spent the night there as their guest. Kurt went up to Second Lieutenant as early as 1915— he'd been a cadet, *Fahnenjunker*, then *Fähnrich*—and now he's going from our old regiment, the 63rd, to the Flying Corps.

On the afternoon of *11 March* we separated, and I got a lift back to Aulnoye, a big junction of various railway lines. A huge amount doing there: there's an information centre for troop movements, crammed with chaps on leave and reinforcements looking for their units. Back at Sains in the evening. Meanwhile a very jolly crowd has got together there, consisting of eight second lieutenants, from the most varied branches of the service but all with front-line service, who sit together every evening.

Baghdad, I regret to record, has been taken by the British. This is the first nasty defeat sustained by the Turks.

A revolution is reported to have broken out in Petersburg.

In one month of stepped-up U-Boat warfare, our U-Boats have sunk 780,000 tons.

In mid-March, we start the planned withdrawal of German forces from the Ancre; brilliantly conceived, too, because it appears that the Somme area, with all its shell-holes, would have been an impossible place for our troops to remain in on grounds of health alone. Now, I'm afraid, my well-beloved Noyon is going to move into the firing-line and I shan't see it again.

Now and then we go for long walks, and the nicest ramble is to Avesnes, a clean, petit-bourgeois little French town full of civilians and with many tea-shops—that's the main thing. We visit the little cathedral there, and hear a lance-sergeant playing the organ quite wonderfully.

Outside it's gradually turning to spring.

I am not missing anything at my regiment, because that sector is quiet.

I've never been able to read so much as I can now, and I'm especially fond of the Nordic writers.

The revolution in Russia is still in progress, the Czar has abdicated, and his brother is in office. It seems that the Russian steam-roller, which was going to crush us, has itself been crushed.

The spring weather is so warm that we can lie about in the garden in the open air.

I'm more or less well again now, and hope to take some leave and then get back to my regiment.

On the Western Front, in the meanwhile, the territory between Arras and the Aisne has been relinquished, and with it the towns I know so well: Péronne, Roye and Noyon. The French and British are reporting an advance in their communiqués, but they're certainly not going to get any further than our planned defence position (the Siegfried Line). Our withdrawal is a strategic masterpiece, as the Swiss press calls it, and while we occupy a beautifully-prepared new defence position, the French have to sit in a shell-torn wilderness, where there are no roads and hardly any water.

Von Richthofen has shot down his 20th opponent. It's a pity that Guynemer, the French Richthofen, has accounted for his 35th.

Meanwhile the auxiliary cruiser *Möwe*, with Captain Count Dohna-Schlodien in command, is back from her second cruise, after sinking 27 enemy ships and taking 580 prisoners.

Several of my hospital companions have meanwhile made their way back to their units, and the jolly circle of friends has been torn apart and scattered to the winds— it's 'good-bye' all the time.

And now we've got into April. Time really goes very quickly here. You think a lot about the war; it was actually intended only to be a sort of intermezzo in one's life, and now it will soon have lasted three years, and sometimes everything seems like a bad dream, but one that we have to dream for years and years.

State of war with America. You feel pretty dubious when

you consider that this huge, rich country is now going to furnish active support—both troops and equipment—to the British and French. The economic position at home doesn't seem to look too rosy any more either. But we have to stick it out and win through to a victorious finish.

On *Easter Monday 1917* I steamed off home on leave. It was very hard to say good-bye to my remaining hospital comrades and to the good sisters.

The general situation is that we have occupied the Siegfried Line on the Western Front. Meanwhile, Lt von Richthofen has shot down his 36th opponent, he wanted to become a Boelcke, and he's done so. His squadron has shot down a whole British group over Douai—not one of them got away.

And so I sit in the train, making for Cologne; it's marvellous to be swinging along in an express. The communiqué for the day reports a huge new battle in progress near Arras.

On *10 April* I am in Cologne, and then travel on through Mainz to Frankfurt-am-Main. See my parents, friends and acquaintances once again.

The new large-scale battle in Flanders rages on and on: the enemy has not achieved anything; the attempt at a break-through has so far broken its teeth on the heroic courage displayed by our troops.

Peace is on the point of being declared with Russia.

I go for walks in Frankfurt and revive memories with friends from my childhood days.

Fate once more ordains that I see my friend Kurt Reinhardt here in Frankfurt on this occasion as well, and also my much-respected 2/Lt Reinhardt, but the pair of them are here for a sad reason: their father has been very seriously wounded and is on his deathbed. I go for walks with my father in the beautiful *Stadtwald* [the municipal forest] but nothing has stayed the same as it used to be. A terrible burden is lying on us all, and we are no longer able to be in proper good spirits. Only sometimes, with the aid of drink, do we occasionally develop an appearance of gaiety.

I go on a trip to Karlsruhe to see my brother, who is back at the barracks in Strasburg. He is a lance-sergeant of horse, a *Vizewachtmeister*, with the Hussars, and although he's several years older than I am, he has to walk on my left to comply with regimental orders: but it seems odd all the same.

On the 22nd I leave Frankfurt, as my leave is running out, and I travel with my mother to Berlin, where my sister is also on a visit: Berlin life, and the general goings-on seem to be as brilliant as they used to be—but there's nothing behind it, and the gaiety is only whitewash.

Richthofen has got his captaincy now, he's a *Rittmeister*, and he's shot down his 47th opponent.

On the evening of the 26th I leave Berlin, travelling east, for meanwhile my regiment has gone to the Russian front! I stop a bit at Munich, then off I go in the train, bound for the Eastern theatre. In the train I meet Paul Graetz, the actor, on his way to a guest appearance in Bucharest, and we team up with each other. In the evening we reach Vienna, which is full of people. Can't find a room anywhere, but my luck is in and I agree to share a room with a naval officer.

28 April: Vienna in the rain is rather disappointing. But what a splendid city, and what lovely buildings! I go for a walk with my naval room-mate and get the impression that the war has had less effect on Vienna than it has on Berlin; for instance, the cars still have real tyres, while in Berlin they are nearly all running on iron ones. The difference between rich and poor is much more drastic than it is in Berlin, and what's more, everybody's still got his *Mehlspeise*, his cakes, that is— all the things that you don't see much in Berlin. One thing I did find disagreeable to see—German and Austrian service-men hardly bothering to salute each other, and discipline getting slack here, too.

On 29 April I travel on, with Paul Graetz and Harry Walden, towards Budapest. In the compartment I get to know some Hungarian officers, who seem very good chaps indeed. We travel through marvellous country, and suddenly there is Budapest spread out before me, on the broad Danube. I stop at an hotel with Paul Graetz; I've got two days to take a good look at this beautiful city. The war really does seem to have had even fewer adverse effects here. All the peacetime food is available, and there's an elegance about the place which makes you gasp. And there's no means of telling whether this sumptuous living is genuine or just a matter of dancing on the volcano. Terrific crowds are thronging the splendid promenade embankments, the cafés are crammed, and much of the time you can even sit outside in the warm spring weather.

30 April: I travel on to Lemberg [L'vov]. Twenty-two hours in the train. Really charming, this green Hungarian country, so lush, rich and varied; past the Tokay area, past the Carpathians where the Russians were thrown out neck and crop exactly two years ago. Gradually the country begins to take on Eastern characteristics. The train stops frequently and you get sumptuous food at the stations. The inhabitants are all tumbled together—Czechs, Slovenes, Slovaks—a colourful mixture. The train pants uphill to the Lubkow Pass; gentle valleys and deep gorges, and the River San flowing along beside the track. The Hungarian peasants are interesting; they sometimes do their ploughing with oxen, strange beasts with very wide-spreading horns, or else using the most splendid Hungarian horses. I am really very taken with the Hungarian landscape and all these new things to see, and fall asleep in the train, which carries me into the *1st of May.* Here I am in Lemberg; I clean myself up and walk through this typical Galician town. You see numbers of Jews about with long beards and ringlets, and the town itself looks as old as the hills. While I'm in Lemberg I visit my Cousin Vera, whose husband is a regimental C.O.: he's commanding a Hungarian regiment on the Eastern Front. At mid-day I travel through Krasnoe to Zolochev, that's the last railway station before you get to the front, and from there struggle out to my regiment —to No. 8 Battery, where I've been posted. It's a strange district, consisting of endless fir-woods sprinkled with a few deciduous trees; there are many bogs running through the woods, full of noisy frogs. The tiny Galician villages with low-built half-timbered houses and thatched roofs look quite charming. There are Austrian, Hungarian and German troops stationed here. The gun-positions are sited in a beautiful piece of woodland.

The first thing I find out on joining my regiment is that

Becker, my comrade and former second lieutenant, was killed in action at St Quentin, the very place where we spent such pleasant hours together.

I feel very happy in my new battery; some of my comrades from No. 7 Battery have been posted here too. We have overground dug-outs instead of underground ones—they're half below ground level, half above it—which shows what a peaceful area this has been so far. The O.P. is up in a tree, and Brody lies opposite the O.P., inside the enemy lines. We belong to the 18th Austrian Army Corps and to the Boehm-Ermolli Army. I ramble over to the infantry positions to see our trench O.P.'s—you can take your horse almost up to the front-line positions, because the thick woods shield us from the Russians.

The 10th Hungarian Infantry Regiment is stationed in our sector; the imminent declaration of peace with Russia seems to be coming true, because at the moment not a shot is being fired—the two sides are even bartering goods and newspapers. It gave one a strange feeling to be stationed side by side with our Hungarian allies; they sit in the trenches and play the most mournful songs on a sort of recorder which they whittle themselves. There are anemones and cowslips blooming all about you, and you feel you've been taken back to peacetime; in the evenings the cuckoo calls just like he does at home, and the frogs and birds strike up a marvellous mixed concert. In the little Galician farmhouses, nearly at the front, you can buy butter, eggs, sausage and cheese—and hunting is provided for as well, for here, roebuck, pheasant and heron can all be found. I celebrate a reunion with my friend 2/Lt Kirsten. I can't help making comparisons with the mass death on the Western Front when I see, for instance, our horses cropping the grass inside the gun-sites. I used to imagine that Galicia was nothing but dirt and lice, and it is actually quite different.

The Emperor Charles of Austria is holding an inspection of delegates from all the seven divisions stationed here, at Krasnoe.

I hear that my old comrade from No. 7 Battery, Bombardier Lenne, a war volunteer and an attorney in civil life, has died on the Western Front after receiving terrible wounds. Another of my dear comrades gone; he was a particularly serious-minded person with a wide range of human experience. The news moved me quite exceptionally; I had met him on my last leave, and it seems to me now that he too had premonitions of his own death.

On the Western Front a new, huge-scale battle is in progress near Arras and the Chemin des Dames. The French are running full-tilt at our positions with an unbelievable weight of armaments, with the idea of forcing a break-through.

8 May: I go off on a duty ride through the rear area: I make my way through splendid woods, almost like the wild, natural background to some romantic tale, young fresh greenery everywhere, birds singing and a bright blue sky. Fabulous.

Towards evening I went up into our observation tree and saw Brody lying spread out before me, and Russian soldiers strolling about; behind the Russian front you can see a good-sized château, which belongs to the Czarina and has golden domes on the roof in the Russian style.

2/Lt Schellenberg told me in the evening how dreadful the retreat from the Ancre to the Siegfried Line had been, particularly hard for the civilians as they were being moved from the evacuated villages; many families being torn apart and scattered to the winds as they were shifted to the rear. Stories are also told about the brilliance of the enemy spy operations—but ours are working brilliantly too.

A few days later I had to go on another duty ride towards the rear. I did some shopping for the battery at Sokolovka; this village almost makes you think of the East—all the little houses with balconies in front.

Next day I was in the trenches on O.P. duty with the Austrian Chasseurs, and as I got back to my battery, I received the news that I had been posted to the Fifth Field Artillery Regiment on the Western Front. I was being posted, with a few other second lieutenants from my regiment, to make good the heavy officer casualties suffered by the Fifth in the great new battle, just mentioned above, now raging on the Chemin des Dames. Well—I'm filled with mixed feelings, because I don't like leaving my comrades; and it's a great contrast to move from this peace and quiet into a new battle of battles. I packed my gear in great haste, said farewell to my friends, took formal leave of my C.O., bade farewell to this peaceful fairy-tale country and steamed off on *13 May* with my fellow-officers on this posting, through Lemberg, the famous Przemyśl and Cracow through lovely country to Oderberg; from there, on and on to Breslau; here I parted company with my comrades, arranging to meet them in Frankfurt-am-Main on 17 May to resume our journey to the Western Front, and dashed off for another quick visit to my dear friend Kurt, who was stationed at Breslau with the Eleventh Air Corps Reserve Group. He was quite exceptionally surprised and glad, and we passed some pleasant hours in conversation.

In the evening I travelled on to Berlin. My mother and sister were there on a visit and I surprised them as well—having in fact only said good-bye to them three weeks before, as I was leaving for the Eastern Front. I spent two days with them, then on the *16th* off I went to Frankfurt-am-Main, visited my friends there, and then off west in the train for the great shemozzle on the Aisne. A childhood sweetheart of mine* went with me as far as Cologne; we had a pleasant journey together, the pair of us and my fellow-officers—we were as jolly as though we were off for the summer holidays.

Once past Brussels it was the old route via Hirson to the Seventh Army H.Q. at Marle; then off again at 2 in the morning for Laon, which I reached dog-tired at 4.30 a.m.; and then further, through Ardon, to my new regiment, the Fifth. The road from Ardon to the front presents the well-known picture from my heavy fighting days: troops, troops and more troops. I soon found the command post and reported to my new C.O., Major von Ohnesorge. I've been posted to No. 2 Battery. Report to my new Battery Commander, he's a chap one will soon be friends with. The first impression I receive of the Silesians—who are quite new to me—is excellent, splendid young chaps who will be friends with you at the drop of a hat. I then report to my Battalion Commander as well, and in the evening I'm at the new gun-positions. It starts off properly straight away: the French attack with unbelievable

* Friedl Schneider.

quantities of artillery, and after I've got quickly into the drill, we lay down a curtain barrage and strafe the enemy at an unbelievable rate of fire. It's a dangerous job for the columns bringing up ammo and rations, as all the approach roads are lying under a blistering fire. Making my way out to the battery was horrible for me too, because even if you avoided the heavy fire on the roads, the French were shooting away like fury at the plough and woodland as well; you needed hours to cover a few kilometres towards the front, because you were always having to throw yourself flat on the ground. And so now we go on firing ourselves, and the French don't achieve anything. The enemy put 800 rounds of the heaviest-calibre stuff into our battery area on one afternoon alone: the position looks like a field of craters.

Next day I took a bombardier with me and went on officer's rounds: it was terribly hard getting out to the front-line trenches near Filain, the place I got to know when I visited Kurt there a year ago, still in quite a peaceful state. Whatever does Filain look like now: a mound of rubble! I am the artillery liaison officer, and went along to the Berthe-Ferme, which we had only just re-taken. I report to the Battalion Commander, who puts me in the picture; we relieve each other on observation duty. One day in the large-scale fighting and in the shelled-out trenches, and a bit of time in the battery as well, have very quickly restored my practical knowledge of fighting in the West. I didn't have a very long spell of it on the peaceful Eastern Front, did I—hardly a week! Here it is thundering and banging away: the French want to soften us up with their incredible weight of fire, but we're *not* going to let them through on any account. After my tour of duty we creep and stalk our way back to the battery position— and that's another difficult exercise; the French are just laying down a curtain barrage on the strips of territory in question, and especially in Monampteuil we have a huge quantity of stuff thrown at us. It really does go against the grain to be shelled in a hole like that; we do an about turn, whip back up to the front line in the trenches once again, and finally have to sit for hours in a deep dug-out because it is absolutely impossible to get back to the battery through this crazy shellfire. As things get a bit calmer around midnight, we try again and actually reach the battery in one piece. Next day I have to do the same officer's rounds up to the front as before, and go through another compulsory performance of the same nonsense. However, I have to be back at Battery at 5 o'clock, cost what it may, to relieve my Battery Commander, and I'm hardly back there when the French start to attack on a gigantic scale. Our own counter-attack now starts, on the quarries west of Berthe-Ferme. All our combined batteries lay down a barrage for just a quarter of an hour; then the infantry assault begins. In no time at all we've taken 15 officers and 500 men prisoner. Towards evening yet another quarry is lost and we and the French are shelling in competition with each other.

Those were two days of real large-scale fighting, at times even heavier than action on the Somme and a thousand times worse than it was in Flanders or the Champagne in the early war years. Each new struggle for a break-through sets a genuine new record for massive weight of men and equipment.

I'm only just beginning to be able to take a look at our gun-positions: they lie in a hollow, and it must be a beautiful district, if one can imagine it before it had been shelled! There is nothing left at all of the beautiful trees, not a scrap.

As I foresaw, I soon made friends with my Battery Commander, 2/Lt Knauer, and with Zimmer, one of my fellow-second lieutenants.

The following day the shelling began to rage once more. It's nearly reached a proportion of 1,000 rounds coming back from the French for every 100 rounds we fire—and the calibres of the French stuff!

The evening falls, and the fighting dies down. Once more I make the beautiful and comforting discovery that birds do not worry about all this large-scale dying—they sing and twitter whether the barrage is raining shells or not, and give great pleasure to us, who are now hardly men at all.

Meanwhile I'll soon have been here a week, it's Whit Sunday—there are no holidays for us, of course. Will life as it used to be ever really come back?

Our regiment and our division are completely worn out with

fighting, so we are to be relieved. This actually becomes a fact, and on *28 May*, at 2.30 in the morning, the quietest possible time, we pull out, after the battery which is going into position has occupied our gun-sites. We move off through Nouvion to the camp at Étouvelles, and there is no shelling. We sit about in the open in this little wood, eat our fill, and enjoy the peace and quiet after the last few really dreadful days. I get to know my fellow-officers from the other batteries —most of them have been invited over this evening by 2/Lt Knauer, my Battery Commander, as his guests. We are in a good mood, we chaps who survived that battle, we sing away and don't give a thought to the next battle—when it comes along, perhaps it will be our turn.

And now it will soon be three years since I went to war, and my diary, which I've been keeping since the very beginning, is not only a personal reminder for me; when one of these notebooks is written full, I send it home to my parents for them to read. Actually, however, I should like to think it was meant to be read by others, not only by my parents— sometimes I wish it could be read aloud to everyone who has stayed at home. That may sound presumptuous of me, but all I mean is that the people who have stayed at home— *you* people at home—have really no notion of what it's like to fight this war! And you have even less idea of the incredible performance achieved by every last man of the thousands, millions of German soldiers! And all this with a way of taking their own heroism for granted and with such particular devotion, faith and conviction, such determination and com- radeship, as the world has never yet seen! If you roll all that together you call it duty, and simply doing our duty has produced the situation that right up to this day we have defied a world full of enemies and are resisting successfully. For God's sake hold fast at home with us out here!

So now we are at rest stations; you go into rest stations when the unit has fought itself weary and needs a little refresher to compensate for the losses of men and horses. But the intervals between front-line service and rest are getting longer, we haven't got the same huge reserves as our enemies—they can actually afford to relieve every division after only a few days.

29 May: Starting from our rest stations, we ride to Laon, a fine town on a hill, whose main feature, the splendid cathedral, can be seen from a long way off. 2/Lt Schmidt, known as *Pieselmax*, has been posted to my battery, No. 2, so that with the Battery Commander, 2/Lt Knauer, 2/Lt Zimmer, whom I've already mentioned, *Pieselmax* and me, there are four officers altogether.

31 May: We break camp on a boiling hot day and move along dusty main roads through Ardon to Toulis, where we spend the night. In the morning we had a look at a fighter squadron which was stationed there. I feel more and more liking, enthusiasm and downright longing for flying as time goes on.

1 June: Move further on to Autreppe, good billets; great celebrations at getting proper beds. We can buy eggs here, a rare pleasure; we have a bit of music in the evenings at the village schoolmistress's house, and have a mandoline, a guitar and a fiddle to accompany us.

2 June: Day's march to Etroeungt, quite near Sains du Nord, where my military hospital was. I'm the billeting officer for the battalion, and since so far I've nearly always managed to find billets with proper beds for every officer and man, I receive many grateful signs of appreciation. In the evening I borrow a bike, ride the short distance into Sains du Nord and visit the nurses who looked after me, and my fellow-patients who are still there. A very cheerful reunion!

So now we are deep inside the rear area; you notice what a well-provided and peaceful war you can lead back here if you're an other rank or an officer with a lines of communication job.

We march on on the *3rd* and on the *4th* reach our objective, Roisin, near the Franco-Belgian border. We have fine billets, the village is peaceful and lavishly provided with food of various kinds. We are supposed to be staying here a few weeks. We *Lieutenants* from No. 2 Battery have been put up in a big farmhouse occupied by a middle-aged mother with two daughters aged 18 and 25, and a son in his mid-20's; they are middle-class people with nearly the same manners as townspeople, and we have our first conversation with them; they are friendly, but reserved.

We begin to have our duties allocated. I am in charge of training officer cadets and also have to train the gunners. In these rest days we also get given lectures on all the new technical gadgets and about the lessons learned from the latest defence battles. Every order, every instruction, breathes the spirit of Ludendorff. In the evenings we sometimes have a bit of music, and the daughter of the house sometimes listens; the younger one especially is more confiding and good-natured; it's possible to talk to her about anything.

I get a great deal of pleasure from my duties, especially instructing.

On 8 *June* I played host for the first time and invited most of the officers from my own regimental batteries stationed here: the battery commanders, the battery officers, the regimental Adjutant, the paymaster, and so on. The evening was very pleasant, we had a well-filled menu and of course a decent amount of fluid refreshment; then we improvised a concert, and about midnight we had achieved a pretty exuberant mood and fell into bed with a fair load on board. So there at least I've made my number with all my fellow-officers, and from the very first day I've been with this regiment and among these chaps I've really felt exceptionally happy. I feel I've been with the 5th Field Artillery Regiment for years. What a warm and friendly little speech was made by the regimental Adjutant, Lieutenant Stürken, for my benefit!

Since our Battalion Commander is on leave, my battery commander is acting commander of the Battalion and I'm acting commander of my own battery—for the first time, even if it's only at rest stations. At mid-day the regimental band plays in our village, with our men and the local civilians standing all around, chatting together very peaceably.

Another day we had some shooting practice with live rounds on a range, and since we are to stay here some time, all of us are getting our turn to go on leave. This time I don't feel all that pleased to be going; I feel I'd rather stay here with my regiment. When I'm going on leave on *12 June* and am just saying good-bye to Roisin, the farmer's daughter says: '*Je garderai un bon souvenir de vous.*' I was very pleased about that. I travelled to Valenciennes and from there via Brussels to Cologne.

On *13 June*, about noon, arrived at Frankfurt-am-Main. Joyful reunion with my parents after these hard weeks, and my friends very pleased as well.

I don't know why it is, but when you're a very small second lieutenant, you get to know many more people—and young girls—than you did when you were a civilian. As though tongues were more easily loosened nowadays. Perhaps it's a fact that the ladies feel they ought to be nicer to us when we're in field-grey than otherwise.

King Constantine of Greece has had to abdicate.

I'm spending my free hours with my girl-friend Bob.

My brother has become engaged to a Swedish lady.*

These days I can't help thinking of a poem sent to my sister by one of her admirers when he had seen her wearing a widow's veil after Georg's death, without knowing that Georg had been killed in action:

> *Da sah ich dich wieder, in tiefer, stummer Trauer*
> *Den Witwenschleier um das junge Haupt,*
> *Und mich ergriff ein heil'ger Wehmutsschauer:*
> *Des Kriegs Gewalt hat dir dein Glück geraubt.*

> So now you stood, racked, silent, and did dumbly mourn,
> Your young head darkened by that veil of pain,
> And all my thoughts with solemn grief were torn
> For this your joy that greedy war has slain.

I made use of my leave to go on an outing to Wiesbaden and on another to Homburg, as I love the Taunus and these Taunus cities. On another occasion I went back to school and looked at my *Gymnasium*—but there was hardly a soul there whom one knew, as even the younger boys whom one could hardly remember had turned field-grey in the meanwhile; it made one really melancholy to go back inside the building.

Another day I travelled with my mother to Munich to meet

* Kerstin, the daughter of August Strindberg the playwright.

my brother and his fiancée. We spent two splendid days in Munich, and had a particularly affectionate reunion with my brother.

Two days later I travelled on to Nuremberg, and was really enchanted by this ancient and picturesque city. And then on to Frankfurt, where I gave my father an impression of his new daughter-in-law.

On 27 June my leave was over, and I looked forward once more to getting back to the front, all the more since saying good-bye has become to a certain extent easier and easier every time I come home on leave. My childhood sweetheart went with me, and we travelled in glorious weather on the Rhine steamer from Mainz to Coblenz, and from Coblenz on to Cologne.

28 June: I've seen the cathedral for the first time, just as a mass was being said, and I was, as much as anyone, almost overwhelmed by the power of this splendid building.

I said good-bye to Cologne and the Rhine and travelled on to Brussels, where I discovered at the City Commandant's office that my regiment had gone back to firing positions.

2/Lt Ullmenroeder had just shot down his 30th opponent and received the *Pour-le-Mérite*, when he was himself killed in action. Richthofen has lost Kestner and Schäfer from his squadron, and now Ullmenroeder as well.

30 June: Reached Laon, and took 3½ hours from there to the regiment, which is at firing positions near Sissonne, that is at the junction of the 7th and 8th Army sectors. The limbers are stationed near Malmaison.

I'm just thinking back to the mood which I found people in at home: my impression is that they were depressed, but by no means in despair, and the mass of the nation are patiently putting up with everything as though it had never been any different.

I have already noted that Greece was threatening to go over to the Entente, and now it's actually happened.

A rumour is circulating that the British have put a price on Richthofen's head—£5,000 and the Victoria Cross. Richthofen is the terror of the French and British, and not only Richthofen: his heroic exploits alone are quite enough to induce more and more airmen to train themselves up to his standard.

Although Russia is in a state of revolution, the Entente has managed to get the Russians to attack once more—but they won't really be able to achieve much.

2 July: I reach my gun-positions. We are stationed to the left of the famous, hotly contested *Winterberg*, the 'Winter Hill', about 25 kilometres from Laon, and south-east of us lies Rheims; or, more narrowly defined, our position lies between Craonne and Berry-au-Bac. Our position is well dug in, with deep dug-outs, but we are quite near that lousy Champagne country. At the front it is barren and empty and comparatively quiet—what we people call 'quiet'! We have a reunion party —2/Lts Knauer, Schmidt and Zimmer. We still talk a lot about our last rest stations at Roisin and the family at the farm where we were billeted, and I think of the farmer's daughter who once said good-bye to me in such kind words.

Whenever I possibly can, I go on taking snaps with my little pocket camera, and you might say that I'd been promoted to the job of regimental photographer.

Our Army Commander (7th Army) is an infantryman, General von Boehn, and the General Officer Commanding the Sissonne Group is Lieutenant-General von Schmettow, the celebrated commander of the Schmettow Cavalry Corps in Roumania.

I walked over to our O.P. and went past many French tanks which had been knocked out in the last battle: there are 20 of them lying in our sector, 3 in our lines. One gunner of the battery which was here before us knocked out 6 on his own; 24 hours later he received the Iron Cross First Class, and the day after that he was killed in action.

I'm now seeing these tank monsters right close up for the very first time, and I can understand what a devastating moral effect they have in an attack. Our infantry lines lie in advance of the ruins of Juvincourt village. I was hardly back in the battery lines in the evening when the French started a heavy attack on Winter Hill with gas and artillery fire, without, however, our own batteries being brought into action. The attack was repulsed, of course.

It is not possible to give detailed descriptions of all these attacks, which are becoming routine daily events; you have no time to make so many notes either; and unless I'm writing about heavy fighting days, every day consists of beating off some smaller-scale attack, requiring the same strength of nerve and the same attention to duty—for us it has all become something that goes without saying.

When you think of it, it seems really quite incredible that all the 'heroes' over there can ultimately achieve, with their 32 Allies and their huge masses of men and guns, is precisely nothing: all their attacks for the last few years have been smashed against our living wall.

I've just remembered a little story I was told by the farmer's daughter at Roisin and which bears witness to the Belgians' fanatical patriotism: Until mid-April, 1917, that is, almost three years after our occupation of the country began, a secret Belgian newspaper appeared in Brussels in spite of the most rigorous control and censorship. The paper incited its readers against us and preached liberation. The German civil administration had been unable to discover either the editors or the publishers of the paper by last April, when in fact the raw materials for its existence ran out, and in the last number which appeared, the editors took leave of their readers with a solemn appeal for liberation.

The first American troops have landed in France.

A short while ago I recorded that my enthusiasm for flying would soon drive me in that direction. I should so very much like to do this, and have so far only held back because of my parents, although it's no less dangerous down here. But now I really am going to do it.

To our regret, our regimental Adjutant has been posted to the Brigade.

2/Lt Dossenbach has been killed in action—another famous airman gone.

Evenings in the dug-out are agreeable, and we spend the time playing *Wattepusten* (which involves blowing tufts of cotton-wool) or *Mauscheln* (the army gambling game).

9 July: I have struggled through at last and sent off the following message today:

> To Sub-Group III: I respectfully request permission to be posted to the Flying Corps for training as a pilot.
>
> (signed) Sulzbach
Second Lieutenant, Reserve

My enthusiasm for flying is not a matter of yesterday and today; as I have said before, it dates from Count Zeppelin's first beginnings, from the I.L.A. (the International Aviation Exhibition of 1909) and the Prince Henry flights. I have sent off my message, certainly, because Ludendorff has pointed out in an order published today that in view of America having joined the war, we shall be obliged to form a large number of new units, flying squadrons particularly, and that there is an urgent requirement for air pilots. I hope to be posted away for air training soon.

In the evening our Division mounts a small-scale attack for the purpose of taking prisoners, and I put down 308 rounds of rapid fire. 2/Lt Knauer is soon going on leave and every evening is accordingly a farewell party. All four of us sleep in one dug-out, and as far as this goes things really couldn't be more pleasant, although you often have to turn out at night and do some shooting.

On the *11th* Lieutenant-General von Schmettow inspects us in our positions. 2/Lt Zimmer reports to him as senior officer present (2/Lt Knauer being on leave), and the General seems very pleased. He is a giant of a man.

In the next few days we mounted several more operations without any large-scale battle developing.

Our U-Boats have sunk a million tons of shipping in June and our planes have shot down 220 enemy opponents.

There are political squabbles at home: Capelle, Helfferich and Scheidemann* are threatening to go, and Bethmann-Hollweg's position is in danger.

---

* Admiral von Capelle, Tirpitz's former collaborator and his successor as head of the Reich Admiralty Office, Helfferich, the currency expert and Vice-Chancellor, and Philipp Scheidemann the leading Social Democrat, had various reasons for opposing the upright but ineffective Chancellor Bethmann-Hollweg, whose dismissal was forced

My regimental commander has put his 'Approved' on my application for flying training, and has written me a character testimonial which I find really moving. I have copied it here because it is a document of enduring importance for me:

> *Leutnant* Sulzbach, Reserve, has belonged to the Regiment since 22 May, 1917, when he was posted from the 15th *Landwehr* Field Artillery Regiment. In the short time that he has belonged to the Regiment, by reason of his impeccable conduct both on and off duty, he has justly merited the entire satisfaction of his superiors and the high regard of his fellow-officers. The Regiment will be most unwilling for *Leutnant* Sulzbach to leave and has only supported his application for flying duties because the requirement and the need for flying officers is exceptionally great.
>
> (signed) von Ohnesorge
> Major, O C Regiment

15 July: I travel to the rear to the Flying Duties Selection Board via Valenciennes, where I made an appointment by wire with a former fellow-patient at the military hospital. Next day I travelled through Roisin and visited my dear friends at the farm, who truly and sincerely beamed with pleasure at seeing me again. What a welcome they gave me! —they are after all fanatical haters of us Germans, but the one German who has won their respect has in fact become their friend.

Bethmann-Hollweg has resigned. Behaviour in the Reichstag has been really scandalous.

Dr Michaelis is now Reich Chancellor. The foreign world is rejoicing over our internal dissensions, and they will give more power to our enemies' elbow. Bethmann-Hollweg is being accused of responsibility for being unable to prevent America from entering the war.

I take a large number of letters to the civilians at Roisin, entrusted to me by good-hearted gunners from my own unit and others, for in many cases true friendships had sprung

on the Kaiser by Hindenburg and Ludendorff with the concurrence of practically every political voice in Germany.—R.T.

up, and when I left I was given a pile of replies to take back with me. Here, therefore, a great deal has been done to give the Belgians a different impression of us Germans from the one with which they have been inoculated. Everywhere I take these German letters I have to translate them for the Belgians, and everyone who receives one of these letters from our gunners is sincerely pleased. *Kleinchen*, 'Little One', as they used to call her, from my farm said good-bye to me and gave me a slip of paper on which was written:

> '*Il faut que cela finisse avant que cela ne devienne trop difficile—n'écrivez plus à moi—je vous prie.*'

('It must stop before it gets too difficult for me—don't write to me any more—please.')

At Roisin a captain of a Frankfurt battalion very kindly placed his car at my disposal, and I drove on to Aulnoye.

At Sains I paid another visit to my nursing sister, who invited me to a meal, and then I drove on to Vervins, where I spent the night; next day I went on to the Examining Board, and there, believe it or not, I found 100 7th Army officers and N.C.O.'s, who had all applied for flying duties and who all had to be examined. When my turn came to see the Medical Officer and he was examining my ears, I suddenly felt completely faint and only came round to find myself lying on a bed. What the cause of this faintness was I've no idea, but apparently something had affected my heart, so I had to go back for another examination a week later.

The new Russian offensive, which I mentioned earlier, has had no success whatever.

At Vervins, by the way, sitting next to me in the officers' club, was a young second lieutenant wearing the *Pour-le-Mérite*, and I recognized him: 2/Lt Rackow, who captured Fort Vaux at Verdun.

And now we have started a large offensive operation in the East ourselves.

In the Reichstag they are talking about a negotiated peace.

22 July: The following wireless message comes through in the evening: 'The 7th/11th Russian army retreating in total disorder; quantity of captured material too great for assessment.

24 July: I travel to Vervins once more for another visit to the Flying Duties Board. My fellow-officer, 2/Lt Schmidt, *Pieselmax,* tells me 'I wish you all the best—but between ourselves, I hope you don't get through.' This small, jolly, forthright Silesian is a faithful friend.

When I reached Vervins I still had time to spend the evening in a 'Front Cinema'; I was particularly impressed, less by the film than by the people in the audience: how charmingly and childishly they did enjoy themselves, these Musketeers of the 214th Reserve Infantry Regiment, what rough wit they displayed with their comments in Holstein Low German *Platt,* and what a sense of humour they've got; next day they were taken off in the train to Flanders.

25 July: The examination went off quickly and painlessly. I'm a hundred per cent fit for flying duties, and very happy about it. After that I walked through the little town; a very great number of people were standing in front of the church, servicemen and civilians: the great bronze bells were being brought down to be melted at the foundry—these bells of peace were being made into cannon! The civilians stood watching with tears in their eyes.

On the Eastern Front, in Galicia, Tarnopol has fallen. The advance is flying ahead along a 300-kilometre front.

Here on the Western Front a new battle is raging in Flanders, and the communiqué, referring to the artillery fighting, says: 'of hitherto unsurpassed severity'.

Siam has declared war on us.

In the latest Russian military communiqué, if you read between the lines, it looks as though the Russian Supreme Military Command meant to say, 'I can't help it; I can't stop the soldiers running away and not obeying orders!' So that was the Russian steam-roller, that was.

Our Kaiser and the Emperor Charles of Austria have gone to the great battles in the East.

The battle in Flanders rages on.

In Eastern Galicia 10,000 square kilometres of territory have been evacuated by the Russians in eight days.

On *29 July* our planes shot 35 of the enemy down in a single day on the Western Front. *Oberleutnant* Dostler was given particular mention in despatches.

Kurt has written in a very good humour saying that he and I are now brothers-at-arms, and that he hopes we shall be able to get into the same flying group.

1 August: It's three years now since that day at 5.30 p.m. when the official mobilization of the whole of the Army and the Navy was announced—the endless cheers, thundering through the streets, still ring in my ears, and I remember how I marched through the city with the jubilant crowd. In the cafés you saw all those scenes which you would never be able to forget, and it really seemed as though all Germany were standing united for the first time. Of all the many who were singing then and hurried to the colours as volunteers, few are now left alive. You often scratch your head and ask yourself whether it's still you, and whether you're still the same person.

So today the fourth year of war begins. The noisy enthusiasm has died down, but we stand unbowed, unvanquished, and keep a whole world at bay.

For a few days I'm now in a camp, in a wood, with the limbers, and have another chance to look at a book; I've been deeply impressed and charmed by *The Honeymoon* by Charles de Coster, which Martha* gave me.

I'll mention a small, apparently unimportant event which nevertheless brings out the character and attitude of our good-hearted soldiers: An order came out that mail going home was to be checked, and while I was doing this, I noticed that one gunner was sending 50 cigars home to his father; cigars and cigarettes are what our men long for most, but nevertheless this splendid chap had saved 50 and was sending them to his father, because the old man couldn't get any at home. I was so much moved by this that I bought this kindly man 30 cigars from the canteen myself.

Fliegeroberleutnant von Pechmann has received the *Pour-le-Mérite*. He is the first air observer to receive the *Pour-le-Mérite* for 400 flights against the enemy and decisive reporting.

Meanwhile I have been made temporary acting battery com-

* Martha Dreyfus, *née* Koch, later Frau von Hirsch.—H.S.

mander. Sometimes I am the only officer left in the battery and come into closer contact with my gun-crews, very pleasant chaps. I really feel like shaking everyone of them by the hand, once I've got to know their wonderful attitude and their first-class character through conversations or sitting together in the dug-out.

I made a rough estimate today that since the beginning of the war I've been in over twenty different gun-positions, and how many times I've been in action, how much fighting and how many battles, just can't be totted up at all.

2/Lt Gontermann has shot down his 25th and Sergeant Müller his 21st opponent.

In this sector you often see our airmen diving at French captive balloons; then you see the balloons plunging in flames, while our airmen do their best to scorch back to our lines at top speed.

My regimental Adjutant, who regards me as a Rhinelander because I come from Frankfurt, has given me the job of buying some wine for the regiment on the Rhine or in Frankfurt, and I'm to be off in a few days; I'm pleased, of course. I travel once more through Hirson to Sains du Nord, visit the people I know there, and this time, find the little town of Sains quite different: One is accustomed to looking at everything through war-time spectacles, every village, every town, every meadow or wood or hollow—you see it all from the point of view of a theatre of war: and suddenly I saw Sains as a little peace-time town, and the landscape round it pleased me two, three times more than before; and here I must say a few words as well about what goes on in the rear areas. Scornful things are often said about the rear echelon, but every man, here as well, is genuinely doing his duty; and the organization of rail-way traffic, to name one branch particularly, has developed immense achievements which have never been equalled before. Look at the perfect way it works behind the front: the leave trains, the troop movement convoys, the ration trains and ammo trains; all this tangle is sorted out like clockwork, and these are achievements which no one talks about and which are nevertheless quite exceptional.

I travelled on through Brussels.

The battle of Flanders has come to life again, and it is getting noisy along the entire Western Front. The beautiful cathedral at my well-beloved St Quentin is in flames.

On to Cologne, and thence, at 8 o'clock, off in the train to Frankfurt-am-Main. It sounds so stupid if you talk about girls, but I just have to mention a little episode. In the train from Cologne to Frankfurt there was a girl, quite young, and she was wearing mourning, and looked infinitely sad.* There was such an awful crush that we couldn't speak to each other, so that it was only at the last minute (in Bonn, where she got out) that I was able to press a little note into her hand bearing my name and a few kind words.

Arrived Frankfurt-am-Main in the afternoon; joyous reunion once more, and I start my purchases as a 'travelling wine sales-man'. I had had permission to take a friend with me, a bombardier from my own battery.

I'm very happy to have received a postcard from Bonn, which is connected with that ride in the Bonn–Cologne express.

A new wave of hostilities, the 11th Ilonzo battle, has begun on the Italian–Austrian front; more of the same on the Western Front at Verdun, and in Flanders it has never stopped.

I've finished my shopping and two days later travel back to the regiment. In the train between Bonn and Cologne I meet a man I know; I went through the Champagne winter battle with him in 1914–15. When I get to Bonn, 'she', the one from Bonn, is waiting at the station, we have a short conversation and make an appointment for next leave. On again via Brussels and by evening, via Laon, to La Malmaison. The cases have arrived in good order, and I hope that my C.O. is satisfied with what I've bought.

My former class-mate Richard von Maurig, who was in the Imperial and Royal Austrian Air Force, has been killed in action.

Our limbers are stationed at La Malmaison; I go up to the gun-positions, and meanwhile 2/Lt Knauer, the Battery Commander, is back from leave. He is very cross with me for wanting to join the Air Force.

China has declared war on us.

* Fräulein Gustl Bähr.—H.S.

Terrible rows again in the Reichstag. It's enough to drive you crazy, with this really ideal military situation, to have politics at home in this fearful muddle!

Meanwhile we've come to the end of August, and a mad hail of fire has been directed on Winter Hill. It's moving across to our sector and spreading out about four or five divisions wide. Red, yellow and white Very lights keep bobbing up, it's a stormy, rainy night, and we lay down curtain fire like nobody's business—you can hardly hear your own voice giving the orders. It degenerates into a barrage, the kind we really do know enough about. Towards daybreak it eases off. We ourselves had no casualties.

On 28 *August* there arrived with my mail from Frankfurt an anonymous letter containing a little gold medallion and a white sheet of paper just bearing the words 'May God protect you'. I was overjoyed with this and I'll certainly wear the medallion. I can imagine from whom this affectionate talisman has come, and I'd love to thank her for it and tell her how moved I've been.

Richthofen has shot down his 59th.

I am being given great pleasure by reading particularly nice letters from Bonn.

After this we had some more very lively days. Heavy strafing, feint attacks and harassing fire on all our batteries. For our part we lay down a barrage on the French trenches; in spite of all this, no infantry assault follows from either side.

I have now spent over three years in the field, and sometimes feel that my need for warfare has been satisfied. Life only really begins at twenty for a young man, and what began for us at that age was the war, and it has turned us into different people; sometimes one has a feeling that one will never be able to laugh again.

I'm often on night duty, and these nights are soothing and inspiring. Then you only have a bang here, or a bang there, from time to time—otherwise a veil of complete silence lies over the broad landscape, and you can hardly believe that under this veil stand thousands of cannon, and hundreds of thousands of soldiers with their rifles in their hands; you can hardly understand what purpose it is all supposed to serve.

And then suddenly, on a quiet night like this, there's a humming overhead, and the big bombers sweep across behind the French lines to drop their 'greetings'. When they've been gone ten minutes you can soon hear the rumbling and banging in the French rear areas.

Riga has fallen.

We are supposed to be leaving this sector soon.

Richthofen has knocked down his 61st.

My brother is getting married soon, and since we are in fact being relieved here, I may perhaps be able to go to his wedding.

Lt Schaller has been posted to us.

Sergeant Müller of the Air Corps, whom I have mentioned before, has gone up to second lieutenant. He is incidentally the first officer promoted from the ranks to have received the *Pour-le-Mérite*.

8 September: We have been relieved and move into the Marchais rest stations, which are just tents and wooden huts in the middle of a wood near Marchais village and the Château de Marchais. We second lieutenants have a wooden hut to ourselves with four separate cubicles.

The days in Marchais camp pass quietly; we have a good rest and are really quite jolly. The duties are very reasonable. A fairly big field exercise with the 7th Grenadiers, directed by the Divisional Commander, is most interesting, we practise advancing; a whole battalion wearing steel helmets looks marvellous. The exercise finishes with a parade march past.

Lt Voss has shot down his 46th opponent.

The evenings are pleasant, and we invite each other to bunfights as though we were children. We organize sports for the men and award prizes. It is fine weather to end the summer. I start a new war diary and can make my notes in peace and have time to think and have feelings. When shall I be able to start the last war diary?

I'm sitting in my cubicle in the camp in the wood; the trees are oaks, and the sky above me is deep autumn blue; the planes are humming up to the front and back again, and I can hardly wait to get into the Flying Corps.

1. The author in Picardy, Summer, 1915.

2. Pieselmax with his horse.

3. Friends of the author moving up to the front by train for the second time, 1915. On the sides of the trucks are floral tributes from wellwishers.

4. Gunner Lenne on the Somme, Autumn, 1916.

5. Lt W. Reinhardt (*nearest camera*) with two other officers, 1915.

6. The author (*standing*) with two nurses at a hospital near Sains du Nord, March, 1917.

7. (*Below left*) The author and 2/Lt Kurt Reinhardt on leave in St Quentin, 1916.

8. (*Below   right*)   Kurt Reinhardt standing in front of his plane with a flying NCO at an airfield near Ghent. Reinhardt was shot down a few days later over Dunkirk.

9. Hungarian troops near Brody, Galicia, 1917.

10. The author fording the River Dniester on the Eastern Front, 1917.

11. One of the first British tanks to be knocked out in action, 1917.

12. Friends of the author washing their feet in a bomb-crater, 1917.

13. The author on a machine-gun course at Beverloo, Belgium, Autumn, 1917.

14. 2/Lt Hans-Ado Freiherr von Seebach, with two infantry dog-handlers, Summer, 1918.

15. 'Baby' Scholz-Babisch, the youngest officer in the Regiment, as an officer-cadet in 1917. His brother Friedrich was executed in October 1944, for taking part in the plot against Hitler in July of that year.

16. The author sitting on the shoulders of Lt Knauer, with Pieselmax (*left*), and Lt Zimmer, in 1917. The author was the only one to survive the war.

17. Valentine (*left*) at Les Petites Armoises, 1918.

18. A street in Noyon, after heavy shelling, 1918.

19. A comrade of the author's looking at the debris of the plane in which 2/Lt Pernet, Ludendorff's stepson, was shot down in April, 1918.

20. The author on leave in Frankfurt, 1918.

21. The author as a Private in the British Army, at Tidworth, 1943.

22. The author on leave in London, 1946.

23. The author as a captain in the British Army with a group of German prisoners-of-war at Featherstone Park Camp. General F. Heim is seated on the author's left and on his left is Major Rosenhauer, later a general in the post-war German Army. On the author's right is U-Boat Sub-Lieutenant Herbert Schmitt, later Editor-in-Chief of Associated Press in Frankfurt.

Here and there around us the infantry bands are playing, just near me our chaps are cooking themselves something special, dear old Lt Knauer is stalking round the camp on his long legs, other chaps are playing a card game called *Doppelkopf*— the whole place is really idyllic.

One morning I was sent on duty to Colonel Zechlin's brigade to take command as orderly officer. It was an exercise, just as interesting as the one we had recently, and I watched the Grenadiers perform their infantry assault. I was also able to take part in the critical assessment, and was struck with admiration at the way the Staff commanded the exercise: sheer genius! God knows we've simply *got* to be unconquerable. There are an endless number of divisions exercising here in order to be classified as 'thrust' divisions for attack purposes. They'll soon be off again to some ticklish place.

Another day we went to a concert in the church at Liesse, which is quite near; our divisional commander, General Weber, was sitting behind me.

20 September: Memories of the same day in 1913:

> *Keine Schwalbe bringt dir zurück, wonach du weinst—*
> *Doch die Schwalbe singt im Dorf wie einst!*

> Weep; what thou weepest for no swallow brings,
> But as of yore the village swallow sings.

The news of the heroic death of *Oberleutnant* Wolff, until his death in command of the famous No. 11 Fighter Squadron, has deeply moved me once again. He was the man who shot down his first air opponent on 6 March, 1917, and as early as 6 May accounted for his 29th—for which he received the *Pour-le-Mérite*. His fighter squadron alone has brought down 200 opponents in seven months.

So far as any closer friendship was possible between fellow-officers, or between officers and other ranks, these have deepened since we've been here. It gives me real pleasure to train my men.

We hear that our merchant U-Boats act as bases for our fighting U-Boats, and often supply them with fuel and rations on the high seas.

When you look at the German newspapers, you feel surprised from time to time to see how, in some respects, everything is the same as it was in the old days: they actually have racing, and Pergolese* is just having a real triumph! Oh well—they have to have that too.

The new offensive in Flanders has been brilliantly repulsed by General Sixt von Arnim's troops.

We often have exercises for us gunners alone and others with the infantry.

On 26 *September* I hear by wireless that my brother is being married soon; I shall be getting leave to go.

Lt Voss, the air ace, has now been killed in action: he got up to his 50th air victory, so that he too has equalled Boelcke.

28 *September:* I receive news that I am *not* being posted away for flying training, the High Command explaining its refusal by stating that a serious shortage of artillery officers exists, and that such officers cannot be spared from their units in the near future. I have to put up with the news, and the others make this refusal an excuse for a big party—that makes me feel all right too!

29 *September:* The French Richthofen, Captain Guynemer, has been killed in action.

I go on leave to attend my brother's wedding, reach Brussels on the evening of the 29th, and travel on next day, the 30th, to Bonn in the first instance. The reunion there was something quite different from other reunions. We went for a walk together, and then this person of the feminine sex whom I really only knew from letters told me the story of her life, and heart-breaking it was to hear it; it was a most difficult task to give any comfort at all, to live up to what was expected of me. But there was something about this walk—you could only call it something soft, something tender—which made one quite a different person. Then as evening came on we sat by the splendid Rhine, opposite the Dragon's Cliff, the *Drachenfels*, and the illuminated gardens were just like a fairy-tale. Many, many years ago, when I was a child, I had been here with my father, and now that first time seemed centuries ago. Even the porter

* A famous race-horse from the Weinberg stable.—H.S.

at my hotel knows me from earlier times; he, too, is in field-grey and only here on leave.

I travelled on, and my thoughts were filled with the tragic misery which had been brought to my notice in this woman's story. She went with me in the boat as far as Boppard, and I reached Frankfurt in the evening. Hardly two hours after my arrival a small war broke out on the spot—there were rumblings and bangings, and it almost made me feel at home to hear French Air Force bombs whizzing down on the peaceful city of Frankfurt.

2 October: Hindenburg's 70th birthday.

3 October: I met 2/Lt Reinhardt, my friend and former battery commander, who is on leave here; it was a great joy for both of us.

4 October: To Munich for the wedding, which took place on the 6th, and suited the times we live in by being very quiet.

On *7 October* back to the front, this time via Ulm, Stuttgart and Metz—on the morning of 8 October I was in Charleville, and when night fell I was already in Liesse. My battery is still in the wooded camp at Marchais; so I haven't missed anything.

12 October: The fighting in Flanders goes on unceasingly. Many chaps from my old regiment, the 63rd, have been killed in action.

In the Reichstag, sensational revelations by Capelle about a mutiny—which has been thwarted—in the Navy (von Capelle is Secretary of State at the Reich Admiralty Office).

Our 9th Infantry Division is soon going to be sent into action. On *15 October* we march off, to the north of Laon.

At this point orders arrived that several of our officers are to be ordered away to attend a machine-gun course, one lieutenant from each battery; I'm selected for this too, and nine of us travel to La Bouteille, and then make our way on foot to Landoucies la Cour, where we report. Some of us are billeted in the neighbouring village, Les Ninelles. Here we are with the Divisional Machine-Gun Training Company. I am billeted with a fellow-officer from one of our other batteries. Duties start straight off the following day, and the course of training is to last several weeks. The idea of providing us gunners with machine-gun training is that each German battery is now being issued with two machine-guns for defence in hand-to-hand fighting. The infantry and the artillery are getting closer and closer to being a single unit. When I get back I will pass the training on to my battery. At home they are supposed to be turning out over 10,000 machine-guns a month.

The famous fighter pilot, Lt Dostler, has been reported missing.

German troops have landed on Oesel Island in the Bay of Riga, with naval support—a new and brilliant exploit by the Army and the Navy. From the island we command the sea to the north, and Petersburg is threatened.

In the first nine months of 1917 our airmen have destroyed a total of 1,962 enemy planes.

Our machine-gun duties here start with theory, and we second lieutenants are given some idea of this sister weapon; we have to strip it and clean it as well, of course.

Meanwhile a new and massive attack has been mounted by the French between Soissons and Vauxaillon, that is, exactly where my regiment is at present stationed. You almost have a bad conscience, being here on a course instead of being able to fight at the front with your battery, but we'll be out there soon enough.

A masterly exploit by our Navy has been reported from the North Sea, where our ships have destroyed a convoy of thirteen enemy vessels.

A great sensation has been caused by the execution in Paris of Mata Hari the dancer, a Dutchwoman alleged to have been one of our agents. How ever could the French have been justified in organizing such an outcry back at the time when we were obliged to shoot Miss Cavell after a trial by court martial? Miss Cavell was a spy, proved to have been an agent of our enemies.

Here at the village lives a 75-year-old veteran who fought against us in 1870; I talked to him, and he thought I was only sixteen or seventeen because he just couldn't believe I was already in the field, and pointing to my ribbon, he said: 'Ah, *vous étiez dans la bataille, vous êtes guerrier!'* ('Ah, you've been in action, you're a real soldier!')

At home the 7th issue of War Loan has brought in twelve and a half thousand million.

Meanwhile the whole archipelago in the Gulf of Riga is in our hands.

Up at the front, in our sector, the battle continues; the noise of the terrific barrage rumbles over to us, and I think of the chaps I know and like who are in the fighting.

On their way back from an air attack on England, four Zeppelins have been lost: they were forced to land in France.

Meanwhile the second lieutenants posted here from the Second Battalion have been called back to the Regiment: it was on the cards that this would happen. Among them was 2/Lt Peters, a particularly cheerful soul.

Far to the rear in the lines of communication area, a rear reserve position is being built with incredible speed by our sappers. It is to be ready by 1918.

My sister has become engaged to Captain Sandkühler.

The military communiqué writes in some detail about the heavy attack mounted by the French at the front here, at Vaux-aillon and the Chemin des Dames. Convoys of troops and ammo are rolling past us here unceasingly on their way to the front.

We are attacking on the Italian front. It is incredible that in spite of their massive attacks, the enemy have not succeeded in depriving us of the initiative; we attack wherever we plan to do so, whether the enemy pours very large forces into an attack elsewhere along the front or not. The military communiqué for today reads: 'Yesterday, as loyal brothers-at-arms, German, Austrian and Hungarian troops struck out side by side in the campaign against our former ally.' The Italian front was penetrated—on the Isonzo, once again—with the precision of a military exercise. The communiqués describing the fighting on my own front culminate in the expression: 'A hurricane of fire so far unequalled in intensity.'

The offensive in Italy has so far brought us in 80,000 prisoners.

From my own front sector, however, very sad news items are coming in, for our regiment has suffered terrible losses: all the officers of our No. 6 Battery have been killed in action, including my dear friend Lt Zimmer, who was in No. 2 Battery with me in May. His brother was killed in action in 1914. Eight gunners were killed in the same battery. My friend *Pieselmax* sends me regular reports about No. 2 Battery, which thank God has so far had no fatal casualties.

One neighbouring battery was overrun by the French, but they did not get any further forward.

In Italy our troops have reached the outskirts of Udine, and the number of prisoners taken has reached 120,000.

Michaelis, the Reich Chancellor, has been forced to resign; that was a short period of office.

1 November: The number of prisoners taken in Italy has reached 180,000.

It is All Saints' Day. My thoughts go back to a lovely day's outing to Rohrbrunn in the Spessart many years ago today. You almost have to make an effort to dream your way back into the past.

I've been a second lieutenant for a year now. We are firing with live ammunition, so I'm already a marksman and will soon have finished my training.

Count Hertling has become Reich Chancellor.

The following Sunday brought us, as on several other occasions, some front-line leave in Brussels, where I met a remarkable number of old friends from Frankfurt. It's still the same scene in Brussels, everyone sucking a bit more life into himself: after all, we are now what you might call one-day flies, nothing more.

One of the pleasant things at this post is mail which arrives nearly every day from my friend *Pieselmax*, who writes as faithfully as if he were my son. Luckily things are all right up at the front.

2/Lt Gontermann, the captive-balloon specialist, has been caught in his turn, killed in an air battle.

I receive pleasant news from Kurt in Galicia, where he is flying; he writes with great enthusiasm to tell me about *his* first air battle.

We have an immeasurable victory in Italy, now along the

Dolomite front as well. The number of prisoners taken has risen to 250,000. The Italian general Cadorna has been fired. We have reached the Piave. In Russia the revolution is boiling up again, all the ministers have gone, and Lenin is demanding peace.

Now we have a week of highly exacting duties, and gradually we are getting perfect at handling the machine-gun.

My C.O. on the course lets me have two days' leave to go to my sister's wedding. The ceremony was on *19 November*. The whole of Frankfurt is still shocked by a dreadful explosion at the Griesheim-Elektron chemical works in Griesheim. The station is full of people who have escaped from the disaster. On the *21st* I am back in La Bouteille.

In Russia it's the fall of Kerensky, and the Bolsheviks are offering an armistice.

At our sector on the Western Front the British have had a local success between Cambrai and Péronne and have pushed us back a few kilometres; once again the tanks must have had a very great effect on our infantry and artillery; but the British did not succeed in using their local success to achieve a strategic victory. *Rittmeister* von Richthofen has shot down his 62nd opponent, 2/Lt von Richthofen his 26th, and 2/Lt Bongartz his 25th.°

The British are attacking again at Cambrai and Passchendaele.

Our course here is finished, and off I go back to the regiment via Brussels. On the journey I met Flight Lieutenant Rolfes, who was at school with me and is in command of 32 Fighter Squadron. For the first time I was given a fighter pilot's personal account of his experiences, from the last battle of Cambrai, watching attacks made by tanks, infantry, even cavalry, and heard how much personal pluck and daring you need in an air battle.

30 November: Our counter-attack at Cambrai wins back all the ground which we had previously lost.

° Manfred, the best-known of the Richthofens, was promoted to *Rittmeister* (cavalry captain) while flying, on the strength of his own mounted regiment. *Leutnant* von Richthofen was Manfred's younger brother.—R.T.

I'm with the guns again, back at my own well-beloved battery. We are stationed between Nouvion and Laval, so we are on the Chemin des Dames. Jolly little 2/Lt Peters, who was with me on the machine-gun course and was taken off it at the start of the battle of Vauxaillon, has also been killed in action; we have a new second lieutenant in the battery now, 2/Lt Exner. I'm on O.P. duties again, stationed in the front-line trench on a sunken track between Monampteuil and Chevregny. In front of me lie the ruins of the two villages, Filain and Pargny, which I've mentioned before. An air battle finishes sadly for us, once again; our plane crashed in the enemy artillery lines.

3 December: At 3.40 p.m. a report arrives that the armistice has been concluded with Russia. This may be the decisive factor for us—now we can release huge numbers of troops for the Western Front, and perhaps we shall manage to achieve what the enemy nations have been trying to do for three and a half years: a break-through, and then out of this dreadful static warfare at last, and into a mobile battle!

5 December: Armistice with Roumania. The situation is looking more and more doubtful for the Entente. Our counterattack at Cambrai has brought us in 9,000 prisoners. When the British had their partial success there, they celebrated it with peals of church bells and described it as the start of the breakthrough offensive. This British 'victory' is now ending with a great success for us.

2/Lt Müller has shot down his 36th.

Our observation planes report heavy troop movements in the enemy sector opposite us and heavy detraining activity at the railway stations.

2/Lt Exner, the new officer recently posted to us, suits us down to the ground, and we live in real harmony. This makes us co-operate, so that one's duties in battle become much easier. The N.C.O.'s and men feel just as happy.

I've been a week up at the front here on O.P. duties; we are doing comparatively little shooting and are not getting much fire in return either; now and then we get a visit in the evening from the chap we call 'Baby', little Officer Cadet

Scholz-Babisch, and then we generally sit down in the deep dug-out with our fellow-officers from the infantry.

I've been given temporary acting command of No. 5 Battery and am really very pleased with my varied responsibilities.

Now I must add a brief report of how matters are going on in our colonies: in German East Africa General von Lettow-Vorbeck has actually been able to hold on up to now with his little band of heroes. Cut off as he is from the outer world, he has been slogging his way through against a very large numerical superiority; but now his ammunition seems to be nearly exhausted.

In the East, Jerusalem has fallen into the hands of the British.

Meanwhile, in our sector of front, we have dug in what they call a battle-gun, which is only fired in the gravest emergency. The theory and practice of anti-tank training is being taken further all the time. At the moment I have an unbelievable amount to do, on the go from morning till night, and for weeks I've only had a few hours' sleep, several of my fellow-officers being on leave, and several others away on a posting similar to my machine-gun course. I have to do it all by myself: appointments, reports, firing, and in between, lectures to the men, because even on the gun-sites and in lulls between the fighting, the men have to be given a varied programme of training—allowing, of course, that they have time for rest between-whiles. In addition, I have to shuttle to and fro between the battery, the observation post and the battle-gun; I've made friends in no time with the chaps on No. 5 Battery. Meanwhile our second lieutenants are occasionally being posted to a flying corps group in order to get to know what range firing is like from the air; this is because we are getting into closer and closer contact with the observation pilots as time goes on.

The latest Battle of Flanders—you really can't count how many there have been—has finished in its turn, and in a struggle lasting over three months, our 4th Army has victoriously resisted the attacks of the entire British army, further supported by French divisions.

'Baby,' our 'youngest' from No. 2 Battery, visits me every day and tells me what is going on there; he is only eighteen, but modest, conscientious and right-thinking both as a human being and a soldier.

Our fourth Christmas is nearly upon us, and thank God, the front-line spirit still stands supreme above any feelings of doubt. What countless numbers of people one has come to know in these years; what boundless knowledge of human nature one has acquired. Meanwhile the weather up here has turned really quite wintry, and I'm still alone with my No. 5 Battery; actually, one has learnt everything in the course of these years almost without seeing or touching anything, and you command a battery as though you had done it for years. One evening I take a walk round the battery, that is, I give the guns another check, although there is no firing. It gives me great pleasure, and I find it most impressive, to see the men unobserved; there they sit in their dim underground passage, reading, talking to each other or playing the mouth-organ, practising *Silent Night* or marches and folk-songs. Even without hearing them speak, you recognize their convictions and their true spirit of comradeship. It seems that all we have up at the front is good, decent people! On the *17th* I was able to announce to the men that the armistice with Russia has been extended to 14 January, 1918—that is, between all the Central Powers and Russia—and that peace negotiations are to be initiated during this period. On receiving this joyful news, the men were beside themselves with enthusiasm, and now it really is our Western Front's turn to get a word in. We have had a fall of snow, and meanwhile my battery has a second gun at the extreme front on anti-tank duty, so that I have one section here at Nouvion and one up at the front with the infantry; this means double the work and twice the number of arrangements to make.

It is of course impossible to talk about individual hostilities or artillery battles—we are a living wall, and the chaps over there are a living wall too; we are a fortress thousands of kilometres long, in which each of us does his war service, silently, taking the job for granted. There isn't much talk any more now when casualties occur—all the arrangements follow automatically. Nevertheless, every single thing you do requires, and requires again and again, the commitment of your entire being. And the good times, the occasions I've already described, come back as well, again and again. When it's quiet, someone provides a bit of music, and then a thousand chaps hang on their 'blower' to listen in—telephone exchanges, groups, batteries, companies, even the small staff H.Q.'s.

So far as I could do so with the aid of newspapers and the military communiqués, I have kept a running note of successes scored by our airmen. The list is of course headed by *Rittmeister* von Richthofen with 63 victories; then 2/Lt Müller, whom I have often mentioned, with 36 victories; but these are followed immediately by 2/Lt von Richthofen, Captain Berthold, Lt Schleich, Ritter von Tutscheck, Lt Loerzer, 2/Lt Hess,* Kissenberth, Lt Göring,† Menckhoff and Udet.‡ These are all men who have been mentioned in despatches, that is, who have scored several successes; some of them have already received the *Pour-le-Mérite*, and some are certain to be given it in the future.

Two or three times a week my sergeant comes up to the battery from the limber position, the men are given their pay, and other formalities between the sergeant and me are dealt with. On *21 December* he came up once more, drove off in a good humour, and ten minutes later a unit lying a little further to the rear rang me up to say that my sergeant had been killed by a direct hit; so there, once again, I've lost one of my best-hearted men. All my men were very upset, some of them having been with him since the war began. Meanwhile we have reached the depths of winter, 8 degrees C. below zero, deep snow, the woods are sparkling, and the guns are completely snowed in under their artificial trees. How innocent, how peaceful this landscape looks in the lovely snow; and to think of all the things that have passed over it!

And now it is Christmas Eve again, the fourth in France, the fourth in the field; the last one, on the Somme, was much worse. We have a short service at the gun-sites, in a deep dugout, with a Christmas tree bright with candles, and the gunners standing round, helmet in hand, listening with great devotion

* Possibly Rudolf Hess, later Hitler's deputy.   † Hermann Göring.
‡ Carried on his flying exploits in World War II; he inspired Carl Zuckmayer to create the character of General Harras in *The Devil's General*.

to the chaplain's words. It is impossible to describe a wartime Christmas service in a dug-out—especially the expressions of these good men, such really good people they are. After a little service like this you do, you just must, feel more than ever convinced of final victory. Then the men go to their own dug-outs, each with its own candle-lit tree, and they sit round it in deep thought for a while, but soon start to sing. The weather could not be more Christmassy; all this snow is quite unusual for France. Whether you look at it from the guns, or from the sentry-posts, the landscape looks more and more innocent. It sparkles everywhere, you see the ruins of what used to be villages in the evening light, and far away, Laon cathedral; and you feel very moved. Late in the evening the mood turns to jollity, everyone has plenty to eat and drink, and we don't have to do much firing, so it is a harmonious Christmas Eve.

One day I get a visit from some other people—my fellow-officers of No. 2 Battery—and however glad I am to be here, I do hope that I'll soon manage to get back there. If this could be done, I'd be glad to give up the honour of being a Battery Commander. I have a faithful factotum here, my Herrmann,* who speaks the broadest Hessian you could imagine. When he received a big Christmas parcel from home yesterday, he said, 'Sir, 'ere's something decent for us to eat!' It goes completely without saying for these chaps that every parcel is divided with one's companions. One quiet evening I entrust the battery for a few hours to my lance-sergeant, having been invited to have a drink with my Battalion Commander; but it finished up with a great many drinks.

New Year's Eve, 1917/18: So we go into a new year for the fourth time; however, this evening was no kind of celebration at all, as I stayed alone in my No. 5 Battery.

Once more a year reaches its end, a year in which we can really be proud of each other, since what we have stood firm against on this Western Front can never be described in words; in fact, it will perhaps be understood even less by the people at home.

* My batman, Herrmann Müller—H.S.

V

1918

The St Quentin Offensive

MEANWHILE the peace negotiations with Russia are in progress at Brest-Litovsk. Kühlmann's* declaration that we are prepared to enter into discussions with all governments for a peace without annexations of territory or payment of reparations, has put the enemy powers to the test whether they are going to stop the slaughter and reveal truthfully what they are fighting for. They have refused straight off, and the hypocrisy of the few neutrals in the world could not be demonstrated more clearly.

People are talking a lot just now about a big German offensive which is supposed to be coming off in France; we are already keyed up, and hardly dare to hope for it. But there are so many preparations to be completed for an operation like that, it obviously can't be launched just yet.

2 January: I'm really speechless, not pleased at all in fact, about having to go on a course at the Artillery School at Beverloo in Belgium. Duties at a barracks, which is what I'll be going to there, are not what I like at all. People are telling me, of course, that it's an honour, because it means being re-trained for the great battles to come. I have a party to say good-bye, in my No. 2 Battery, but I don't miss anything up at the front because the very day I steam off for Beverloo,

---

* Richard von Kühlmann (1873–1948), Foreign Secretary in 1917–18, represented Germany at the Treaty of Brest-Litovsk. An open advocate of peace by agreement rather than by trial of arms, he was forced to resign in 1918.

the whole division at our sector is relieved and goes back to the rear to be trained for mobile warfare. It would be just unbelievable if it actually came to any mobile warfare! Before taking my leave I get invited, with 2/Lt Knauer my battery commander, to the regimental staff H.Q., get given another few days' leave, travel on *4 January*, through Cologne once more, with a splendid reunion, and then on to Frankfurt-am-Main.

It is really providential that wherever I am, I get opportunities to see my faithful friend Kurt, or, to express it better, we make it possible to meet either on leave or at the most impossible front-line sectors. And so we celebrate another reunion on *10 January* in Frankfurt-am-Main. Meanwhile he has left Galicia and is with the 2nd Air Photography Section at Ghent, and he tells me a lot about flying, although it makes me sad that I failed at the last minute to get into the Flying Corps. On *12 January*, in a restaurant, I met *Rittmeister* Freiherr von Richthofen with his brother. It made a quite overwhelming impression on me. He has truly become a national hero; people seemed quite paralysed with respect for the two brothers.

In Frankfurt itself it has got really quite dreary, and quite early in the evening the streets have to be shrouded in deepest darkness, because French planes come over only too often. The consequences of three and a half years of war are weighing heavily on the home country, and you see a great deal, in fact a never-ending amount of distress.

The crisis in our internal politics keeps smouldering along.

Flight Lieutenant Müller, whom I have often mentioned as having risen from the ranks, has been shot down after his 38th air victory.

Since my leave was not yet finished, I travelled to Berlin and visited my relatives there, and then my sister in Wünsdorf.

On *18 January* I travel to Cologne, where I find, believe it or not, 18 letters which the Battery has forwarded to me there at my request. Here the sad news reaches me that my friend Cameron* has been killed in action in the course of an infantry assault in Flanders. I feel I have to mention him

* A German of remotely Scottish descent.—H.S.

because he won the Iron Cross First Class so very early, while he was a corporal in the infantry, and also because he was the man who on 29 June, 1914, after the murder at Sarajevo, was absolutely certain that a world war was coming.

Meanwhile I've wound up at Beverloo, after meeting Lucy Hoefner at Louvain; the place is swarming with young officers who are here to learn all about the latest technical achievements in the world of artillery. My faithful Herrmann is here too. Beverloo Camp is a well-known Belgian firing-range. I have quarters in a wooden hut, which is reasonably comfortable. The following day we are split up into different battalions for firing purposes; then the General, the Camp Commandant, gives a talk, the formalities are completed, and off we go to our new duties. Our instructor is a captain with a temperamental and very lively way of teaching. My God, what an incredible amount we've still got to learn! That's the first impression you get. On my course there is one of my mates whom I marched out of barracks with on 2 September, 1914, and whom I haven't seen since—from the old No. 1 Battery when I was under 2/Lt Reinhardt. There are plenty of pleasant young second lieutenants here, whom one is certain to get along with. It's almost painful to have Brussels so close. Everybody, after all, has these training periods and training duties—the men too, of course, with a different kind of training. One day, a few days later, we were already firing with live ammunition, and on 27 *January*, the Kaiser's birthday, a parade. I think back to the parades we used to have on the Kaiser's birthday in peacetime, when we were children and used to go and watch the show on the Opernplatz in Frankfurt, and had no idea that anyone would ever wear field-grey. The church parade on 27 January was fine, very solemn. Several hundred officers and thousands of other ranks stood drawn up in a large square, and listened to a fine, quite unemotional talk by the chaplain. It was impressive as the General gave three cheers for the Kaiser, we saluted, and a 101-gun salute was fired to the strains of *Heil Dir am Siegerkranz*. In the evening we dined together at the mess in the Kaiser's honour.

The following days and weeks at Beverloo pass smoothly,

the evenings are spent pleasantly with my comrades, and duties in the day-time are strenuous and interesting. On Sundays we can take leave to Brussels or wherever we want to go.

You feel anxious, however, when you hear the news from Germany: strikes—yes, really large-scale strikes—and disturbances, and of course, huge rejoicing over this among the French; while our front stands firm as a rock. If the people at home could only hold out at the present time when we have a huge job to do in the West after getting our hands free in the East!

Trotsky is apparently spinning out the negotiations at Brest-Litovsk to an interminable extent.

My birthday is of course celebrated in a highly liquid fashion.

A special peace has been signed with the Ukraine.

On the *18th* a special party: after these few weeks I go off to my regiment, stopping for an equally gay reunion with Kurt in Brussels.

Even if you enjoy all this madly throbbing life in Brussels, rather as though you were tipsy all the time, and partly because it makes a conscious change from the front, you still feel disgusted with it all when it's over, and begin to long for the German style of being clean, I mean thinking in a clean way. And then I have to think about the words I have had from Bonn, in the latest letter:* 'My love will give you power, courage and strength for everything which is in store —it will care for you and protect you.' And it is genuinely true that if you are an individual and are conscious of something like this, it has an enormous effect on you and gives you very great strength.

Meanwhile in the East our troops have taken Reval, and Estonia is entirely in our hands.

Well, here I am back with my regiment, at Le Hérie. It was an indescribable pleasure, and a splendid reunion with my comrades and faithful friends. There is no end to the troops stationed here, no end either to the troops moving past all the time, and you get the impression that we are

* From Gustl Bähr.—H.S.

on the brink of the most colossal action the history of the world has ever seen; it's the start of the greatest advance, and the preparation for the greatest battle that has ever been fought. While I was away in Beverloo our division has been here continuously, and nearly every day they had exercises and other forms of preparation for the great battle. The roads look the same as they did in 1914; we belong to General von Hutier's new 18th Army. 2/Lt Knauer, my battery commander and friend, was not going to be put off celebrating, in fact 'wetting' my return to the unit with a large-scale party. The speech he made moved me so much that I was hardly able to say a word in reply; nearly all the gentlemen from the other batteries and staff H.Q.'s were there, and *how* they were there!

3 *March:* The final peace treaty has been signed with Russia. Our conditions are hard and severe, but our quite exceptional victories entitle us to demand these, since our troops are nearly in Petersburg, and further over on the Southern front, Kiev has been occupied, while in the last week we have captured the following men and items of equipment: 6,800 officers, 54,000 men, 2,400 guns, 5,000 machine-guns, 8,000 railway trucks, 8,000 locomotives, 128,000 rifles, and 2 million rounds of artillery ammunition. Yes, there is still some justice left, and the state which was first to start mass murder in 1914 has now, with all its missions, been finally overthrown. Courland, Livonia and Estonia are ours, and Finland and the Ukraine have become independent states. While on this subject I recall the words of a song, and if I mention it here, I do so because many Germans do not themselves realize to what extent France, which is always putting the blame for the World War on to us, has been agitating for decades, preaching revenge for Sedan in 1870. The song I remember was one I heard on my journey to the North African colonies in 1913; its chorus ran: '*Alors, petit soldat de la république, préparez-vous pour le combat!*' ('Now, little soldier of the Republic, prepare for the battle!') You can hardly imagine the hullabaloo and general enthusiasm at the end of the song. This event is highly significant in proving the agitation for a war of

revenge, which thus reached right into the furthest corners of the French colonies.

On 4 *March* we are at Guise in the afternoon. The scene there is once again troops, troops, and more troops. There is a small cinema in Le Hérie, which we go to sometimes. The most amusing thing there is the remarks made by the soldiers in the audience.

Incidentally, all of us on the Western Front have been equipped with gas-masks.

A new second lieutenant has been posted to the battery; and we keep doing exercises to practise the tactics of mobile warfare.

From far and wide, every emplacement and every hole and corner is being filled up with troops, and it looks as though we have Austrian troops here as well. The traffic on the roads is unbelievable.

A few days later we have a large-scale exercise with one other division.

I've been posted as acting Adjutant to the 2nd Battalion, and even if that is supposed to be a kind of distinction, I'm still really rather unhappy to be leaving my No. 2 Battery just now before the big offensive. And I'm even happier when, twelve hours later, the order is cancelled.

Flight Lieutenant Buddecke has been killed in action; he was one of the Knights of the Order of *Pour-le-Mérite*, and particularly famous for his air victories in the Dardanelles.

If any increase in the masses of troops marching through here were possible, one would have to make a note of what went through today!

15 March: Von Richthofen's 65th air victory. Our airmen on the Italian front have bombed Naples, while Paris has once again been given a substantial 'blessing'.

We get the first secret orders for the attack; and again and again you have to gaze in wonder at this careful work which the Staff people are putting in, working things out right to the last detail—after all, that is the secret of our greatness. I don't want to write anything about it here, because it is forbidden to do so, and because there is also the real danger that one might be taken prisoner, and secret notes like these might be useful to the enemy. The whole thing can only be compared with the gigantic general mobilization of 1914 in volume, but concentrated on a comparatively short front; and on top of that, all the things which did not exist in 1914 in the way of new weapons, new equipment and unbelievable masses of men, and with the difference that in 1914 an advance was completely taken for granted, and all that counted then was to win the battle; whereas here and now, it is a question of our being successful in breaking through the enemy's gigantic fortified line and then winning the battle afterwards: in fact, it's a question of two victories. Shall we be able to achieve this immeasurably great objective with just a few divisions, and with our own troops no longer fresh, having regard to the enormous masses of men which the chaps over there have available? The enemy facing us are supposed to be mainly British. We'll be giving them good service, with a large number of new specialities. The preparations are getting more and more urgent, sleep is getting more and more unthinkable, every battery commander and every battery officer is a miniature General Staff. Even if you were tired, the excitement and enthusiasm wouldn't let you sleep anyway.

16 March: We are already being moved up to the front, the roads are pretty well impassable.

17 March: Hauteville, where we move into billets, i.e. bivouac beside a hedge, because this little place, which may have had 700 inhabitants in peacetime, is sheltering about 15,000 people. Around the village there is bivouac after bivouac, battery after battery, battalion after battalion. At the moment I am sitting up here on top of the village church at Hauteville and trying to get my impressions together. It occurs to me that I forgot to record a little scene which made quite an impression on me as we were pulling out of Le Hérie: Among the detachments moving past was one marching with in-struments playing and drums beating; it only consisted of corporals and sergeants, and they too had been on a course and been discharged to get back to their regiments. The music was playing '*Muss i denn, muss i denn zum Städtle hinaus . . .*'

('Must I go, must I go, must I leave the little town . . .') They marched on, waved to us one after the other, with such a nice look on their faces that you felt warm and enthusiastic: but then suddenly you felt an icy shudder run over you and thought: 'Which of these good men, and which of us for that matter, is going to come home from this battle which lies ahead of us?'

18 March: It is sunny and warm, and I've slept on the roof of Hauteville church with 2/Lt Knauer, Baby and Herrmann. The church itself is stuffed full of troops all fast asleep down there like herrings one beside the other.

They keep on moving through the village to the front, only a few kilometres away, and as they pass we see the latest self-propelled guns, long-barrelled giants on 100-horse-power chassis which have front-wheel drive and back-wheel drive at the same time. These great things will be ready to fire in two hours' time—they look to us like monsters raging across the country; as they drive off, the men wave at us and cheer as enthusiastically as if it were 1914.

18 March, evening: I've been working with 2/Lt Knauer until 2 o'clock in the morning, getting out a mass of orders, particularly for the creeping barrage.

19 March: Early in the morning I rode over to the survey section and could hardly get along the roads—it's a mass concentration of troops completely impossible to describe. The columns making for the front are moving up the roads four abreast. Thank goodness the weather is dull and no enemy planes are coming over, so that so far there is no danger that the British will have noticed us moving up.

Our kicking-off point for the offensive is going to be the 'Island Suburb' of St Quentin and that was once a gay, pleasure-loving rear-echelon city, and now it's pretty well a front-line position: but it will soon be in the rear again! Every house in St Quentin that is still standing has received two or three direct hits.

The British are firing into the city every day, with sweeping fire, and now and then one of our ammunition depots goes up.

We have moved into our emplacements in the firing line, and the limbers are already going into their waiting positions, so it can only mean a day or two at most before the huge offensive starts, but the date and time will only be passed through at the last second. We are already imagining what it will be like when the order comes: *'Protzen heran'*—'prepare to move!' We are most conscious of the greatness of the moment, and have got into a terrific state of tension, and even when we have any time for rest, we genuinely can't sleep any more, not for a second.

20 March: I fetch the firing lists from the Divisional Artillery Commander and today ride once more a little to the rear through slush and mud; there are still troops, troops and more troops moving up to the front. The weather is still in our favour, it is dull and cloudy, and raining as well, and thus very unsuitable for enemy observation activity.

The operation of bringing the troops forward and deploying them into position must have been completed by now. The infantry have been concentrated, and you see a number of units with messenger dogs.

On *20 March* in the evening an order arrives from Sub-Army Group, Central Sector which I have transcribed as it stands:

> After years of defence action on the Western Front, Germany is moving to the attack; the hour eagerly awaited by every soldier is approaching. I am certain that the Regiment, true to its history, will enhance its reputation in the days which lie ahead.
>
> This great objective will call for sacrifices, and we shall bear with them for the Fatherland, and for our loved ones at home.
>
> Then forward, into action! With God for King and Fatherland!

So it was at 7 in the evening that we had this order through by telephone. It says quite enough. *21 March* has been fixed for the start of the barrage. There is a terrible lot of work to do, we are in the highest possible spirits, and everybody lends a hand in distributing the huge quantities of ammunition.

21 March: The artillery fire begins at 4.40 a.m., and at 9.40, that is after a five-hour barrage, came the infantry assault and the creeping barrage. Meanwhile the evening has come on, and I'm sitting on a limber and can hardly collect my impressions of today. I'd like to write volumes about this day; it really must be the greatest in the history of the world. So the impossible thing has been achieved; the break-through has succeeded! The last night of the four years of static warfare passed, as I have said above, in the greatest possible excitement after the starting time had been fixed for 4.40 a.m. The exact time, down to the last second, was given through three times. 4 o'clock. The darkness begins to lift, very, very slowly; we stand at the guns with our gas-masks round our necks, and the time until 4.40 crawls round at a dreadfully slow pace. At last we're there, and with a crash our barrage begins from thousands and thousands, it must be from tens of thousands, of gun-barrels and mortars, a barrage that sounds as if the world were coming to an end. For the first hour we only strafe the enemy artillery with alternate shrapnel, Green Cross* and Blue Cross.† The booming is getting more and more dreadful, especially as we are in a town between the walls of houses. Meanwhile an order arrives: H.M. the Kaiser and Field-Marshal von Hindenburg have arrived at the Western theatre in order to command the battle of St Quentin in person.

So we are stationed right at the most decisive place, and the hottest.

In the middle of this booming I often have to make a break in my fire control duties, since I just can't carry on with all the gas and smoke. The gunners stand in their shirt-sleeves, with the sweat running down and dripping off them. Shell after shell is rammed into the breach, salvo after salvo is fired, and you don't need to give fire orders any more, they're in such good spirits, and put up such a rate of rapid fire, that not a single word of command is needed. In any case,

* 'Green Cross' was a gas shell containing Diphosgene, a liquid with an unpleasant smell.
† A 'Blue Cross' shell was two-thirds filled with high explosive. The remaining one-third contained a glass bottle filled with Diphenylchlorarsine, which caused sneezing.

you can now only communicate with the gun-teams by using a whistle. At 9.40 the creeping barrage begins, and under its cover the thousands, and thousands more, and tens of thousands of soldiers climb out of the trenches, and the infantry assault begins: and the infantry assault has now succeeded.

The limbers come up, and we reach our finest hour when 2/Lt Knauer gives the order *'Nach vorwärts—protzt auf!'*— 'To the front—limber up!' We move through St Quentin at a trot, and the British are hardly firing. And now come the scenes of the advance, the scenes of the ravaged, shell-torn battle-ground that we still have in our memory from 1914. Everything has gone brilliantly, the sappers have already thrown bridges across the British trenches, the whole supply column is working successfully. We move forward in the second line of advance, and columns and troops on the move are blocking the advance routes, which of course we ourselves have largely shot to craters. The first prisoners are coming through, well-built chaps, with very good uniforms and equipment, in hard training for field sports, all thorough-going 'Tommies' walking along cheekily with a fag in their mouths. I had a quick word with a few British gunners, they had been completely surprised and were speechless at our massed infantry assault. We spend the night of *21–22 March* in readiness outside Essigny-le-Grand.

22 March 1918: We move on through Essigny, but there is such a traffic block in the town that we hardly manage a kilometre in three hours. On our right and left flanks it's the same situation, all the troops pushing forward, taking the advance for granted as well, as though static warfare had never existed.

However did we people, who have been enduring a starvation blockade for a good four years, manage to do the *very* thing that the chaps over there couldn't do in some 50 pitched battles? We pass the first British battery emplacements, and we're soon in their second-line positions.

Now we get along at a trot to positions near Artemps, and put up a short burst of fire in support of our right-flank neighbours, the 238th and 5th Guards Divisions. From our observation post I can see the fighting in progress; our infantry support planes are coming in quite low to attack with machine-guns, the fighter planes keeping above them to protect their colleagues. The advance has got moving to such an extent that even the captive balloons at our rear are being brought forward. We are not able to judge where the line is to our right and left, nor how far the divisions next to us have advanced, but the position near Arras is supposed to be favourable.

General Foch is said to be marching against us with the well-known French Reserve Army. Incidentally, since 21 March we've had the most beautiful spring weather—it might have been laid on specially, and our men are in splendid spirits. We are still second-line troops and now only occasionally join in the fighting.

23 March: Five of us spent the night in an ammunition trench lying on the ground; we were all wrapped up in blankets, but were still cold, and dripping with dew in the morning.

Our first-line troops have taken Ham, and we shall soon have made enough progress to reach the old position we were in before the 1916 retreat; we have only sustained slight casualties. There is now less of a jam on the roads and you can advance at a better pace. The 5th Guards Division moves at such a lick that soon we can't keep up with them. We bivouac right in Artemps, which was a British camp, and suddenly we're in another world. English posters, sign-posts and name-boards. We take a lot of prisoners and spend the night in a British officers' dug-out.

24 March: Our Sappers build a bridge over the canal, and we pass some really very heavy British guns. Then we move on to Dury. We are still second-line troops. In the first three days the offensive in our sector of the front alone has brought in more thousands of prisoners than you can count.

We've been made front-line troops now: the Division is following on in order of march. But the pace is pretty slow up to Ham, a little town which I passed through in 1916 when it was a rosy little rear-echelon station. Now it's a pile of rubble; we forage, and find some splendid British supplies. There's really everything you could think of. Plenty of oats for the horses and tinned food, bacon, cheese and wine for us. There are huge masses of troops rolling forward again towards Nesle.

25 March: Official news arrives that Paris has been shelled with 150 rounds of the largest-calibre artillery ammunition. Yes, shelled, not bombed! So there we have perfected a technique enabling a long-range gun to fire a distance of over 100 kilometres. It's just unbelievable, and what an impression it must be making on the morale of the people in Paris!

We bivouac on the road and enjoy the wonderful British grocery supplies, which even include biscuits, ginger, whisky and English cigarettes.

For the last few days I haven't got round to making notes on the same day; today is *Good Friday, 29 March.* I am sitting in the gun-emplacement near Montdidier, in a chalk-pit. Since I last put pencil to paper, days have passed, days full of great deed and events, and victorious actions fought by our 9th Division, and our Battery, which you just couldn't record in detail. So I'll go back:

On *25 March* we halted near Eppeville and spent the night sleeping down by the water and freezing.

On *26 March* we moved on at 4 a.m. At Nesle, taken by our infantry assault in the course of the morning, I requisitioned three pigs and several hens for our cookhouse, out of a burning house; at the pace we are going, of course, our supply column can't keep up, and we have to look after ourselves. At Carrépuis we move into firing positions to the left of the village. Our infantry are bringing large numbers of British prisoners past us on their way to the rear; and a few French among them as well. The British must really have run like rabbits. It appears that the French who were thrown in to support the British were brought up from Paris at top speed in motor-cars. The first French prisoners whom I speak to ask me anxiously whether it is true that Paris has actually been shelled by our guns.

I must record a highly expert trick performed by a British pilot: Among other installations, we have occupied a British airfield (in fact, we have pushed so far into the British positions that we have reached the British Air Corps' living quarters), just a few hours ago. We are riding past it, and what do you think, a plane takes off nice and comfortably from the airfield; we are just thinking it was pretty daring of our own Air Corps to occupy the enemy airfield so quickly, and then suddenly, in view of the whole division, the plane reveals itself as it climbs to be not a German one—not in the least, it was a British plane which had been left behind; the pilot had hidden, jumped into the plane, and before our very eyes there he was off and away!

At Carrépuis we get our first dose of air bombing from an enemy squadron which has also been shooting away at us like mad with machine-guns. Among other casualties in this attack, our Battalion Commander, Captain von Schleicher, has been wounded. In an advance you are quite helpless against being bombed from the air, and it is a much more uncomfortable feeling than being bombed in static warfare when you have decent dug-outs. The casualties were correspondingly greater.

Our 9th Infantry Division has taken Roye. We spend the night on the gun-site.

27 March: What used to be the old French position before our retreat in 1916 has now been taken in a really splendid infantry assault by our 7th Grenadiers. The pace is getting hotter and hotter. The enemy have been on the run for six days. We push on at a mad pace, keeping as hard on the heels of the infantry as we can manage. Laboissière gets taken by the infantry, and the enemy only halt beyond Etelfay. We are holding many prisoners, and the battlefield presents a scene of the most hasty flight. We have to pass the bodies of many dead Frenchmen and Englishmen. Our own losses are comparatively light. Now we move into firing positions, first at a trot and then in our excitement actually at a gallop. We lay down some fire at 700 metres and some at 2,000. As we hurry through the village of Laboissière at a gallop, the

French open up for the first time and lay a heavy barrage in front of the village, so that we take our lives in our hands to ride through and get out of this hailstorm. We had, thank God, only two men injured when an ammunition limber turned over. We had the devil's own luck, as in shelling like this we might easily all have been done for. I led the battery through a double curtain of fire, and now there was a proper textbook illustration of a pitched battle going on. The enemy were still on the run. We are now advancing nearly level with the infantry, and our battery is ahead of the infantry-gun batteries. Our morale is splendid, as could be expected. Our great objective seems to have been achieved, that is, to separate the British army from the French.

27 March (continued): We move on to a point beyond Faverolles. It's going at such a pace that I'm afraid our neighbours won't keep up with us. We, that is the 9th Infantry Division, the 7th Grenadiers, the 19th, the 154th, and our own 5th Field Artillery Regiment, maintain our high record of achievement with an infantry assault on Montdidier, and this brings the fighting for 27 March to a close.

Now, however, strong enemy fire started up to make it difficult for our reserves to advance, and a shocking business it was; we turned back, got behind the village, on the northern perimeter, in a state of readiness, and stayed the night there in French wooden huts. The enemy has even sent dismounted cavalry into their trenches, or actually thrown them into action, so short of reserves they seem to have become. The only really dreadful thing still is the sight of all the dead from both sides. Faverolles village is completely undamaged, so we are deep in the French rear area; everything seems peaceful here—masses of supplies, but the civilians have all fled at the last minute.

28 March: I manage to get hold of a copy of the newspaper *Le Matin*; it gives a comprehensive account of the shelling of Paris—the Parisian population seem to be immensely surprised.

We receive the first official German military communiqués: we have captured an incalculable amount of equipment and

stores in our sector; the 2nd and 5th Armies have been beaten
—but the most important thing is still to come.

Paris has once more been shelled—for seven and a half
hours.

We go into position north of Montdidier, and the advance
is to be halted for two days until our right and left flank
neighbours have come up. Our division advanced attacking
for 15 kilometres on 27 March alone, and now we need a
little rest. I go into the town of Montdidier with Dr Dankwardt
to do some requisitioning; there are few civilians left in the
town, but all the more supplies, so much that you don't know
what to choose. It's full of military parties who, like ourselves,
are requisitioning for their companies and batteries. A French
pilot, however, observes the comings and goings in the town,
unloads a few heavy-calibre bombs into the middle of it all,
and caps it by letting off his machine-gun at us. Everybody
dodges into the houses and cellars. Meanwhile the pilot has
told the French artillery about us, and now Montdidier starts
getting shelled; this means that the requisitioning parties are
caught in the cellars, and we have to squat there for hours.
We sit surrounded by cases of wine, tinned food and all kinds
of delicacies; there are several grenadiers in the same cellar,
and one gives the next man something which he hasn't got
himself; and another one hunts out the best possible things
for his wounded second lieutenant, and nothing seems good
enough for him. Whatever situation you are in, you are always
coming across little incidents like this, really quite touching,
which show what comradeship, in fact almost friendship, there
is between officer and man at the front line. We were sitting
down there for five hours before the fire slackened off. Meanwhile my Battery C.O. had sent four more men from our
battery to hunt for us, and we soon found a small cart to
take away our goodies in. I fastened myself between the
shafts, and we trotted off, blessed by the loving attentions
of the French artillery, through the town to our position,
where there was naturally great rejoicing at our return.

I must, however, mention one thing: anybody who maintains
that our U-Boats are starving the Entente out is ill-advised,
and he ought to come to Montdidier or other towns or villages

which have been recaptured, and take a look at all the luxury goods. Our U-Boats have certainly been reducing the enemy tonnage appreciably, but I do not believe that we can starve out our enemies with U-Boats.

29 March: It is Good Friday. We get into a rather sad mood and feel worried because our people cannot have heard from us for quite some time and are bound to be worried about us. In the afternoon a strong French attack starts up from Le Mesnil, and they advance in seven or eight waves; the answering fire, steered from our observation post, is splendidly accurate, and our infantry take free aim from a standing position. The attack has been beaten off in half an hour. The French must have been moving fresh divisions to the front to throw them into action.

I go out on a recce in the evening with Captain Walter to look for new positions. We are back at 10.30 in the evening, but at midnight it starts up again. We get fired on at St Medard because we are so near to the French that they are bound to have heard our horses trotting. I ride back and move the three batteries of our battalion further forward: that's for the attack which is supposed to be coming off on the 30th. There are houses on fire in the town of Montdidier, just for a change, it's terrible to see, but very pretty, especially with the moon hanging above it.

30 March, Easter Saturday: It is evening, I'm writing down my impressions of this day, which must have been the nastiest of any blessed day in the whole war, full of many dreadful situations, each one following closely on the one just before: At 7.30 our infantry attacked, and by way of a reply to that a hail of machine-gun fire comes out of Le Mesnil, worse than I've ever known; our command system breaks down; at 8.30 a.m. my Battery Commander, 2/Lt Knauer, rides forward, in spite of the heavy fire and the fact that on a horse you make a beautiful target for the French, to look for a new position. I bring the battery up behind, and now we've got so much shrapnel rattling down on us that you can hardly hear or see anything. The machine-gun fire, chattering away at us from only a few hundred metres distance, keeps on as heavy as ever. All hell has been let loose. The French seem to be transformed, they must have thrown completely fresh, properly rested troops into this sector, and a large number of them too. Among others, my good old Herrmann has been wounded. We pull up a steep track on to a plateau, and there is our No. 3 Battery next door to us. And up there it's a witches' cauldron, compared with which the business we had before was child's play: machine-gun fire and small-arms fire so strong that it might have been thousands and thousands of enemy gun-barrels being trained on our one Battery. The concentration of fire is so heavy that all we can do is lie on the ground beside the guns, with the infantry hardly 300 metres in front of us; and we haven't reached the peak yet, because suddenly we start being fired on from the right and left flanks as well, and it looks as if we are on a pointed wedge of ground offering a marvellous target for the French on all three sides. Times like this are really unbearable, as you haven't any way of seeing how you're ever going to get out of this witches' cauldron. Our own attack never gets off the ground, and now it begins to rain in torrents, and we are already very tired from the efforts of the last few days and from not getting a second's rest last night; and just in front of us, 2/Lt Mayer of No. 8 Battery gets killed in action; that's the tenth officer our Regiment has lost since 21 March. Now it gets even 'lovelier'. Our infantry start coming back, in groups or singly, because they can't stand it any more up there at the front, and finally there they are lying between the guns. Now comes the moment to bring up the limbers, but however are we going to manage to bring back the guns in this fire without very heavy casualties? They come tearing up at a gallop, and in a few quieter moments we actually manage to drive the guns back to the hollow by St Medard. It was high time indeed, because a few minutes later the French would have been inside our battery position and beyond it. In the early morning, incidentally, a French plane crashed in flames just in front of us, and the pilot fell out—he was dead when he hit the ground—just a few paces from our position.

Meanwhile, in spite of the bad weather, enemy planes have been appearing over our lines, flying at a low altitude in heavy swarms of twenty or thirty in a bunch. We are not having a much better time of it in the hollow, which is being swept with fire by French guns of every calibre. In the pouring rain the hollow has become a morass, so that after our unsuccessful operation our morale is a bit dismal. While waiting for orders we aren't doing much shooting. Later we were able to sit down in some old wooden huts which had belonged to the French, and everybody was so dog-tired that they all fell asleep. It would make no difference to us what happened, as the huts offer no protection against shelling, and if the French put a shell inside, we should all be done for. In fact a piece of shrapnel does come through the hut wall from a shell-burst nearby, and wounds one of our chaps. Now it's got round to 5.30 p.m. and we get word that our infantry has to move to a position further back. So for the second time today we have to do a high-speed move to the rear. One battery, lying a few hundred metres in front of us in the hollow, can't be brought back; but next day we get it back by mounting an infantry assault for the purpose. The enemy are so near that we should have been firing over open sights, but we have no time for any firing. We move back through Montdidier town to the old position which we were in to start with.

Easter Sunday, 31 March: We are sitting in our chalk-pit, six of us together, thinking about yesterday, and there isn't much chance of an Easter atmosphere. Then I go on observation duty, watch a number of dog-fights in the air and admire the splendid way our new triplanes are operating. Nimble, lively, highly manoeuvreable and incredibly fast, they climb almost vertically to take on one enemy plane after another, and our triplane's victories, in fact its very superiority, are overpowering to watch; but it's still dreadful to see the final act of one of those dog-fights, especially when the enemy pilots crash from a height of some 800 metres. The dog-fights go on in the afternoon; our squadrons have knocked down five enemy planes in the course of today in our sector alone. Meanwhile Montdidier is on fire, blazing from one end to the other. We don't attack on 31 March, and after yesterday's efforts the French, too, have had enough.

1 April: It isn't an April Fool joke, but early in the morning an order comes in that I've been appointed Adjutant of the 2nd Battalion. I'm really very unhappy to be leaving my well-beloved No. 2 Battery for good, even if it is promotion or what they call an honourable appointment. There is another point, and it doesn't give you a particularly pleasant feeling either; nearly all previous adjutants of the 2nd Battalion, 5th F.A.R. have been killed in action, and the reason for my own appointment is that my most recent predecessor, 2/Lt Jonas, died a hero's death yesterday.

'Baby' of No. 2 Battery, 5th Light Artillery Regiment, has been gazetted a second lieutenant. I say good-bye to my fellow-officers and my men, and go off without any ceremony through Montdidier to my new Battalion Commander, Captain Knigge, who has his H.Q. on the road to Faverolles. The funeral of my predecessor, 2/Lt Jonas, is just taking place in Lignières. 2/Lt Pastowsky is my staff officer. Captain Knigge is a splendid chap, both as a person and a soldier, very good at his work, and highly confident, as well as being a pleasant fellow-officer, and I get the immediate impression that I'll be able to work well with him. I have a pleasant surprise, a telephone call from the Regimental Adjutant, Lt Stürken, to congratulate me. An entirely new subject has now started for me, more varied than before and perhaps involving more responsibility.

2 April: My staff of the 2nd Battalion is being relieved, and two of my batteries, No. 4 and No. 6, as well. The other battalions are staying here and taking part in the artillery preparation for the attack on the 3rd; then the whole regiment will certainly go to rest stations, because they're worn out with fighting and have done a huge amount of work. Our 18th Army has thrust 60 kilometres deep all told, and in this sector alone has taken 1,100 guns and a huge number of prisoners. It is difficult to see how it's going to continue. In any case we are no longer east of Paris, but practically north of the city, and we hope our Army will have the good fortune to get the job of breaking through the enemy line to the south; except that it appears, as I foresaw, that we have pushed much further ahead than our neighbours to the right and left; this means that we have pushed out in a big wedge, very tempting to the French for the purposes of a flank attack. We learn from the military communiqué that we distinguished ourselves to the highest degree in the shemozzle on 30 March: we, in fact, the 9th Division, beat off the attacks made by three fresh enemy attacking divisions.

None of us has any idea what the Army Supreme Command is planning, but we all feel overwhelming confidence in Ludendorff and Hindenburg.

In this area we call the new triplanes the Air Hussars. Richthofen is working above our sector. We receive our first mail after these days of fighting, rush for the letters and newspapers, and read with great enthusiasm what the reports and commentaries are saying about our victory. Reports seldom sound so full or so enthusiastic, and our Army (Hutier's), our Corps (Webern's) and the place-names of Ham, Roye, Nesle and Montdidier are names that are going to stick.

Ludendorff has received the Grand Cross of the Order of the Iron Cross, and Hindenburg the Star of the Grand Cross of the same order.

Paris has been shelled once again with the 120-kilometre gun, and the world is trying to solve the mystery of this piece of artillery.

Richthofen has knocked down his 73rd opponent, and Bongartz his 35th.

The communiqué writes this about us gunners: 'In the course of the advance, the German artillery is showing a hitherto unequalled spirit of daring.'

My staff (God knows, not a rear-echelon staff!) has moved into quarters in Lignières. This means that we are a little way back from the front because, as I said before, our division is gradually being relieved. On the day I left my No. 2 Battery, it suffered quite exceptional casualties. I have been sad, really shaken by the news. The offensive cost 100 men, 13 officers and 200 horses from our Regiment alone.

The supplies—rations and ammunition—are now gradually able to get forward, mainly by lorry and by freshly-laid railway spurs. Positions are being surveyed, listening and flash-spotting sections are at work, and the whole business will soon be starting up again.

In the East, a combined German and Turkish offensive has begun against the British.

Our 1st Battalion is still in position and has been unfortunate enough to suffer further heavy casualties on 6 April, seven men in No. 1 Battery alone, and a warrant officer, *Offizierstellvertreter* Nikolaitschek, is dead.

On 6 April General Weber, our Divisional Commander, inspects detachments from all formations and expresses his most deeply felt thanks to the Division for their achievements since 21 March.

You can now gradually feel the approach of spring, the bushes are already green, and in woods which we walk through after the inspection, the handsome red and white anemones are out once again. And once more, memories from my childhood.

I record the full text of Regimental Orders dated 5 April:

> Days of supremely important action lie behind us. The Regiment has done what it promised to do. Every individual has given of his best. The things which the Regiment has done belong to History. With sorrowful but proud hearts we mourn our heroic dead. We wish a speedy recovery to our wounded. With eyes fixed on the way ahead, we gaze with rock-hard confidence into the promised land of the future!

7 *April:* The sun is out, and meanwhile other units who are being relieved are coming back from the front and stopping temporarily in Lignières, which is itself only a bare five kilometres behind the front, so it is not a rest station for divisions exhausted with fighting. But the infanteers of the 36th Regiment, returning from real hell at the front, start straight off by playing gay marches fit to make you cheer, and round the band as it plays stand the good-hearted musketeers and gunners, who—God knows—leave no doubt on their faces of their fidelity, confidence, pride, and certainty of final victory. When you look at these men, and several of them are already wearing the Iron Cross First Class, it seems such a natural

thing for us to win that you acquire fresh confidence in final victory.

The following original text of an order issued by the French High Command needs no comment:

Ordre A.O.K. 18. la/N.O. 1491.
28 Mars, 12.45. Copie Ordre Général No. 104:

L'ennemi s'est rué sur nous dans un suprême effort. Il veut nous séparer des Anglais, pour s'ouvrir la route de Paris coûte que coûte. Il faut l'arrêter. Cramponnez-vous au terrain, tenez ferme, les camarades arrivent. Tous réunis vous vous précipiterez sur l'envahisseur.

C'est la bataille, soldats de la Marne, de l'Yser et de Verdun, je fais appel à vous. Il s'agit du sort de la France.
                                        sign. Pétain

(The enemy has thrown his forces against us in a supreme effort. He wants to separate us from the British in order to open a route to Paris, whatever the cost. He must be stopped. Take a firm hold on the ground; stand firm; your comrades are on the way. Once united with them, you will charge against the enemy.

This is the decisive battle, soldiers of the Marne, the Yser and Verdun, for which I call upon you. It is a question of the fate of France.

(signed) Pétain)

Meanwhile a few comparatively quiet days go by at Lignières. I have been getting on very well indeed with Captain Knigge since the first few days, and have been working my way into my job as Adjutant.

Rittmeister von Richthofen has meanwhile notched up his 78th air victory, so that with his brother he now has over 100.

In Finland, incidentally, the German troops have beaten the Red Army and gone into the offensive near Helsingfors, fighting for Finland's rights and Finland's freedom. We have troops all over the world! And wherever they are, they are winning! Down in the Ukraine, heavy fighting with marauding enemy bands still continues; my first regiment is over there, and I hear from them now and again.

Up at Armentières in Flanders, the second act of our offensive has started, and the communiqué states that our troops are proceeding in column of march in pursuit of the scattered groups of British and Portuguese troops.

The days of spring weather here at Lignières are warm, sunny and full of sentimental memories. Once more you dream your way back into the past, and the daily round of peacetime living seems now, as I've mentioned before, just like Paradise!

One afternoon I was walking with Captain Knigge through the village of Lignières, and we went into the church. Captain Knigge sat down at the harmonium and began to play. Four old *Landwehr* men were standing there with their caps in their hands, old soldiers with beards; and they listened, devoutly and with pleasure, as our Captain played.

Armentières, where my unit was stationed in October and November, 1914, has been recaptured by the enemy. *Fliegerhauptmann* von Tutscheck has been killed in action.

I receive a very happy letter from my friend Kurt; he was over Flanders, flying on observation duty at 6,000 metres, and in a dog-fight with six Sopwiths he shot one down in flames, and got the Iron Cross First Class for it next day; he's terrifically proud of himself.

Army Orders published a few days ago contain (under Item 7) a brief request for a search to be made for the whereabouts of a German pilot recently shot down. A considerable number of German pilots are being shot down in any case, so I find this order surprising.

20 April: Czernin, the Austrian Minister-President, has resigned because the Emperor Charles is supposed to have written a letter to France behind his back.

21 April: We pull out of Lignières, so at last we are going to have a well-earned rest. We move into quarters at Quiquéry, a pleasant spot on the road from Ham to Nesle; our men rush about like a swarm of bees, hammering and carpentering away, and in a moment a dirty French hut gets turned into a clean German one. We only stay a day here anyway. In the evening we get a visit from the Battery Officers of my Battalion, that is, No. 4 Battery, No. 5, No. 6 and the light ammunition columns belonging to them; and I make the acquaintance of these fellow-officers as well. Being the Adjutant, I shall, both at rest stations and in the future fighting, have to deal much—in fact, solely—with the Battery C.O.s of my Battalion. It is evening now, and more German planes than you can count are flying, heavily laden with bombs, into the French rear areas; when we get a quiet time, that's the signal for it to start properly up above, because the amount of air fighting done at night has become very considerable.

22 April: Helsingfors has been taken by German troops.

We hear of unpleasant incidents connected with Prince Lichnowsky, the former German Ambassador to London; but who knows what there is behind it.*

Rittmeister von Richthofen scored his 80th air victory yesterday.

My old enthusiasm for flying is starting up again. I should so much like to have another try at getting into the Air Corps. I have hardly read about Richthofen's 80th air victory, when a rumour begins to fly about that Richthofen has been shot down: that would be a dreadful thing indeed. And curiously, although I feel moved every time an air hero dies, I just couldn't imagine what it would be like if it happened to me.

I receive a letter from my old regiment in the Ukraine: 2/Lt Schellenberg sends me interesting details of the way the war is going on down there: the infantry and artillery ride on a train, and when bands of Bolshevik marauders are reported, a few companies or batteries detrain, scatter the enemy and then get back on the train and travel on.

On the *23rd* I visit my own No. 2 Battery, which is stationed nearby. Other troops move through here, and I meet an officer I know, Otto de Neufville, who is with the 109th, the *Badische Leibgrenadiere.*

We are now posted away from the 9th Army Corps and

* In 1916 Lichnowsky, a strong supporter of Anglo-German harmony, wrote a pamphlet, *My Mission in London, 1912–14,* which was published in Berne, perhaps without his knowledge, in 1918. It circulated in Germany and expressed views shifting guilt for the war from Britain to Germany. L. was forced to resign from the *Herrenhaus,* the hereditary Prussian Upper Chamber.—R.T.

receive particularly warm thanks from the Commander, to which he adds his heartfelt wish that he will have us under his command again.

In the evening an order arrives from Army H.Q. that one Lt Pernet, a pilot in Flying Group 29, has been missing since the first days of the offensive, and that a high reward has been offered by a very senior person for information leading to 2/Lt Pernet's whereabouts; this seems to be about the same pilot whom I mentioned the day before yesterday as appearing in Army Orders. Well, here at Quiquéry, where we shall soon have been stationed for three days, I read this Order from 18 H.Q. and suddenly remember that on one day of the advance, on 23 or 24 March, a month ago, I saw a burnt-out plane lying beside the main road. We have certainly seen plenty of crashed planes, particularly in those days; but this particular plane must be quite near, close to our present quarters, at the place where we were stationed back in March; so I take a spade, walk along the road, and a bare 100 metres from my quarters I find the remains of the very same plane. I feel really most astonished when I discover on a piece of wreckage the very identification mark mentioned in the Army Order. I also find a little silver purse; I race back, report my discovery by W/T message to the unit concerned—Flying Group 29—and hear that the missing 2/Lt Pernet is Ludendorff's stepson.

Czernin's successor* is Burian.

The 8th issue of War Loan has brought in 14½ thousand million marks.

On *24 April* the Regimental C.O. orders a discussion of tactical, supply and personnel matters, which the three Battalion Adjutants are also ordered to attend.

Richthofen has really been killed in action! I am completely shattered by the news. No words will suffice to do justice to his deeds, or to describe the grief which every German feels at the loss of this national hero; it is just impossible to grasp; he has been buried by the British with the highest military honours, for he crashed in the British lines. Six British flying officers bore his coffin, and a British chaplain preached the sermon and sang his praises as an enemy hero; a British plane

* As Austrian Minister-President.—R.T.

with mourning pennants circled round the burial-ground during the funeral, and showed the highest honour to this fallen enemy. The British are indeed truly chivalrous, and we must thank all of them for honouring our great airman.

25 April: We march away from our cottage at Quiquéry. We could really have put up with it a bit longer, but we are going back into the deepest rear area. How precisely everything has been worked out! How well everything works—Ludendorff style down to the last detail! Even these relief operations require an immense amount of work. Traffic on the road is very heavy in both directions. On the march I get to know Captain von Rabenau,* the senior General Staff Officer with our division. We move past Italian, British and French prisoners working in the rear.

Towards evening we are in Happencourt, quite near the area where we advanced exactly a month ago. I talk to a rifleman from No. 18 Sturmtrupp, and am very pleased with his splendid morale; he was with Hutier at Riga, Jakobstadt and Oesel Island, and now he is under his command again here. I hear many interesting details about all the places where the war is being fought.

26 April: We move on through the devastated area where we did such throrough work in the retreat of 1917.—There's not a tree left standing, not a bush, and the scraps of rubble, which is all that remains of the houses, are already overgrown with grass and weeds—this is really horror brought to life! We pass a combined German–French cemetery with graves dated 1914, 1915, 1916, 1917 and 1918—there is one cross inscribed *'für sein Vaterland'* and another bearing *'Mort pour sa patrie'*. They were all doing their duty to the same degree; we feel that all this murdering is unworthy of the human race. This was really a place where no bird sang, and not even a rat or a

---

* Captain von Rabenau rose to the rank of General and was Chief of the German General Staff at Potsdam in the 30's. Herbert Sulzbach had to leave Germany on 25 May, 1937, but kept in touch with Rabenau, who was arrested in 1944 for his involvement in the conspiracy against Hitler culminating in the bomb plot of 20 July, 1944. After sharing a cell with Pastor Dietrich Bonhoeffer, Rabenau, a man of dedicated religious conviction, was executed in April, 1945.—R.T.

mouse would find anything to eat here. We move through this desert and gradually reach a rear area that looks more peaceful. There are actually civilians in the villages again. We move past a party of British prisoners at work in the area; a British corporal gives the orders 'Eyes—right: eyes—front'. The civilians regard us as an unavoidable hardship, and even though we are always decent to them you get the feeling that they will go on cursing us for ever, and that after the war they will hate us just as much.

27 April: We move on to Landifay; we are already many kilometres behind the front.

Unsuccessful attempt by the British to land at Ostend to destroy our harbour installations.

28 April: We ride on, and as we pass through Le Hérie, where we were at the beginning of March, I pay a visit to the family where I was billeted. It was a great pleasure and highly moving to see each other alive; I told them how bravely their own troops had been fighting, and they were very pleased at this and wished us *'tout de mieux jusqu'à la fin'*. The whole civilian population was out along the road as our 5th marched through. We have really made some friends here. In the evening we reach our permanent quarters where we are to stay at rest stations: Lemé, a straggling, very clean village, nice and peaceful, surrounded with lush fields and meadows. We move into good billets, all in one road, and the telephone exchange is set up in a house quite near mine. I've been billeted on pleasant people, have a clean room and, what a blessing, a proper bed. Our three infantry regiments move through and past us to the neighbouring villages to which they have been allocated, and a wonderful sight it is to see them march with bands playing, as though they were on manoeuvres. In our village there are another two battalions of our infanteers.

We shall really be able to have a good rest here. On the first evening we sit with the civilians in our billets and begin to talk to them. Every one of us does his best to help the work of serving our cause, and wherever we go, to enlighten the people by explaining that all the stuff that has been put into their minds about the German 'barbarians' is nothing but lies and

168

deception. For the first time in weeks we sleep without our uniforms.

In the magazine *Die Jugend* today, the title-page carries a drawing of Arnauld de la Perrière, the U-Boat commander. I mention him because he is a proper example of our sea heroes; he came to fame by making a voyage to Spain, and by sinking a very large tonnage of enemy ships; he is also a Knight of the Order of *Pour-le-Mérite*.

1 May: I come back from a session with the 1st Battalion, F.A.R.5. It is late at night, and I had a lovely ride over the countryside on this spring evening. I step into my billet and find a very large envelope waiting for me. I tear it open, and inside is a large photograph, and with it a hand-written letter —from Ludendorff. I just can't describe how excited I was about it. Just like the letter, the envelope is written entirely by hand, by Ludendorff himself; at the top is written 'by despatch rider'; at the bottom, on the left, 'via A.O.K.'; 'on via A.O.K.7'; on the right, '9th Division, sender Ludendorff'. The back of the envelope bears the large awe-inspiring seal, 'Chief of General Staff, Armies in the Field, Operations Section'. The text of the letter reads:

> My dear Lieutenant,
> I wish to thank you for searching for the body of my son who was killed in action. I have in fact been able to discover the grave, which was near the plane.
> Please accept this photograph as a token of gratitude from a father who has suffered a great loss.
> Ludendorff

I must have looked at all this a hundred, or perhaps a thousand times, rejoicing to myself there in the middle of the night. Whoever else in the Army is going to possess a portrait like that with a letter from Ludendorff? And I woke up my mates and showed it all to them, in the middle of the night.

Tavastehus [Hämeenlinna] in Finland has been taken by General Count von der Goltz.

In Flanders we have taken the famous Kemmel Hill in an infantry assault.

2 May: I reply to General Ludendorff and write exactly what I feel, that a soldier at the front could wish for no higher decoration than to possess his portrait signed by his own hand.

General news: We have taken Sevastopol on the Black Sea and Taganrog on the Sea of Azov. In Finland, the whole of South-West Finland has been liberated, and German and Finnish troops are fighting shoulder to shoulder; fighting is going on in Mesopotamia against the British, and in Persia our Allies the Turks have occupied important positions.

2/Lt Knauer, my Battery Commander, has gone up to Lieutenant.

6 May: We celebrate the Crown Prince's birthday. My friend *Pieselmax* of No. 2 Battery has been given the Iron Cross First Class.

We are having some really peaceful days here, with lovely weather, and our duties are quite tolerable too.

In Berlin there is a row going on in the Reichstag about voting rights.

General Foch has become Commander-in-Chief for the Entente on the Western Front.

7 May: The peace treaty has been signed with Roumania.

We receive orders issued by Ludendorff about experiences gleaned in recent actions, and these orders are so clear, precise and brief, hitting the nail on the head so accurately and invariably, and clarifying every action which is faulty or capable of improvement, that when you think of Ludendorff you can really feel struck dumb by admiration.

I've now been an Adjutant for six weeks, and even if these weeks, except for a few days, have been quiet ones, I really have worked my way well into my job, and can say for my own pleasure and satisfaction that I feel damned happy in the job. I get on famously with my C.O., and the same with all the officers of all the batteries in the Battalion.

Once again one has time to think things over, and I feel a strong desire to keep letting the people at home know about the great things which are happening here. I should like to tell the story of all the deeds that are done out here, both great and small, and the devotion to duty, the comradeship, the loyalty and the thousands of different examples of heroism. I still feel as keen and dedicated as ever, and I should like to transfer my own spirit to the luke-warm people and inject them with the idea that they too can feel pride—in fact, that they should have the proudest feelings that anyone could possess.

I quote a passage, in fact the final words of a newspaper article written recently by my friend 2/Lt Reinhardt, who was also once my Battery Commander:

> At such moments those who are responsive are moved, shaken and inspired to an overwhelming degree by proud happiness at being part of such an industrious, creative nation.

Guatemala has declared war on us—that won't bother us much.

A few days later we had a big exercise with our infantry, and Captain von Mutius in charge. There was a long session for criticism and appreciation, in the presence of the G.O.C.

Once again we receive secret orders, reminding one of the days before 21 March. Lectures on exterior ballistics are given to all officers in the Division, and cross-country runs over obstacles are organized for the batteries.

Lt Knauer of No. 2 Battery has developed T.B. and is going to hospital. Saying good-bye to him moved me very much. When I had just arrived at the Regiment he was like a father to me, and I have a huge amount to thank him for.

I have been a year with the Regiment now, and love it with all my heart. After one lecture I ride back alone, on a wonderful May evening; nightingales and blackbirds are singing in competition, and the little villages, surrounded by hedges, meadows and woods, are peaceful and enchanting. Our men are sitting or standing outside the cottage doors, some with French girls. It all looks like scenes from large-scale manoeuvres. It is charming to see these bearded German soldiers, who have families of their own, cradling the little children of Frenchwomen in their arms.

18 May: Last day at Lemé. Preparations for a new offensive have been completed, and for the first time I shall be going into action as an Adjutant; I have a thousand things to think of, and must take great care of my batteries. This evening a lance-bombardier arrives back from leave and brings me a letter from my parents: I can't believe the news: Kurt Reinhardt is dead! I had never wept before in the war, but I did then. I never had a friend like him. He was such a wise, warm-hearted person, so easily aroused to enthusiasm. I pulled out of the depot with him in 1914, we had our first dose of heavy action together, we understood each other from the very first moment, and we were, if you can't find a better word, really soul-mates; we shared everything between us, and when we were separated, went out of our way to see each other in every nook and cranny of the front, as well as meeting on leave at home. How proud his last letter was, just after that air victory—and a few days later this most faithful of all friends was killed in action himself. His poor mother, who has now lost her husband and her only son as well! I think of the poem which one of von Tutscheck's comrades dedicated to him (I've mentioned his flying exploits before) when he died:

> *Ein treues Herz ist hier gebrochen,*
> *das Freundschaft nahm und Freundschaft gab.*

> Here is a true heart broken,
> That friendship took and friendship gave.

In my unending grief I went that last night for a walk in Lemé, and thought of all the beautiful things, all the wonderful nights in May that our well-beloved Kurt would never see again, and the final victory of our armies that he would never see again either.

When he was at the flying school in Warsaw, he wrote to me after his father's heroic death in action:

Warsaw
2 May, 1917

I feel so lonely. You can't believe how provokingly sentimental it makes you to live in such a huge park which reminds you of by-gone splendours, all perfumed with heady scents and fragrance. I've just come back from my evening walk through the park; after the thunder-shower which has at last freed Warsaw from its oppressive sultriness, a drowsy scent of jasmine and limes is pouring through the wide open windows. Remembering a theme from Bach, or a person whom you love, brings you to the edge of despair. I believe I can never be really cheerful again, everything that faces me seems to be either hostile or indifferent.

I shall be celebrating my birthday with Murnau, the actor who was with Reinhardt, out in the park here, very quietly.

All the best, with all my heart
Your faithful
Kurt R.

Another letter from Warsaw, dated 13 June, 1917:

... not a trace of war here: everything is in the shops, only terribly expensive. Streets, shops, cafés, theatres, civilians, women, magnificence and poverty make up a bewildering, many-coloured scene.

You saunter through the streets, quite aimlessly, until a child dying of hunger wipes the happy look off your face.... Churches swell in unbelievable splendour among the fresh greenery, and neither the luxury nor the poverty can touch them. And if I keep talking about Warsaw, this throbbing foreign city, I still have to think of you and the time we stayed in Lille and other French towns, and I regret that we can't enjoy it together....

After I had applied for flying duties, he wrote to me from his home on leave:

Frankfurt-am-Main
17 July, 1917

... I received your kind letter, about your having become one of my brothers-at-arms. How pleased I am! All the best of luck, with all my heart! And my sincere admiration to you for wanting to go straight into a fighter group!

After being posted to No. 2 Air Photography Section at Ghent in Belgium, he wrote:

Thielt

15 January, 1918

... First of all, there is our hero and leader, Lt Fricke, who is a Knight of the *Pour-le-Mérite*. This small, distinguished, quiet man hasn't got anything heroic about him, and with his round horn-rimmed spectacles he looks more like a man of learning than a regular officer. I always feel tempted to call him *Herr Doktor*, especially yesterday when I had a learned discussion with him about Kant, space and time, and life and death. He is very easy to talk to. He wears his decoration with a perfectly justifiable, rather childish pride, and he has certainly earned it; he has been flying since October '14. ...

Then came the letter dated 2 April, 1918, from Thielt:

... Imagine what incredible luck I had: on 12 March I was on an Army Group flight, at an altitude of 6,000 metres over Ypres, when I was attacked by six Sopwiths; and by using telescopic sights and incendiary bullets, I managed to shoot one of them down in flames! It all went so quickly that I was not conscious at all of what I was doing; but I was after all taking action in an emergency. Since apart from that I brought home a good report, Fuchs and I were awarded the Iron Cross First Class by the A.O.K. on 18 March, which was Fuchs's birthday. ... So this is how you become a top dog overnight and hardly know how you got that far (perhaps rather like the maiden lady getting a child!).

What do you say to the splendid way things went at the start of our offensive—recapture of Roye, Noyon, Evricourt and so on? Where was your regiment at the time? What action did you see? Write soon, and let me know particularly that you are in good health. You'll get something much more detailed from me soon. There are great tasks ahead for both of us. I shall only be able to go on leave in May or June—how about you?

Ever your
Kurt R.

And then, dated 16 May, 1918, came the letter from his friend and comrade Ottfried Fuchs:

My Dear Sulzbach,

I have to fulfil the sad task of informing you that our dear friend Reinhardt has died a hero's death. On 9 May, 1918, at 5 in the afternoon, dear Kurt was fatally wounded in an air battle not far from Dunkirk, so that he died on the same flight. By some miracle his pilot was unwounded, and we have to thank his presence of mind for bringing back the body.

So that was the great thing that was waiting for him after his last letter. Going on leave—to eternity.

These few letters show what an unusual person died in him. Isn't it shattering that after his first and last air victory he makes a kind of apology for taking the life of a person—for our enemies are just that, people—and nevertheless expresses, with all the gift for enthusiasm which he was ready to show for anything, the devotion to duty and the idealism embodied in victory itself?

VI

1918

The Assault on the Chemin des Dames

19 May, Whit Sunday: At 4.30 a.m. we march off and leave Lemé; the people at our billets looked after us so well that early as it was, they had already got up and made coffee. We rode off into a wonderful May morning, but all my thoughts were on Kurt.

By 10 o'clock we had already reached Barenton on the way to Serre, and called a halt. I have managed, by the way, to have a particularly keen officer, whom I always liked very much, posted from No. 1 Battery to the Staff to be my staff officer; he was transferred to me on regimental orders today; 2/Lt Freiherr von Seebach. In the evening secret orders arrive: creeping barrage, means of communication, cover names— in short, it's soon going to start up again along the Chemin des Dames. We belong to the old 7th Army again.

20 May: At 3.30 a.m. we march off for Athies; moving off in the very early morning like this shows that they are trying to conceal the troop movements from the enemy Air Force.

21 May: The mighty cathedral of Laon rears up in front of us once more. It was exactly a year ago that I arrived here in the middle of that terrific defence battle, and here we are now starting a new offensive. So many of my comrades have been killed in action in this last year.

Our men are digging up the asparagus at Athies as expertly as though they were all farmers. On *21 May* at 11 p.m. I ride off on a recce with my Captain Knigge through the Monampteuil area, well known to us of old. It is a hot night, and the moon has risen high above us; there isn't just one nightingale singing here, there are thousands of them, and the frogs are croaking as though it were high summer. We ride through the spooky ruins of Bruyères village, then Vorges via Laval and the 'Snake Road'. Now we are so near the front that we have to dismount, stumbling about on foot until 4 in the morning, looking for the command post which has been allocated to us. We are almost exactly at the spot where we had defence positions a year ago. The enemy hardly fire at all during the night, just a little searching and sweeping fire. They seem not to be noticing anything, in spite of all the columns of ammunition being trundled up to the front; many batteries will be moving into positions partly in advance of the infantry lines. The croaking of the frogs in the Aillette area is so powerful that it drowns the rattle of the ammunition columns; so the frogs are what you might call our latest allies. I daresay that after this the French will be saying that the Boche have been bribing the frogs to do it! We get back from our recce at 6 a.m., and the same day, 22 *May* that is, we move on. We look for our immediate superior, Major Leonardi of the 1st Battalion, 28th Saxon Field Artillery Regiment. We have quite a selection of batteries under us. In the evening we set up the communications to our higher command and to our tactical batteries. I have a huge amount to do with administrative and tactical orders. This work of deploying troops for action is enormously exciting, and this time it is on just as great a scale as the preparations before 21 March. Everything gets worked out, conceived and calculated down to the smallest detail. The barrage is going to be laid down on the very second—and it is going to last seven hours! Once more the most exacting demands are going to be made on every officer and every man. Once again, every shot fired will have to be estimated. We have to think about telephones, signalling lamps, runners—in fact, all forms of communication, so that after the rolling barrage begins, the break-through will operate successfully. The transformation from static to mobile warfare demands unbelievable accuracy and far-sightedness, and I'm kept at work until 3 o'clock in the morning.

Next day 2/Lt von Seebach joins us, a lively, cheerful, sensible chap and a good comrade.

24 May: One can hardly keep level with the work, and sleep no longer bears thinking of. In the evening I receive a letter from one of Kurt's flying companions, giving me some more details about his death. I still can't believe it. But the war goes on and makes no allowance for feelings; new impressions come rolling in, new people, events pass in a long succession and obliterate the scenes gone by. The things which you once thought were overwhelming are now forgotten and have long since been succeeded by new facts and details—you keep moving on and on, and on. But I shall not forget Kurt, never.

Orders are now tumbling in, and the new offensive is going to be given the code-word *'Turnstunde'*—'Physical Training Period'; everything has been marvellously well worked out, and it's going to succeed! We shall be stationed right up near the front; we'll lay down our barrage and follow up as second-line troops, and then, on the second and third days, we'll have the job of pursuing the enemy who by then, we hope, will be in flight.

27 May: Once again world history has been made, and just as I did on 21 March, 1918, beyond St Quentin, I am sitting now in our bivouac in the evening after this splendid victory, with Chavignon behind me: but with a completely different feeling from the mood we were in on 21 March. That time little 2/Lt Schmidt, my *Pieselmax,* was sitting beside me on the limber, helping me to make my notes; and now *Pieselmax* is dead. Only yesterday he was charging about in his battery, as keen, cheerful and lively as ever; he was one of our most daring chaps, and for four weeks he had worn his Iron Cross First Class, awarded for conspicuous gallantry; but now he is lying in his grave near Monampteuil. Yesterday, shortly before the attack, he was killed, and a lance-sergeant with him, by a direct hit; and my pleasure at the thought of the offensive left me entirely. Now he is dead, our companion who was always gay and always eager for hard work. I think back over how many of my comrades and school-friends are no longer there—it's just unbelievable! And apart from this, we had other losses before the barrage began. I will go back.

Last night at 8 o'clock we rode out of the little village of Athies. It was a splendid scene on the main roads—the typical final stage of a deployment on a huge scale; battery after battery, column after column, and infantry at the ready; then, for the first time, I saw chasseurs and mountain machine-gun battalions brought up for this hilly terrain. Outside the village of Laval the French were putting down harassing fire on the road, and we got into a patch of this, but by another piece of extraordinary good luck, we galloped through it without sustaining any losses. Then we dismounted and marched over the Siegfried Ridge, well known of old, to our command post near Chevregny. The French were putting down more harassing fire over the whole area. Our lads were in splendid spirit. Again and again, when we passed other troops, the men would shout 'All the best!' or 'Make a good job of it!' to each other. And every one of them was a picture of confidence that we would win.

Telephone lines were now laid very rapidly from our command dug-out to all the batteries. Then came the weather report, to work out the exterior ballistics. Very soon it was 2 a.m. on *27 May*, and at exactly 2 o'clock the barrage began, from thousands of gun-barrels. The guns roared, and in a moment the enemy harassing fire had slackened; dozens of different Very lights were going up, and we were shooting Blue Cross and Green Cross* and shrapnel. It all works marvellously, there isn't silence for a moment, it just went on uninterruptedly, rumbling and banging away; rapid fire of every calibre was rattling down on the French, and we hoped they still had no notion of what was coming. Not a single battery had done any range-firing, but our shooting was a masterpiece of accuracy, all worked out and plotted according to the latest principles of ballistics. Communications with the command posts and batteries were functioning very well indeed, since nearly all the telephone lines were still intact. The times laid down for the barrage passed, and at exactly 4.40 the rolling barrage started, cloaking the infantry

* For the contents of these gas shells, see footnote to p. 150.—R.T.

assault, which rushed over the Chemin des Dames and beyond with unbelievable impetus; and there were the first 5,000 prisoners in our hands, and more guns than you could count. Regrettably, our regiment once again suffered a few casualties, including four officers. There was talk of our offensive having been betrayed by deserters. Hence the strong harassing fire on the evening of the 26th. It hasn't helped the enemy, but it's a terrible thought that the villainy of these criminals has led to many of our comrades—*Pieselmax* among them—having lost their lives. Certainly not even the enemy could have any respect for such scoundrels.

In general it was an exact repetition of the pattern of 21 March, except that the terrain here was more difficult because the Chemin des Dames is a range of ridges: the French sat on them, and obtained very strong rear support from the natural configuration of the ground; but even that advantage could not hold out against our barrage and the victorious thrust of our infantry.

Towards evening we bivouacked with our 18th (Colonel Zechlin's) Infantry Brigade, to which we belong, since my three batteries of the 2nd Battalion are now support battalions for their infantry. Each of the three batteries is allocated to one of the three infantry regiments of our Division, so that now, for direct operational purposes, I am only working with the infantry. It is a particular feather in our Battalion's hat to be a support battalion; you have to be particularly keen on this job, because we have to advance with the infantry. I cannot think of any better relations between infantry and artillery than those which have now been established between our two branches of the service in this Division.

We have hardly bivouacked when our valiant signalmen lay lines one way to the regimental C.O. and the other way to the infantry command post, with immediate communications through these posts to Division and to the three infantry regiments; where communication is not achieved by lines, lamp signals take over: we have red light signals today, and white for the infantry.

I have to pick out the signallers for particularly high praise: they have a job which never lets them take any rest, and is almost more dangerous than ours, as they always have to be out when there is any shooting—or rather whenever the lines are cut by fire; they are a very carefully selected body of men.

28 May: The offensive proceeds at 3 in the morning. For me it's my first offensive as an Adjutant, and the issue of orders for the second day of the advance is particularly interesting. We are now front-line troops and so will be in the front line today, whereas yesterday we were second-line troops even after the barrage had finished. At 4 a.m. we have a dose of enemy air bombing, and the enemy pilot adopts the most unpleasant technique of dropping flares and illuminating the terrain in order to take better aim. To the accompaniment of the usual, if highly disagreeable, hissing noise he unloads quite a packet of medium-calibre bombs which by good fortune do not score any hits on us personally.

We belong to the Wichura Corps, the von Böhn Army, and the German Crown Prince's Army Group; to our right are the 14th Infantry Division and to our left the 14th Reserve Division. Our Infantry Brigade Staff is particularly daring; they keep right on their regiment's heels; for a Staff, that is almost *too* daring. With von Seebach, my staff officer, I keep taking messages from Brigade to my Infantry C.O.'s and again to my batteries, and all of a sudden we are right in the middle of a proper battle command; you can see how the individual attacks develop and how everything is thought out and prepared down to the tiniest detail. Meanwhile we have once again taken some prisoners, including the battalion commander of a French battalion of Chasseurs. I try to have a word with him, but it remains merely an attempt: he refuses to say anything at all and just stands in front of me, proud, serious-faced, not saying a word, bent in body and broken in spirit; he is wearing the Cross of the Legion of Honour.

Our infantry attack, backed by our artillery, goes on and on, always forward, as though there were no other direction.

We have taken Soissons. Regrettably, we have lost three officers in just a few hours; that makes seven officers from our regiment in these two days.

Fort Condé has been taken.

The second day of this splendid offensive is drawing to a close, and we are spending the night in Bregny.

29 May: Our command post is in the Montagne-Ferme, where I receive a highly important job: I am required to move the whole artillery—that is, not only my own battalion—to new positions, and since the regimental C.O., Major von Ohnesorge, has been right up at the front with the infantry, I take on the job myself. Near Missy there is a very heavy traffic block; crossing the Aisne has been made much more difficult because the enemy had time to blow up all the bridges; but the obstacles are already being removed, our splendid Sappers are running up emergency bridges in no time. I guide the artillery round Soissons and ride on from Missy to Venicel along the Aisne: an enchanting valley. In front of me lies Soissons, which is already in our hands, and all round me are signs of very hasty flight: packs, rifles and greatcoats lying about in thousands. At Billy we come across the first civilians, and we do some requisitioning there. The prisoners of war and the civilians whom we talk to are very downcast about this new German victory, and everyone makes the occasion a cue for cursing away at Britain and America. I meet my regimental C.O. near Noyant; there is heavy fighting in progress just now. You can see the French riflemen pouring back; enemy batteries moving up to the front; and overhead, planes engaging in dog-fights. After such unheard-of successes our general morale could only be compared with August, 1914. It's wonderful to see the present look on the faces of our valiant regiments as they advance in an assault; they are almost laughing for joy, and all they can see is victory. If you people at home could only see it!

Then I meet a fellow-officer from the infantry, who tells me proudly that he and his men alone have taken 1,200 prisoners.

Meanwhile I have made friends with 2/Lt von Seebach, my staff officer; I've certainly picked a good one there, and believe I have found a chap who is as fine a comrade as he is a vigorous, hard-working officer.

We spend the night in Billy and have done some splendid requisitioning; the good-hearted civilians are giving us everything they can, or bartering what they have for cigarettes. They take it for granted that we are just doing our duty.

30 May: A duty ride takes me to our Divisional Commander, General Weber, and to the General Staff officer of our neighbouring division. One notices in this sort of work how closely communications to one's right and left are maintained in the new mobile warfare. Both in the eyes of the Divisional Commander, the Brigade Commander and the individual regimental C.O.'s, not only my Infantry Support Battalion but the whole 5th Regiment enjoys the greatest popularity, and every infantryman you meet tells you something nice about how keen our batteries are and how well they are commanded. I keep admiring the really expert way in which different branches of the service co-operate. In the afternoon we are in Noyant, where once again we capture huge quantities of supplies. My command post is on the side of a steep slope. In our sector we have taken 35,000 prisoners so far; the Conta Corps has crossed the Marne, and the François Corps is advancing near Coucy le Château. We have a Zouave division facing our sector, with Moroccans and Arabs, and have taken some of them prisoner; I have made some quick snapshots of them passing. Nearly all the Regiment's batteries are moving past us here, and we are pleased to see each other and exchange good wishes.

31 May: We stay in Noyant for the night. Strong enemy counter-attacks: the enemy suddenly bursts out of Chaudun with a large number of small tanks, what we call 'Babies', followed by exceptionally strong forces of infantry. For the first time the enemy Air Force is also particularly active. Today their planes appeared to have intentions regarding our captive balloons, which have been moving up behind our assault with conspicuous promptness. The first attack made by one of these planes was unsuccessful in so far as our observer got away by parachute: we could see it clearly here up at the front. The second attack, unluckily, achieved its object: very suddenly, four planes dived down on our captive balloons from a very great height, no one saw them coming, the ack-ack began firing too late, and two German balloons hurtled towards the ground, shrouded in huge bursts of flame; the two observers jumped clear with their parachutes, and appeared to make a safe landing. The enemy squadron then came up forward and picked us as a target, but fortunately a few German triplanes made a sudden and welcome appearance, you heard the usual tack-tack-tack, and we cheered as two of the enemy up there were 'taken apart'; one in fact came down in three separate pieces.

Our regimental C.O., Major von Ohnesorge, has been wounded. We feel sad and depressed; we always had such unlimited confidence in this daring, really brilliant leader, this extraordinarily just man, who always preferred to be in advance of his unit, nearer the enemy than they were, rather than the other way about.

I really have to say something more about our Signals network: first of all there are the carrier-pigeons, which carry the messages in a little sheath hung round their necks; the pigeon handler is with the troops up at the front, with his birds in a box. Yesterday, for example, I saw the General Staff officer from our neighbouring division, who had come up to our sector, bringing carrier-pigeons with him; he obtained from us the information which was important for his division. The pigeons were released with the message, flew round the point of release a few times, and then made unerringly for their home base. Then there are the messenger-dogs, who are enabled by a similar course of training to carry the message to their home base. Each messenger-dog has two handlers, known as the Reporter and the Receiver, with whom it is trained. Then come the mounted messengers and runners, who dash across the terrain day and night; mounted, as far as they can be, and otherwise on foot as their name implies— doing this very difficult job with extraordinary fidelity and iron determination. And then, lamp-signalling, which I have mentioned before. The lamp-signals are given in Morse code from the most advanced command post to Brigade, and relayed from there to Division. And in addition we have the W/T aerials, sometimes mounted on vehicles, sending wireless messages crackling through the ether to the receiving stations. The oldest and crudest communication system is still our field telephone network, which has to function between the most advanced infantry position, where the artillery O.P. is, and the batteries or lower command posts.

If all these signalling techniques had been working as well as this in September, 1914, we might perhaps not have got into that miserable Battle of the Marne. Now, of course, the supreme role in the world of signalling, is observation from the air.

When our regimental C.O. had to go back to the rear because of his wounds, he stamped his feet angrily and really lost his temper at having to desert his regiment in the middle of this offensive. When he said good-bye he shook hands with every one of us, and once again gave us these words to think about: 'It is no dishonour to lose the guns—we must not retreat, we must never desert our infantry, we must keep on firing until we have drawn our last breath!'

Meanwhile the French are making further attacks: apart from the tanks and the close-packed lines of riflemen, they are throwing quantities of cavalry against us. Our artillery and machine-gun fire are taking a heavy toll. 2/Lt Pumplun takes his No. 1 Battery in front of the infantry lines and knocks out two tanks straight away; what's left of them is now standing there. Other tanks get hit and brought to a standstill. The remaining tanks do an about turn, all our batteries are firing over open sights, and it's splendid to earn praise from the infantry—the best compliment we could wish for. The Brigade Commander immediately says he wants to report to the rear that our quite exceptional performance should be mentioned in the Army communiqué. 2/Lt Mazur, commanding his No. 4 Battery with outstanding gallantry, has made an outstanding contribution to today's success.

Towards evening my Battalion Commander, Captain Knigge, took over the First Battalion, this re-arrangement having been made necessary by the departure of the regimental C.O.; I went with him, while von Seebach stayed behind. We moved through Bercy, and above the village encountered a typical scene of a battlefield in the middle of heavy fighting: German dead, whole ranks of Zouave infantry mown down together, lying dead in a corn-field in the same order in which they were advancing; dead horses, smashed vehicles, all kinds of equipment—all jumbled wildly together.

I'm at the observation post, where all the Battery C.O.'s have gathered. I'm sitting in a hole in the ground with two telephone operators from my dear old No. 2 Battery, and we are in high spirits at meeting again for the first time in weeks.

At 8.15 p.m. the French attack again: they advance in waves, in the closest possible order, with the French company commanders on horseback—this is the way they are going to try to push us back. Our batteries slam down an absolutely splendid barrage, the kind the French wouldn't have dreamed of; they retreat with enormous losses, and our infantry cheer loudly to us. Then the French attack again at the 14th Reserve Division, and our batteries get the range there too, and mow them down. Now a dose of heavy French artillery fire starts to come down on us, with the heaviest stuff landing in front of our O.P., and behind it too—they've got us nicely in a pair of tweezers! We retire into the corn-field, and it gets very noisy there indeed. We come through all right; gradually it gets quieter, and night comes down after a heavy, very heavy day, which ends in glory for us; for we have repulsed a French counter-attack—which one hopes was made in desperation—of very considerable size and weight. The day has cost our regiment heavy casualties; two officers apart from the regimental C.O. and the regimental M.O., and many horses killed. Night has fallen, and at 11 p.m. I walk as far as Noyant, by now very hungry indeed; then I hunt for my command post. First I land in an infantry field dressing station where four rather prim German medical orderlies are sitting very comfortably, eating and smoking with some French who have just been taken prisoner. These chaps have hardly been captured before the German and French soldiers are comrades. I chat a bit with the French; they are intelligent, amiable fellows, who admit the superiority of our troops in a very sporting style. But they say they are not fighting 'pour la France, mais pour les autres' ('for France, but for the others');

they are still being told stories about our killing prisoners, and they are agreeably surprised that it isn't happening!

I then spend the night in a cellar in Noyant, united once more with Captain Knigge and 2/Lt von Seebach. The cellar is so large that it is almost like a cave, and a number of civilians from Noyant have taken refuge here, clutching a few belongings, waiting to see what is going to happen to them. What a wretched life for these poor people! They are terribly anxious about their relatives, some of whom are separated from them. It was strange, incidentally, to hear what a Zouave told me: wearing his yellowish-brown uniform, he was particularly frightened of being taken for a British soldier and being badly treated on that account. They seem to know which people we are particularly cross with!

The Adjutant of our Brigade is Lt von Drabich-Waechter, one of the most good-natured and hard-working officers that you could imagine. His whole style, even his appearance, reminds me vividly of my brother-in-law who was killed in action in 1914. I meet him a good deal because of my job and my particular duties.

The Commanding Officer of the French tank section has been taken prisoner.

In the course of this night we receive order after order, one taking over from the other, and there is a bustle of activity such as I have seldom seen. You don't even get time to think of sleep or rest, that's obvious! Arrangements are made for regiments, about reserves, and concerning attack and defence, messages are exchanged with our neighbouring division, and details are prepared for the day ahead. And in all this, each individual is contributing his entire personality to the whole effort needed for victory.

The latest newspaper we have been able to get hold of uses quite overwhelming language, but of all its reports and articles, one point inspires us most: 'The masterly performance by the Field Artillery on the Chemin des Dames and the untiring, death-defying advance by the Infantry with their faithful comrades-in-arms', and that's us.

1 June: The day begins with a heavy rumble from both sides.

The fighting sways to and fro. We have two casualties right at the start, Captain von Mutius of the infantry being wounded, and his adjutant with him; he was the man who took Montdidier on 27 March. I am with our Brigade Commander, Colonel Zechlin, who is as courageous as he is good-natured. I have to attend tactical discussions now, to deal with problems which arise in the course of the fighting.

I have to add here that yesterday 2/Lt May of No. 5 Battery had to put his guns out of action when the French counter-attacked; and today he took his men out and brought the guns back again, unluckily losing his courageous Sergeant Faller, who was killed in action.

We have been supplied with two messenger-dogs, who arrived with four dog-handlers—the two dog-leaders and their opposite numbers.

Meanwhile we have got as filthy and unshaven as we were in 1914, but in the mad rush of duties to perform we completely forget about this lack of personal neatness.

Paris has been shelled once again by our famous long-distance gun, the French having reported it as having been destroyed some time ago! The official military communiqué for 29 May writes once more of the 'tirelessly advancing infantry and artillery'. A further official report, under the headline 'Fame achieved by the German Artillery', describes the brilliant performance achieved by every single Battery Commander since 27 May.

The day closes without our having been able to advance any further, but also without the French being able to record the slightest advantage obtained from their counter-attacks.

2 June: Heavy attack by our neighbouring division. Chaudun, which is not in our hands yet, is riddled with machine-gun nests. The French put on an attack; and in the afternoon, with some hard fighting, our infantry at last take Chaudun. The supply columns are operating fantastically, e.g. when my No. 5 Battery obtained replacements, three new guns for three of theirs which had been knocked out, within a few hours. I really feel I must correct the remarks which are so often made against Staff people: I can see it here myself;

even General Weber, who is commanding a Division, is very frequently up here with us, and during the attack the Brigade staff are up with the regimental and battalion staffs, in some places in advance of the batteries.

Chaudun has fallen into our hands through the single-handed daring of one corporal and five men. Prisoners were being taken back to the rear, and as one of our men saw these young Frenchmen, in the pink of condition, he said to one of his mates, 'All they need is our officers, and they'd be the best soldiers you could want!' The day closed without any substantial gains having been achieved.

3 June: Missy is in our hands. It seems that the attack—or the whole offensive—has achieved its objective, and that we are not moving any further forward for the moment. We march back to Ploisy and pass through the ruins of Bercy. It all looks really dreadful here, worst of all up on the road to Chaudun. Seasoned fighting men that we are, we can't help being shaken at the sight of all these bodies which have been torn to pieces, and then cut up over and over again; friend and foe, white and black, all jumbled together. It is also very hot, and the stink of corpses is more than one can bear, but we have no time to bury the dead now. There has been very heavy fighting round Ploisy—this place where I am sitting and writing was once a splendid château. From up here you get a view into a pleasant valley, with steep slopes and hilly meadows—it reminds me of the Black Forest; and over-head, the bluest of blue summer skies, and birds singing away; the most lively picture of Nature, and just beside it all, death, decay and destruction! The château itself has been honey-combed with direct hits, and even though the outer walls are still standing, the whole interior is just a dreadful mess, and the whole building is as good as a ruin; but fresh red roses are blooming in the garden.

We, the 9th I.D., are at last being withdrawn to the second line after seven of the heaviest days in the first wave. There are a lot of prisoners coming through Ploisy again, including arabs and negroes from Martinique—black as coal those chaps are. I shouldn't like to be taken prisoner by them!

4 June: So our Division is going to rest stations, we are being billeted at the rear in Billy; the casualties among our horses have been very great indeed.

5 June: In Billy. Marvellous day. In the evening I go with 2/Lt von Seebach and visit some gentlemen at Brigade, and we sit with them until 2.30 in the morning in a fabulous garden, talk about the last few days, and have rather more to say about the days ahead.

New flying stars have appeared in the Flying Corps sky: Udet has got to his 26th, Menckhoff to his 31st, and Löwenhardt to his 27th.

The dream of going to rest stations has now been dreamed, and on *7 June* we are moving away from our pleasant quarters in Billy to go back to the front with the whole 2nd Battalion; we are being brought into action for fresh preparatory fire and a new attack. We stay another night at Ploisy and reconnoitre the positions east of Missy.

8 June: We move to a command post to the north of Chaudun, in a narrow sunken track. For the moment I am alone with Seebach. The telephone lines are laid at once, the batteries move into their positions, and we set up house here with our runners. We dig a large hole in one bank of the sunken track: this is our quarters. The battlefield up at the top is a dreadful sight: the knocked-out tanks stand about barren and deserted, and there are more corpses lying about than you can count; a truly blood-soaked landscape. It looks as though there is going to be some large-scale action here once again. The infantry belonging to our Division has been withdrawn, and ahead of us we have other infantry regiments; or else we belong temporarily to another Division.

Our regimental Adjutant, Lt Stürken, has pneumonia and is going to hospital—the whole Regimental staff is gradually breaking up. Our officer casualties since 21 March, 1918, have been 28.

The general morale among the troops, including the new chaps whom we shall be fighting with here, is quite exceptional. Evening is falling, and the columns are bringing ammunition up to the front very quietly; there are a few fresh graves around us; in spite of the hurry and the fact that we are right near the front, they have been laid out with loving care.

9 and 10 June pass in our sunken track; we spend the time waiting, with a few minor artillery skirmishes on both sides. Hope it's going to start again at last!

Our next-door unit but one is stationed outside Compiègne. At 10 p.m., as it is very quiet, I walk out of our sunken track with Seebach, and we walk to and fro up forward as though there were no front. It is one of these marvellous summer nights. The columns are moving along further to the rear on the high ground, and the silhouettes of men and horses stand out beautifully against the night sky. Men and beasts, trotting along on the everlasting iron path of duty, taking it all for granted; somewhere someone presses a button, and the whole thing begins to operate. A High Command—or the Supreme Command—gives an order, and it filters down through a thousand lower commands to the units and columns. It's pleasant chatting this evening, and Seebach and I have become good friends; we never disagree, either on tactics, or about our duties, or in our private lives.

I must note here that another new type of plane is flying over our sector: a Fokker biplane. In spite of the enemy's superiority in numbers, our tactical superiority in the air is simply overwhelming; the engineers and technicians at home are working away all the time, improving and improving—to say nothing of the perfection achieved in chemical research and development! Our new Yellow Cross gas* is a nasty one; we fire it sometimes in shells, and it holds out in the ground for weeks. Incidentally, we are under orders to fill the great forest of Villers-Cotterets with gas, and then to skirt round it.

11 June: I have to go down twice to Ploisy, the adjutants having been ordered to attend a discussion there. Stürken's successor on the Regimental staff is 2/Lt Strelocke. Everything has been worked out for a new attack, preparation fire for

* Yellow Cross gas shells contained Dichlorethylsulphide, known as Mustard Gas. See footnote, p. 150.—R.T.

90 minutes, creeping barrage and start of the infantry assault at 5 a.m. In fact, only three or four divisions are going to take part in the attack.

12 June: The fireworks start at 3.30 a.m.—and it's still 86 batteries, or 350 guns in round figures. It bangs and thunders away, as is our custom in our repeated offensives; but it isn't the same as it was on 21 March or 27 May. Not even 'quite a small' event compared with those two.

But the infantry regiments don't get off the ground after the creeping barrage; they don't seem to be regiments like ours were in the 9th Infantry Division. All we take is the village of Doumiers, and the fighting sways to and fro, but our men don't get into a proper fighting mood. The French have concentrated a lot of troops here to frustrate any further offensive. It is evening before Saint Pierre Aigle gets taken— now we do seem to be moving forward at last! A plane circles over us, a German plane; he comes down close, just above us, circles again, and throws down a huge bundle of newspapers right near us—a marvellous present!

Late in the evening a Würtemberg infantry regiment comes past our sunken track. They are reinforcements, and I mention it here because I was able to take a good look at every one of these splendid chaps as they moved past: strong, youthful, healthy and cheerful! What a picture, to see them moving into battle, one behind the other, with their steel helmets, their heavy packs on their backs, and their light machine-guns —once again the same inspiring scene, and every one of them the incarnation of the highest devotion to duty. I watch them walking past their comrades' graves and the dead still un-buried, and see some of them look at each other, and they look serious . . .

At 9.30 p.m. we receive orders that we are moving to the rear after all.

So, after these laborious weeks, we are going back for a well-earned rest. We do a night march to Chivres through Noyant and Billy. It's a beautiful warm summer night, with large-scale activity in the air, as might be expected; you can hear our bombs going off in the French rear area and heavy fire from

192

the French ack-ack batteries. We march in the direction of the 1st Army's rear echelon.

13 June: We spend the day in wooden huts at Chivres, and on *14 June* move on through Billy and Fismes, on the splendid Route Nationale between Soissons and Rheims, to Courlandon. We move into quarters on a small country estate belonging to a French senator who must be highly devoted to art, and also has a splendid library of the best French, English and German works. Among writings of a high intellectual level, however, this well-educated man has placed scurrilous works of the meanest sort, published in the pre-war years to attack Germany and the person of our Emperor, so base and filthy that one simply cannot reproduce them. When we see this stuff, any sorrow or sympathy we might have felt for the destruction of enemy civilian property soon evaporates, and we feel that the only proper attitude to have is a ruthless determination to win. We find crate after crate of these inflammatory pamphlets, and also leaflets appealing to our soldiers—which have in the meantime been dropped by French planes—and forged Reklam paper-backs.* Our men will never fall for these crude forgeries; I'd like to have the job of showing these pamphlets to the troops—and then every single man whom I showed them to would demonstrate his unshakeable German attitude in the clearest possible way.

15 June: We move on, marching and riding, to Varennes, on a road completely churned up by traffic. A huge amount of motor traffic, one column of lorries behind the other. We move into quarters at Guyencourt, in the local school. In the evening the band of the 351st puts on a concert; they give a most sensitive and artistic performance; I talk to the bandmaster, who in civilian life is a conductor at the Chemnitz City Theatre. Our old area of 1917, from Juvincourt to Corbeny, is quite near here, except that we are now stationed in the area which we were then shelling.

16 June: Rest day. I go off on a very pleasant walk to Roucy,

* The firm of Reklam published then, as now, a huge range of well-printed books in very cheap paper-back editions.—R.T.

where I get a lovely view over 'Winter Hill', once so hotly fought for. I think back to my times in the Juvincourt area a year ago with my No. 2 Battery and my three mates, of whom 2/Lt Zimmer and *Pieselmax* have now been killed in action, and Lt Knauer, my battery commander, is in hospital —why ever am *I* still here?

17 June: We move further back into the rear area, through Cormicy and the whole desert representing the static war along the Aillette, between Juvincourt and Berry-au-Bac. It's miserable to look at, everything churned up and shot to pieces, like the whole French theatre of war. We approach the desolate Champagne area, north of Rheims, and take up quarters in a hutted camp which has been extended a bit, with block-houses for men and horses. It is known as Hindenburg Camp, and has been got ready for troops in reserve or those in need of rest. It has been fitted up in the latest style; one hut has been turned into a reading-room, with a piano and a canteen.

We hear that the Austrians have made another attack on the River Piave.

18 June: We move on to the place called Pilnitz Camp, near Neuville.

There is an epidemic on, what they call Spanish 'flu, so that even leave has been stopped. We are quite near now to Pont Faverger, of happy memory: spent Christmas here in 1914. Back then, I went for walks with Kurt, there, and we talked about war and peace, but we didn't think of death.

In a written message of thanks from Wichura Group, our Division is picked out for quite exceptional recognition, not only for its brilliant infantry attack but also for its heroic defence after 30 May; the artillery is then mentioned in the following words:

> The support batteries showed tireless energy in overcoming the exceptional difficulty of the terrain and keeping level with the front-line infantry.

We are not all that far now from my well-beloved Les Petites Armoises, where I was stationed for several weeks after the battle of the Champagne country in 1915, billeted on those nice French people.

The Austrians have in fact crossed the Piave.

19 June: I'm sitting in—Les Petites Armoises! And Mademoiselle Valentine is milking the cows, as she did over three years ago. Les Petites Armoises! The village with the mild, sweet, peaceful atmosphere—how often I've longed to be back there! Today I made it come true and rode 80 kilometres out of my way to see the village and my French friends again. I rode alone through Machault and Vouziers, and there I visited Sister Agnes Braunfels, who is in Vouziers now, and whom I visited before at St Quentin—a most joyful reunion. I then rode on along the old road through Quatre Bas and Chatillon and then, there is Les Petites Armoises spread out in front of me! With my heart beating with anticipation at the joy of reunion, I trot into the little village and stop by the Vesserons' house. Valentine and old Mother Pauline rush out, crying:

'*Erbère! Non, c'est impossible, mon Dieu, mon Dieu!*'
("Erbert! No, it can't be—my God, my God!')

It is impossible to express the joy felt by these good people at seeing me alive again after all these years; I had not been able to send any kind of message. They asked about all my comrades of the old days, especially about Kurt, and they were overwhelmed by the news of his death. I have really never known joy like this. My horse and I were as lavishly entertained as if it were peacetime; then they dragged me round to the other local families, especially to the Mayor, Monsieur Bertholet, who nearly collapsed with surprise. All of a sudden the good old chap nipped up a ladder, groped on a shelf, and produced a tobacco-tin; it was the one I had brought back for him from Frankfurt in May, 1915, after I had been on leave, and I had completely forgotten about it. I strolled on through the broad, clean village streets, and then went for a walk with Valentine to the old mill. Back then, Valentine had been sixteen and I had been twenty. Today she is prettier still, frank and jolly, with coal-black hair and big brown eyes, a real village beauty. We strolled along, chatting arm in arm, and walked back to the village, where we met someone else, the old deaf and dumb man from the old days, and he recognized me and made signs to explain just where my artillery limber horses used to be kept. By great good fortune, war and its real horrors have not yet visited this village and its people, for all that they live anxiously, laden with cares. Valentine gets the little room ready which I had in the old days; it still has the names chalked on the door: Bombardier R. [Kurt Reinhardt], D. [Duden],* W. [unidentified] and S. [Sulzbach]. Late in the evening I look out of the window, but nothing has changed, it's the same peaceful, unsuspecting outdoor scene. I think back to those practical jokes we played—that time we put hundreds of cockchafers into old Mother Millet's bed.

20 June: I rode off at 4 in the morning after tearful good-byes; Mère Pauline and Valentine had been so excited that they hadn't slept a wink.

Five hours later I reached Mesmont, our rest station, where our regiment had arrived in the meanwhile.

Here we received the sad news that Lt W., who by the irony of fate had been run over by a gun-carriage during the advance, had died of his injuries; a day before he had been awarded the Hohenzollern House Order; he had once been Adjutant of the 2nd Battalion too. We spend some restful days at Mesmont, and I make another trip from this rest station to Les Petites Armoises—just as pleasant and harmonious as the first.

The Austrians have relinquished their position on the banks of the Piave.

* The brother of Lilo Milchsack (*neé* Duden) who founded the *Deutsch-Englische Gesellschaft*, the Anglo-German society based in the Rhineland in 1950, a year before the foundation of the British-based Anglo-German Association of which both the author and the translator are members. Frau Milchsack was created a D.C.M.G. by the Queen in 1972.

VII

1918

The Third German Offensive at Rheims

Our rest period doesn't seem to be lasting long, as the war of written messages and orders is already starting up, and there is a tremendous amount to do, every evening until 3 a.m. or so. We badly miss Major von Ohnesorge, our C.O.

Reading between the lines of the new orders, you can tell that we shan't be staying here long, that something new and big is in store for us, and that our mob will be an assault division once more.

We really must have become a crack corps for them to come and fetch us every time they mount a big offensive! In the next few days we have highly exacting exercises, and my batteries move into position as support batteries with their infantry regiments.

On *28 June* a few officers and other ranks are allowed to proceed on leave.

Kühlmann's speech has attracted a huge amount of attention at home. Some people said he was just whining for peace, but it seems to me that after our overwhelming victories, the others would have a reason to stop fighting before they were completely wiped out. The disgusting, unworthy behaviour in the Reichstag is however soon going to mess up the effect of our splendid victories.

1 July: There is an incredible amount to do. The latest orders are hinting that the balloon will be going up in the next few days in the same style as 21 March and 27 May. Orders to march off have already come in, leave has been stopped, and officers called back.

The Spanish 'flu still hasn't run its course. We are expecting replacements, both men and horses, to make good substantial shortages. We are already having to go up to the front to study the ground and make calculations; the first party to leave consists of the staffs, the Battery Commanders and one bombardier and 20 men from each battery; we leave Mesmont on *2 July*.

In the afternoon we were in Rethel; a few German girls were walking past us down the road, and one of them called after us 'I know that chap, he comes from Frankfurt!' She was what they call a 'front-line actress', and used to be at the Frankfurt Theatre. At 11 p.m. we moved on, with very heavy traffic on the road and a lot of activity in the air. At 5 a.m. on *3 July* we arrived at a camp near Pont Faverger. We just lay down, dog-tired, and slept all day.

So here I am once again in the old 1914 district, and keep thinking of Kurt, who is dead; what a moving occasion it was, that first Christmas Eve we spent together.

We, the 9th Infantry Division, are now poised for the third time face to face with very large-scale events. The latest offensive is to be launched here, and the break-through, in mid-July. There are some shock divisions which consist of particularly good troops, and who always get thrown into action where the fighting is hottest.

We stay here in camp and complete preparations for the offensive.

Sixty new fighter groups alone are supposed to have been equipped with the new Fokker biplane, said to be superior to the Fokker triplane.

For the moment we are under the command of the 26th Infantry Division, and the 80th Reserve Division is training three assault divisions. Our batteries are being increased in strength from four to six guns for barrage purposes—but only for preparatory barrage fire. We hope very much that this offensive will take us to final victory. We are supposed to be making a direct spearhead attack on Rheims.

Orders are piling up; the following Armies are going to

attack in this sector: Our 1st Army (von Mudra), the 3rd Army (von Einem), and the 9th Army, which will be put into action again between the 1st and the 7th.

The amount of artillery being concentrated here is enormous. We are under the command of the Gontard Corps. Gasmasks for horses are already available. A recent, and disagreeable, development is the French tendency to fire Yellow Cross gas shells into the rear area. A few devices do exist to combat the new French Yellow Cross gas, and they are being explained to the troops in many different kinds of regulations and orders.

7 July: I go up to the front with Captain Knigge to mark the gun-sites and to take bearings. The whole sector has been surveyed. On the way back we go through Pont Faverger, well remembered from the old days; then it was a flourishing little village; now all that remains are scraps of the walls. Yes, this village is dead, dead like my friend Kurt. In the afternoon we are back in our camp in a wood, and hear a talk from a Major M.

I've just remembered a remark passed by a captured French General Staff officer about the way our infantry and field artillery work together: *'Inimitable!'* he said.

We keep receiving new orders, both tactical and administrative, and hardly manage to eat or sleep. By now the Gunners must know practically as much about the Infantry and their fighting technique as they do about their own branch of the service; but they must also know just as much about signals communications and air operations, since these have become completely indispensable.

2/Lt Udet has shot down his 40th opponent.

8 July: Another day filled with hard work; now it is evening, one of the many splendid summer nights out here. I sit writing in my little cubicle, while behind me, infantrymen are singing melancholy songs.

In the *Die Woche* magazine (No. 26) there is a picture of the tank which our 2/Lt May, No. 5 Battery, knocked out at Chaudun.

9 July: We hear that Count Mirbach* (our Ambassador to Moscow) was assassinated there on 5 July.

I have a further mass of work sorting out orders, because in addition to general orders I have to write supplementary orders for my batteries, and extracts from orders have to be made and handed to the orderlies. It looks as though it will take a few more days before the large-scale business starts.

The evenings are sultry, our camp is in a forest, and you go for walks through the cuttings and rides, they are fir-forests right through, and the ground is as white as chalk; column after column is stationed here under the trees, some of the horses out in the open, you can hear our gallant four-legged friends munching away; they are waiting for it, just as we are. The roads are full of traffic, the depots are chock-full, and the ammunition columns are shifting the ammunition up to the front and into the depots. Every battery position is receiving 4,000 rounds.

Kühlmann has resigned, and von Hintze is now Secretary of State.†

12 July: Our whole regiment has arrived at camp in the meanwhile. Our own column is also taking ammunition up to our battery positions every night. Last night poor 2/Lt Hildebrandt, in command of our light ammunition column at Pont Faverger, was killed in action. The French keep up a constant harassing fire on the approach roads and on the villages lying close behind the front. The gunners of his ammunition column have knocked up a coffin in the middle of all this daily round of duties, and Hildebrandt's faithful dog keeps running round the coffin; he sees exactly what has happened, and can't leave his master for a moment; Hildebrandt had him for two years and he stayed by him in any kind of action.

When the mail arrives in the evening I receive my old school magazine and find obituaries for many of my school friends.

* Mirbach was succeeded in July, 1918, by Helfferich the finance expert and Vice-Chancellor, but Helfferich was withdrawn a month later for supporting counter-revolution in Russia against the policy of the German Foreign Office.—R.T.
† Paul von Hintze (1864–1941), previously German Ambassador in Mexico, China and Norway. He remained Foreign Secretary until the fall of the Empire.

13 July: Work is reaching the maximum, and the general excitement grows with it. In the evening I am ordered to see the regimental C.O. in order to fix the disposition of units in my Battalion. This keeps me busy until 2.30 in the morning.

14 July: The camp is full to bursting. Today we go into position.

The attack has been fixed for *15 July,* barrage from 1.10 a.m. to 4.50 a.m., assault to begin at 4.50. Once again, the main effort of the offensive is concentrated exactly in our sector. So far as I know, apart from our own Division, our Gontard Corps includes the 26th Infantry Division, the 3rd Guards Infantry Division and the Reserve Guards Division, all crack units. So now it's going to start, for the third time this year.

On the *14th,* in the evening, I go up to the front-line position. Our command post is near St Hilaire, and just as on 26 May, when we were passing Laval village on the way up to our command post, the French keep up a really heavy fire all over the terrain, absolutely everywhere, so that it costs an incredible effort to get forward in one piece. Our command post is a miserable hole in the ground. All the preparation is gone through again in the minutest detail, and in a few hours the balloon will be going up.

15 July: At 1.10 a.m. on the dot, on a broad front, the terrible brazen roar starts up again from the mouths of thousands and thousands of guns. In just the same way as the three and a half years of static warfare up to 21 March, 1918, became commonplace, these offensives have lost all their novelty as far as I am concerned. You are so sure of your ground that you are convinced that everything is going to succeed—the barrage, and the infantry assault, and the victory!

The barrage makes an incredible din, you can hear nothing, and can't see anything either because of the smoke; once again, the enemy do comparatively little firing, and don't bother us very much. At 4.50 the creeping barrage begins, and with it the infantry attack. My No. 5 Battery has unfortunately suffered heavy casualties. We ourselves have to keep our gas-masks on for a long time, as the French are firing a mixture of gas and shrapnel. We can't get any clear picture of whether the infantry is advancing properly. And strangely enough, we have so far received no orders to move forward ourselves. At 12 o'clock we go to the Dailly-Ferme. The first thousand French who have been taken prisoner are just moving past in their light blue uniforms. As before, I talk to some of them and find it strange to hear that our plans for an offensive are supposed to have been accurately known for the last ten days, including our plans to attempt a break-through on the 15th.

2/Lt Thuns, commanding No. 3 Battery, has been killed in action with five of his men, and 2/Lt Bone and 2/Lt Hübner of the same battery are also dead—that makes thirty-four officers lost since the first offensive this year.

The attack is coming to a halt outside Prosnes: enemy resistance seems to be insurmountable. How is it going on our right and left flanks? We haven't got the same morale that we had on 21 March or on 27 May. The Kaiser is here, at the command post of a General commanding our Army. 15 July passes without our being moved forward. We are very depressed indeed, because if a giant attack like this does not succeed straight off, it is all over.

16 July: We have got some sleep, and the situation is unchanged.

In the evening orders arrive for the 9th I.D.—that's for us—to proceed to the rear! This is puzzling; whatever is going to happen to us? I rush from my dug-out to Brigade command post and take my orders. We are to move back to Torgau Camp. I pass the orders on to my batteries, and the following day at 5 a.m. we are in camp at Torgau. All the huts are full right up, so we bivouac. Our morale is quite terrible, we can't get the faintest glimpse of what is going on, and all we can guess is that this great offensive hasn't come off! We haven't actually had any proper rest since Soissons, because even if it were called a rest period, we started work on the new offensive almost straight away, work that generally went on until late at night.

We hear that our attack has in fact been repulsed by the French in this sector, with heavy losses. We feel really desperate.

17 July: Orders to withdraw to Bazancourt, the craziest night I've ever known: as a reaction from the tropical heat of the last few days, dozens of thunderstorms opened up on us while moving along the road in column of route. At 11 p.m. it was so pitch black that you couldn't see your hand in front of your eyes; a shower of hail belted down, lashing our faces and soaking us to the skin in a second; the horses got restive and started rearing, the endless column ground to a standstill, and there were other troops marching to our front and rear and alongside us into the bargain. No rider could see the man in front of him, and you shouted into the darkness, trying not to lose touch, but in spite of this the unit often got separated into different parties. Then bits of other people's units would push in between, and it all became a hopeless jumble. At Pont Faverger we were standing at one spot for three and a half hours because the roads were completely blocked. If the French had chosen that moment to drop something, there would have been no way out. One man after another lost further interest and dozed off on his horse. We arrived at Bazancourt soaked to the skin after ten hours on the road, having managed to travel fourteen whole kilometres in ten hours.

VIII

1918

The Foch Counter-Offensives

On *18 July*, after getting a bit of rest, we received an order which seemed really sinister; I give the full text:

1. Strong enemy attacks in progress in the Bois de Villiers-Cotterets against left flank of 9th Army and right flank of 7th Army.
2. 9th I.D. to proceed as rapidly as possible to Fismes and Bazoches, at disposal of 7th Army.
3. Battalions will march off 8 p.m. Route . . . to Fismes.
4. Motor-cycle riders will await Battalions on route named and issue further instructions.
5. Arrival to be reported to 9th Artillery H.Q. (direct) at Fismes (enquire whereabouts of H.Q. from local Commandant's office), if whereabouts of Regimental H.Q. not known, otherwise to Regiment. Enquire whereabouts of Regimental H.Q. from motor-cycle riders.

                                                          (signed)

                                                              xxxxx

This order tells us everything, and we are speechless. At 8 p.m. off we go (there goes another night's sleep) and manage the forty kilometres to Fismes. So we are moving along behind the front; it looks as though we are being thrown into the largest enemy offensive of all time—and it was supposed to be *our* offensive! We couldn't even have dreamed that this would happen—never. We seem to be coming to the exact site of our offensive of 27 May, or else into the battlefield of early June. But in spite of everything, it was a lovely night march, cloudless and warm. Although the roads were packed, we made good progress; troops in lorries were passing us continuously; they will be thrown into the new critical position sooner than we shall. And what is the present position?

We are all in the grip of incredible tension, and can hardly speak for excitement and anticipation. And so back we go to our 7th Army.

19 July: After twelve hours of marching through Courlandon, Fismes and Gilles, we have wound up in a bivouac. We find mattresses and drop off to sleep in the broiling daytime heat until the evening. So here, near Soissons, the bastards are at it on a large scale! Taking the 7th and 9th Armies by surprise, the enemy has attacked both with very strong forces, and is said to have advanced six to eight kilometres in the first phase alone. And so the very places have been recaptured which we, the 9th I.D., took with so much effort and paid for so dearly with our blood. Chaudun has been lost. The fact that they are driving us back here at such a pace must mean that the situation has got really ticklish.

Let us only hope that this may be the final display of strength by a desperate adversary!

The French have imitated us in everything, laying down a short surprise barrage on a broad front, and attacking in massive numbers—and numbers are a thing we can't compete with any more.

By great good luck our Commanding Officer, Major von Ohnesorge, is coming back in the next few days.

The military communiqué is similar to the reports of action in the summer.

We move off in the evening, there's another night gone west. Through Bazoches. Enormous amount of enemy air activity. They've kept up the disgusting habit of illuminating the whole landscape before they unload the heavy bombs on us. We bivouac in Lesges at 3 a.m.

20 July: We do a recce in the morning, then move to Muret et Croutes. Captain Knigge is acting C.O. of a heavy artillery battalion, and I'm doing the liaison staff work alone with Seebach. I go up to the position with Knigge and as early as 6 o'clock our division starts a counter-attack in the Parcy-Tigny direction; the enemy forces are very strong indeed. After a short preparation by our own batteries and other regiments, we counter-attack successfully; the operation at least enables us to advance two kilometres.

Our Brigade Commander, Colonel Zechlin, has been promoted to the rank of General.

In the evening we move up to Droizy; there is a battery observation post here, really a very tight position; we are sharing it with the infantry command post. There isn't even room to unfold your map.

We spend the night in a cellar, but this is a restless place too, because at 1 o'clock the French begin to plaster the whole area with fire, and there is really no shelter at all in this shallow basement. We sit here like sardines in a tin, with all the orderlies round us, and get the telephone lines laid.

21 July: I don't know the word indicating the difference in degree required to describe the wholly crazy artillery fire which the French turn on for the attack in the morning. The word 'hell' expresses something tender and peaceful compared with what is starting here and now. I have really had enough experience of barrage in offensives, both our own and the enemy's. It's as though all the barrages one had ever known had been combined to rattle down on us now. At 6 a.m. I do observation for my batteries at the command post, but you can hardly keep going in this massed fire, you can hardly see anything because of the smoke, you have to keep throwing yourself flat on the ground, and you can't understand why you haven't been hit. I don't see how the French have managed *this*—first bringing our offensive of 15 July to an unsuccessful halt, and then, completely unobserved by us, preparing and carrying out an attack on a huge scale, with such quantities of troops and equipment. The Americans must be very strongly represented here, especially with artillery and infantry. It is also a fact that in the War and because of it, the French have grown hugely in strength, energy and morale; they have got tough and developed very considerable endurance.

Our neighbouring division on the right flank has to give

ground; we win the lost ground back again; then the French attack again, and a bitter struggle sets in, a struggle for every scrap of ground, and we cling to every inch of it with iron determination. Patrols are bringing back the most conflicting reports; the telephone hardly ever works, as the lines keep getting shot through. We receive a few messages by lamp-signals too, but one cancels the other out; French and British planes are coming over at us, thirty, forty and fifty planes at a time in waves close behind each other, flying in close formation but strung out in a line, and it's dreadful to know how beautifully they can see everything from up above; the bombers come over as well, chucking down their revolting cargo in the broad light of day; and in two ticks, of course, the French batteries have got our battery positions from the observation planes, and are plastering us with fire. 2/Lt Basonge was killed in the morning, and all our batteries have had a number of casualties. Fortunately reinforcements for our units are on the way.

The Order reads:

> The Army's situation requires every foot of ground to be contested. We must put up a tough defence, without regard for the consequences, until reinforcements arrive.

Never have such demands been made on our men's strength of character, morale and physical endurance as have been made in these last few days: brought in over long distances by continuous forced marches, in hot weather and without rest, and after the failure of their own offensive on which they embarked with great expectations, thrown into a defensive battle of a gigantic scale; they do their duty, they fight, they keep going.

A dreadful day is drawing to its close; it really got on one's nerves, all this uninterrupted raging and roaring, and one is still alive!

22 July: The enemy do not attack; instead we put down some strong fire on enemy-held hollows and woods, shooting at any promising target. We are still in our cellar, except when we are on observation duty. At night we have more shells and bombs sown round our cellar.

Whether the enemy has had enough now, or whether they are re-forming and re-concentrating, we are not able to judge. We hope that Ludendorff will take the brunt off our shoulders by making a counter-thrust in Flanders.

My No. 5 Battery under 2/Lt May (also from Frankfurt) has harvested very special praise from the infantry, and helped yesterday in a most decisive manner in beating off the heavy tank attack; they pulled out into the open in that hellish fire and knocked out several tanks, firing over open sights; yes indeed, one single battery can intervene most decisively in a battle, and final victory may well lie in the hands of a little second lieutenant.

23 July: The quiet time we had yesterday was deceptive. At 4 a.m. a barrage suddenly began: the very earth was rumbling, and it seemed as though the world were coming to an end. You couldn't hear what the next man was saying; it was indescribable. Our hole in the ground was under constant fire, bricks and entire walls were thrown about; it became more and more unbearable. Contact could hardly be maintained between ourselves and the infantry, and with the batteries. When you sent a runner off, you felt you were condemning him to death. It may in fact be very ticklish in our hole in the ground, but as long as you've got a wall round you, even if it's only a paper one, you feel you are safe! The signals equipment is functioning less and less: the lamp-signal messages are not getting through because of fumes and smoke, the W/T set has been shot to pieces; all you can still use, in fact, are runners and messenger-dogs. The messages are getting serious, and we won't be able to hold out here much longer, since it is only a matter of seconds for us all to be shot to pieces; every gully and every track is impassable. I rush out of the cellar and down into a nearby hollow, and we set up our quarters there instead. The 9th Infantry Division has been putting up a splendid resistance to the gigantic enemy pressure. We haven't yielded a single foot of ground. Unluckily, our batteries have suffered heavy casualties. 2/Lt May, in command of No. 5 Battery, the tank hero, was buried by a direct hit with the whole Battalion staff of 1st Battalion, 19th I.R.: they were nearly all dead, and 2/Lt May is just being carried past me unconscious. My No. 5 Battery has now lost all three of its officers in this battle.

The battle rages on: there are knocked-out Baby tanks standing about, we have kept the ground in our own hands, and the victory seems to be ours as well. Anyway, in spite of the incredible forces mustered by the enemy, they have not managed to break through, and it is only after realizing this that one is able to get an idea of what we managed to achieve in our offensives of 21 March and 27 May, and what unbelievably brilliant performances those were!

In the Army communiqué, Hartennes is named as the critical point of this gigantic battle. That is exactly the centre of our sector here; it seems to be turning into the bloodiest and most embittered battle in the history of the world. Really tough fighting is going on for possession of Hartennes and Parcy-Tigny.

Very truly one can say that it is a victory in defence, and should rank equal with our victories in attack!

Your nerves have taken a heavy beating now, you feel physically run down, you haven't slept a second all night, you've been standing in this witches' cauldron for days, but never mind, away with these petty matters! We mustn't weaken with these damned nerves of ours! If someone asked me today when we had anything to eat in the last few days, I could only answer that I didn't know; because all that sort of thing just happens mechanically, and the whole of our thought and our concentration is only turned towards victory. Frenchmen, white and black, Englishmen, Americans, Italians—God knows what mixture of races General Foch has drummed up against us in our sector.

Since it has now come to a defence battle, my 2nd Battalion batteries are as from today no longer under the command of the infantry, but directly under us; since Captain Knigge is commanding the Heavy Artillery Battalion, I am carrying the entire responsibility—with my friend and comrade 2/Lt von Seebach, that is. I have to look for new positions and new targets; our batteries now have to specialize in close-quarters work, including anti-tank shooting and defence against infantry assaults. Apart from the important tasks which these new functions imply for me, I remain here as the front-line liaison officer with the infantry.

On the *22nd* 2/Lt May of No. 5 Battery was mentioned in Divisional Orders for his heroic achievements.

The casualties suffered by the enemy are gigantic. For the first time we had put up massed machine-gun posts, and when the French ran into them, they fell, whole ranks at a time, in this terrible fighting. The fact that we have held the positions and scored a defence victory has restored the troops' wonderful morale.

Divisional Orders of *23 July* state that we carried out a brilliant operation by breaking a triple enemy assault and thus giving the whole front on this sector, which had begun to lose its firmness, sufficient stability to halt the enemy thrust. All branches of the service had contributed equally to this success.

In one day we shot down fifty-three enemy planes.

We long to get a quiet night just once. In fact, the evening of the 23rd was a little quieter. Then, at 12.30 midnight, they put a direct hit into our den which tore the whole wall away; by some miracle nothing happened to any of us, and we moved house for the third time, into another hole.

24 July: We have found a larger den and are now living in it.

Our C.O., Major von Ohnesorge, has come back.

The French are quieter today, just putting some searching and sweeping fire into the rear areas. I am grieved to say that a gunner I liked very much, from No. 2 Battery, who drove a brewer's dray in Berlin in civilian life, has also been killed in action.

25 July: Our gallant 2/Lt May, Commander of No. 5 Battery, has died of his wounds without regaining consciousness.

2/Lt von Richthofen has scored his 31st air victory; he is flying again after being wounded three times. The Richthofen squadron can now notch up its 500th air victory.

Voss, the famous air ace, has been killed in action. The following passage was recently written on the subject of 2/Lt

Voss by an Englishman, Major McCudden (who incidentally has himself been killed on active service):[*]

> As long as I live, I shall be filled with admiration for this German airman who defended himself for over ten minutes against seven of the enemy and damaged all our machines. His flying was astonishing, his courage really brilliant, and in my view he was the most courageous German pilot whom I ever saw in action. My comrades, too, were all agreed that this man had been one of the finest enemy airmen, and we argued about whether it had been Richthofen, Wolff or Voss. Since the triplane had crashed in our lines, we received the news the following morning that he could be assumed from his identification marks to belong to the Boelcke Squadron, bore the name of Werner Voss and was a Knight of the Order of *Pour-le-Mérite*.

Our den is quite acceptable, except that the entrance faces the enemy, so that they can watch every movement by day and have a wonderful chance of firing at us. So far he has not done so, but he has put down the heaviest calibre you could imagine both in front and behind. Our den is the scene of continuous coming and going, receiving orders, cooking, etc.

27 July: A few British prisoners come by. I have the job of interrogating three of them; they don't say anything more than what we know already. With one of them, a corporal, I then have some more personal conversation, and he is particularly pleased that I know his home town.

29 July: Those were two somewhat quieter days; now the French are putting on another hellish attack, and the artillery duel is taking its course. At 12 midnight I get an order to see the regimental C.O. There, we adjutants are given grave and disagreeable news; the front is being withdrawn in this sector; it will be the same here as in the case of the Siegfried withdrawal; it's the Marne down there, yes, the Marne, that's done this to us once again! It began down there with the loss of

[*] McCudden, the air ace and author of *Flying Fury*, was himself killed in an air crash.—R.T.

Château-Thierry, then it moved up to Fère en Tardenois, and now here. We feel terribly depressed and filled with pain at having to give up all that ground which was so dearly paid for, all the more since we held the line here so brilliantly. My God, we thought July was going to be different! But we've got to pull ourselves together; you can't be lucky every time, and even a decision like that, taken by the Supreme Army Command, can be great, in fact magnificent, since it only proves our strength and our ability to cope with any circumstances.

Now there is an endless amount for me to do and very many orders to give, since it is the most difficult thing alive to prepare a withdrawal and to detach one's forces from the enemy, if possible without being observed and without suffering any casualties. Everything has to go back. The first units to be cleared, behind us, are the field hospitals, field dressing stations, ration dumps, ammunition dumps and artillery workshops. After receiving these orders from the Major I go back at 3 a.m., accompanied by a telephone operator whom I had brought with me just in case, to my command post—or rather, I try to get back there. The French, who know, of course, that at this time of night we carry out troop movements and bring up ammunition and rations, are laying down harassing fire on every blessed road, at completely irregular intervals; we chuck ourselves into one hole after another, scrabble out again, hop along a little further and then duck out of the way of the next shell-burst. We rush about like wild animals with a pack of hounds after them, and take an hour and a half to get back this short distance. I then sit down and work till morning getting out the orders for the withdrawal of my batteries.

Once again, several officers and other ranks of our Regiment have been killed in action. This battle of intensive fire, which doesn't leave a single nook or cranny un-shelled, means death for everyone, sooner or later.

30 to 31 July: The enemy are putting the whole terrain continuously under gas. I'm still working without a break on preparations for the withdrawal and am quite alone up at the front here, because Captain Knigge and Seebach have gone off for a few days on a special assignment, presumably to reconnoitre the new positions at the rear. I have finished my preparations, and it has all—let us hope—been so well prepared that nothing, not one single thing, will be left in the hands of the enemy. Our No. 9 Battery has been put completely out of action by gas. I have sent for Officer Cadet F. while Seebach is away. My No. 6 Battery is pulling out tonight.

Today it is four years since war was declared.

I get a visit from a friend in my old No. 2 Battery. Oh dear, there will soon be no one left there whom one knew from the old days. It is evening, and the Engineers are hammering holes in the walls of my den to put the charges in—when we go, even these poor bits of shelter will be destroyed so that the enemy can't nest in them. The Sappers have a lot to do, because everything which could be useful to the enemy is being blown sky-high. Incidentally, we have got completely lousy in this den, and when we have a quiet hour to spend we make bets with the infantry on the numbers involved.

1 August: It is evening again, and once more it is almost impossible for me to report the crazy things which have filled the day at last drawing to its close. The night before 1 August, preparations for this splendidly devised withdrawal movement had been completed, and in some cases the withdrawal had already begun; batteries had been withdrawn to new (one-day) positions, smoothly and without casualties; the ammunition had been taken back, so that there were no further means of conducting a large-scale defence. Thereupon, at 5 a.m., as though the French knew our exact situation, a terrible barrage started up, mixed gas and high explosive, and what gas! And what high explosive! I pull my gas-mask over my face, and it works, but this damned new gas holds on for days; it lies on the ground, you don't know it's there, you can't see it or smell it, it clings to the grass like dew, and does its dreadful work. We have a very large number of casualties, and the poor chaps suffer from temporary blindness and continuous vomiting.

So hell is let loose once again. We have to get ready so

that—we hope—we'll be able to hop it at the last minute. I've never been so near being taken prisoner as I am now; there's hardly any chance left of dodging back to the rear, because the French are putting down a crazy fire on every road, every hill and every exit from every village. I have to go up to the O.P.—a lovely decision to have to take! Over there I can see the French sitting on the heights of Courdoux and Launoy, they are looking you straight in the face, you aren't even ten minutes away from the beggars, and any minute now they could storm the next village. A hail of fire starts coming down on the O.P. so that you can't get away from this rising slope of ploughed field. I keep on the ground with my telephone operator and have no alternative but to wait. Then I rush down to the den—it's only a few metres away—and manage to get there without being hit. Order after order is coming in, each cancelling the last, and I'm carrying the whole responsibility for my entire Battalion. However am I to get my batteries in and save them? Our infantry are still holding out, but to our left the enemy are right into our flank. I try again to climb up the slope above the den to do some observation. Eight tanks are lying out in front there, just smoking wreckage; but once again one can't observe anything else, because the French are putting down all this rotten fire on my O.P. And now on top of it all two enemy planes come over, hardly 100 metres up, we don't know where they're going; it's a dreadful position. Once more I manage to find a quiet moment to rush down to the den and report the few items I was able to observe. This day has cost some nervous energy, and all the waiting as well, and the uncertainty and fear that the French are going to score another success. At times I really felt quite desperate.

Some individual infantry units are moving back separately. We have to look after two things: to carry out the withdrawal, and to hold up the enemy while we do so. In the evening we receive our cue by messenger that the withdrawal operation is to start the night before 2 August. I now issue the last orders and arrange for limbers to be brought up to take the batteries to the rear. How our poor Regiment has suffered again today! All the guns belonging to No. 1 Battery have been shot to pieces, and No. 4 Battery only consists of a few men now, because they are all gas casualties; our regimental C.O. has to send a report that our Regiment is out of action. Just this single French offensive has cost us nineteen officers up till today.

Everything is now ready for the withdrawal, and that has gone off successfully too. Towards evening, with two telephone operators, I am the last man out of the den. We make for the rear, and once more every sense and nerve that we've got is put to the severest test. The French have got our route to the rear lying on a silver salver. We run, throw ourselves down, run, throw ourselves down. Fairly out of breath, we find our way through this revolting fire past Château Muret to the Siège-Ferme. At 9.30 I am at the new rear position, and really and truly, after these last few days, and particularly after the last 24 hours, I feel completely at the end of my tether. You really can't call this the human race any more.

The artillery withdrew in the night, and the infantry have detached themselves from the front positions very neatly, without the enemy noticing. All that is left of each Division at the front is one machine-gun company, a dismounted cycle company, and individual units, known as hunting commandos, whose job is to cause casualties to the enemy as they withdraw in their turn.

We occupied one position for the night of 1/2 August and are to abandon it in the night before the 3rd in order to occupy one further to the rear.

2 August: We are stationed on the Vesle and in the morning have interesting tactical discussions with the C.O., particularly concerned with protection against enemy fire. You get the feeling that every single Staff is inspired with the same ideas and thoughts as the Supreme Army Command.

Gradually the enemy are feeling their way after us; at 2 a.m. they were still putting down a barrage on our empty, abandoned positions. On the evening of 2 August we move on beyond the little Vesle (a small stream which has now achieved fame). This line is to remain our most advanced position. The strategic withdrawal has thus gone off with complete success, even if it can't be denied that any withdrawal, however strategic, is nevertheless the consequence of a defeat, and we don't want to deny that July, 1918, was indeed a serious defeat for us.

Our opponents, however, cannot be said to have achieved their main objective in any way at all: that is, to break through our line or to turn our flank and roll up our front. It was, however, a defeat in so far as the enemy deprived us of the initiative. But Ludendorff will find a way out! It is clear to us, in any event, that we miscalculated, and we have no idea what is going to happen to our offensive now. However, now and then we do have the feeling that it will be barely possible for us to get the better of this giant army of Frenchmen, Englishmen and Americans and their swarms of auxiliary nations, their incalculable quantities of equipment, raw materials and food supplies. But we just have to do it!

And so we have moved into the fifth year of war, and no end is in sight yet.

How well this withdrawal went off once again—another master-stroke of Ludendorff's! In the evening of 2 August alone, four divisions moved back through Braisnes, the traffic was regulated, each Division had its own road, and they all wriggled back across the little Vesle like huge endless worms! There were houses on fire everywhere, villages in flames, châteaux collapsing, bridges and railway tracks being blown up. Let them come on then, the French, let them come! Only it's a pity about the ripe corn which is being wasted.

We stay in Presles, bivouacking.

3 *August:* We've had a good sleep, and now we're having a proper wash-day. Get your shirt off at last: you've had it sticking to your back for the last four weeks!

The military communiqué gives a detailed account of the withdrawal operation which I have described above, from immediately after the heavy fighting near Hartennes.

For a long time now we have been fighting in this 7th Army area. We are now a reserve division with the Schöler Corps, and are moving over to the area north of Fismes in the evening.

We hear that General-Field-Marshal von Eichhorn has been assassinated in the Ukraine. First Mirbach, our Ambassador, and now Eichhorn; whatever is this going to mean? In any event, the situation in the East is exceptionally confused, and we shall certainly have to send troops there again, all the more because the Czechs are supposed to have organized an independent army which is being supplied and reinforced by Japan, France and Britain!

Four years of war have thus been spent in the field. By degrees I've reached the age of twenty-four, and the splendid years of one's youth are being spent on this mad business of killing. The finest time of our lives is tearing away from us. Now and then you have your sombre thoughts—no wonder after these forty-eight months.

4 August: We attract a bit of enemy fire and break our bivouac camp during the night. During the same night an order comes in from the Regimental C.O. that he has put me up personally for the Iron Cross First Class for what I did between 18 July and 1 August. I am so happy about this, of course, that I can't sleep at all.

5 August: We pull back again to a hollow north of Chivy on the crest of the Chemin des Dames. We are still an *Eingreifdivision*, that is, we are stationed quite close behind the front for emergency cases, ready to attack immediately in reserve. The enemy are supposed to have crossed the Vesle in the Etzel Corps sector. We have good trenches here, really deep dug-outs, because a short while ago this was the French front line.

The murder of General von Eichhorn has in fact resulted in our having to send troops to the East; not a very good beginning to this fifth year of war. On the Western Front we can feel the enemy's strength growing all the time because of American support.

The Czechs are supposed to be advancing against Moscow.

Admiral von Holtzendorff, Naval Chief of Staff, has resigned; Scheer is his successor. The Imperial and Royal General von Hötzendorff has also left.

It is fairly quiet in our hollow. We are of course too far

forward for ordinary duties, so we are able to take a rest. Our horses are having quite a good time too, they can graze a bit, and today I witnessed a charming incident: a shell which burst at a fair distance had frightened some horses while they were grazing, and they rushed off at top speed. While galloping one of them fell into an old shell-hole and couldn't get out again; the horse's team-mate saw this, and after galloping some distance further, turned back, stood by the scene of the accident, and would not leave his team-mate's side until two men came and got the other horse out again.

Meanwhile I've had some mail, very gripping letters from some of my wounded companions, including one from 'Baby'.

Meanwhile I have received my Iron Cross First Class personally from General Weber and was then ordered to see my Regimental Commander, who had some particularly appreciative things to say to me and gave me his hearty congratulations. As the General was giving me the decoration, he said '. . . one of the few brave chaps from the Fifth Regiment who is left'. When I got back to my men and my fellow-officers, they were as pleased as though they had been given the decoration themselves.

Flight Lieutenants Menckhoff and Kirstein, both Knights of the *Pour-le-Mérite*, have been killed in action.

On *9 August* I ride to Laon, passing through the battlefield along the Chemin des Dames. My God, what a dreadful desert! I pass the remains of villages and woods. No trace of Cerny at all. At Athies, where we were billeted before the offensive on 27 May, I visit the people at my old billet.

The Kaiser's appeal to the Army and the nation which was published on 1 August to mark the start of the fifth year of war is now lying in front of me; it is a summary of the undreamt-of performance which we have put up against the enemy here on the Western Front.

The Army communiqué of 9 August reports that a new large-scale battle is in progress near Montdidier, where the French, after putting up a smoke-screen, have advanced a considerable distance with great numbers of tanks and the strongest forces imaginable. It is a terrible thing that the enemy's reserves are inexhaustible. But they are not going to get the better of us!

We have had more big successes in the air. Udet has brought down his 47th, von Richthofen his 35th, and Löwenhardt his 51st.

We now have monoplane fighter planes once again.

Our Army Commander, Colonel-General von Böhn, has taken over the command of a recently formed Army Group, and left his trusty old 7th Army.

We hear that the French have advanced 13 kilometres in the Montdidier sector and that unluckily Montdidier is again in enemy hands. All the ground which we, we personally, conquered has been lost again. It seems over and over again that America's entry into the war is capable of tipping the scale not only by its moral effect but by the intervention of its army, which has meanwhile landed with powerful forces.

Fregattenkapitän Strasser, the well-known airship skipper, has been shot down in one of his airships during a raid on England. The whole crew perished in this valiant action.

The British have occupied Archangelsk.

Almost daily one can find news of fresh heroic deeds by our Air Corps in the military communiqué. We can thank Ludendorff for the spirit which our flying men have shown; he it was who demonstrated his clear-sighted forethought in 1917 by issuing his stirring appeal to recruit flying officers for 1918.

Meanwhile the military communiqué has resumed a particularly confident tone, for we are now complete masters of the situation on the Avre. It appears from the communiqué that the French have imitated our practice of bringing a few batteries of light artillery forward immediately behind the infantry during an attack. It also appears from the same source that the enemy have unheard-of numbers of tanks, including new models. It is gradually turning into a complete war of machines.

Italian planes are said to have been dropping propaganda leaflets over Vienna.

So now we have been an *Eingreifdivision* [an élite formation reserved for special assaults] for ten days; we are starting to dig in at a second position.

It's a real August heat-wave, with warm, clear, starlit nights; on one such evening we are sitting outside our dug-outs; the crescent moon is shining over the barren desert of the Chemin des Dames, over the ruins of what were once, perhaps, well-to-do little villages, and up above it begins to hum, and goes on humming; there they are again, those giant birds, lumbering along heavy-laden to carry their deadly cargo across to the French. They seem just like ghosts as they move across the sky, and—as usual—it doesn't last long before we hear the heavy crump of their bombs bursting in the French rear. Next day I walk through the hollow with Captain Knigge, visit the individual batteries in their dug-outs, and also pass through the almost completely obliterated remains of Chivy village. Nearby, according to the map, there once grew a beautiful wood, bearing the name of *Le Paradis*; today, all that remains, as though in mockery, is one small stump. We pass bivouacs and dug-outs belonging to other units lying here in reserve, and all of a sudden there, standing in this desolate place in front of me, is Lothar Mohrenwitz, my brother's best friend! That was a cheerful reunion in this barren district; the last time we ran across each other in a real paradise, on leave in Brussels—a lovely contrast!

Meanwhile, some of our batteries are being sent to join other divisions, and it looks in fact, after those awful weeks, as though we still aren't going to get a proper rest. I ride off to get instructions from the Artillery Commander of the next division to ours; the burning August sun blazes down pitilessly. Riding through what used to be flourishing country you note that through concentrating on the war, you've really lost the ability to look at anything with civilian eyes. You can't imagine yourself being in a place like this without there being a war on. This is an area where there is just nothing left alive: the trees are dead, the animals are dead, the people are dead. All that is left are crickets, chirping occasionally in the undergrowth.

Now I must say something about the kind of operation for which our batteries are once more being brought into action.

220

If it is sucessful, there will be a brief mention in the military communiqué, 'In the course of a patrol operation near . . . we took a few prisoners.' Whatever does the civilian at home imagine when he reads this? In all probability, something quite unimportant, and nevertheless this kind of item, which merely causes the civilian to read on, requires days of preparation by the different staffs. The Group (or Corps) issues an order for the operation to take place, either to improve our tactical position, or to take prisoners with a view to discovering the enemy's intentions, or to ascertain the latest disposition of enemy forces, which of their units are in the front line, and so on. The staffs and subordinate staffs work for days to ensure that everything goes off as planned and casualties kept to the minimum. Even for a very small operation, the Infantry Command collaborates with us—the gunners—to work out everything in the smallest detail. In exactly the same style as is used for large-scale offensives, every enemy battery is shelled with gas and every hill and every path put under fire by our batteries; and every battery is given its precise target. Only then is the plan approved by Division, and at X o'clock on Y-Day the operation starts.

The British are reported to have new giant tanks which have a strong effect on morale.

I have already reported that the enemy have got our Yellow Cross gas. In this connection the following story is going the rounds: a British officer is supposed to have been in Berlin with forged papers, gone on a gas course and thus discovered everything that was worth knowing! It sounds very nearly impossible, and one couldn't possibly imagine how it could be done.

Conditions in Russia seem to be getting worse and worse; Helfferich has returned from Moscow.

Flight Lieutenant Löwenhardt has been killed in action. He reached 53 air victories. Udet is in the lead.

On the 12th a strong enemy air attack took place on Frankfurt-am-Main, in which ten people were killed.

16 August: A discussion has taken place between the Emperor William and the Emperor Charles in the presence of Hertling,

Hintze and Helfferich. Whatever in God's name is going on?

Colonel-General von Boehn has been given a new Army Group and is commanding the Armies between the Somme and the Oise.

The battle of the Avre must have been the maddest that could ever have been fought; between 400 and 500 giant tanks attacked there on 8 August, with hundreds of planes attacking from the air at the same time, and behind the tanks, masses of cavalry and infantry; they say it was dreadful, perhaps even worse than it was for us a fortnight ago at Hartennes. And yet they definitely did not reach their object- ive. It is unbelievable what our troops are still able to resist after more than four years, and what unimaginable moral strength they have in them!

Lt Pütter, another airman with the *Pour-le-Mérite*, has been killed in action.

Army Orders of 18 August report that a German bomber group has dropped 36,000 kilogrammes of bombs over there in a single night, during which time the same group, with the same crews, flew five times there and back, taking on fresh bomb-loads every time they returned to the airfield.

Udet has received a personal letter of thanks from the Kaiser on the occasion of his 50th air victory, and in the meanwhile he has brought his score up to 56. The same communiqué further reports most intense fighting near Lassigny and the Attèche-Ferme, where we were stationed for a long time in 1915 and 1916, and now my well-beloved Evricourt will no doubt have been levelled to the ground as well.

On *20 August* we suddenly get orders to march off for Vorges at 8 p.m. Why so very sudden, one wonders? I manage a quick good-bye to Lt Lothar Mohrenwitz, who is bivouack- ing not far away, and we ride off out of the hollow at Chivy. The 9th I.D. is on the march again; endless columns, shrouded in dust, are marching and riding through the Aillette terrain. My word, we know this area accurately from May and summer '17! The moon is nearly full as it hangs right over us, and this marvellous August night is sultry, cloudless and bright with stars. The ruins look really quite spooky—well, no, all they are is ruined ruins! Just a few bits of wall sticking up in the air, that's all. The marvellous weather puts us in a good humour and makes us feel that there is such a thing as justice after all, a higher power which will not allow Germany to go under. After all, we are still deep inside France, we have faith once more in this higher power and are filled with confidence in victory. You people at home, believe in it a little yourselves, and have some real confidence in your Army, which is still, as always, ready for victory! We are still a match for the enemy, and we'll manage it!

The 9th I.D. is being placed at the disposal of the 7th Army and moved over to the right wing; the enemy is attacking strongly in the 9th Army sector.

23 August: We seem to be staying in Vorges. There's a lot of building and hammering. Here too we are an *Eingreif-division* and are stationed in reserve. It seems no longer possible for us to go back to the rear into rest stations; instead, we are to take a bit of rest up here just behind the front. The scenery is prettier than it is at Chivy, we've got woods and hills, and in the distance the fine panoramic view of Laon. But this pleasant atmosphere is invaded by the rumbling and rolling of the new large-scale battle between Noyon and Laon; it seems to be turning into the fourth phase of the Foch offensive, directed against our 9th Army.

I feel nervous, not pleased with life. Another thing is that now you have to worry about your relatives as well, with the air-raids on Frankfurt occurring over and over again. There were as many as 17 dead after the last one.

Even Major von Ohnesorge, the Regimental C.O., is nervous; there is a lot of detailed work to be done.

Meanwhile the battle has spread to Cambrai, but we are still masters of the situation in spite of the enemy having a ten or twenty to one superiority in numbers. Every defeatist grouser at home ought to get into a large-scale attack like this, just for a minute! Now as ever before, our men are magnificent. Even if they swear—and after all, they are old soldiers—they are cheerful as they keep on pitching straight into the shemozzle. They do their duty, and I can only repeat the same message: you people at home, put your whole trust in Ludendorff and us!

The French Secret Service has listed our 9th Division as a first-class German assault division—and we're damned pleased about it too! That is proof that the enemy appreciates our striking power.

24 August: We're supposed to be going to entrain, but I don't believe it.

Captain Knigge and 2/Lt von Seebach are both on leave, so I hope that afterwards I might get some too.

25 August: In the afternoon we pull out and move to St Croix. We bivouac in pouring rain. In the military communiqué of 24 August, for the very first time, a non-commissioned officer of a Field Artillery Regiment has been mentioned by name for a single act of conspicuous gallantry; this was Lance-Sergeant Bauermeister of a Frankfurt Reserve Field Artillery Regiment.

26 August: We march off through St Erme to Nicy le Comte.

27 August: At Nicy.

28 August: My brother-in-law was killed in action four years ago today. We move on to a spot near Villers le Thour. There, in the afternoon, a long discussion with my Regimental C.O. in connection with a secret paper by Ludendorff on the experiences gained in the last battles. The reason for our defeat is regarded, in the main, as being quite undoubtedly the unbelievable effect produced by tanks. New techniques of anti-tank warfare are therefore being brought out, and the Field Artillery is to become even more mobile than hitherto.

29 August: We march on to the *Kavalierlager*, the 'Gentlemen's Camp' west of the main road from Rheims to Rethel, three kilometres north of Warmeriville. The 9th Division is an *Eingreifdivision* in the Lindquist Group of the 1st Army (von Mudra). Provision has been made for one *Eingreifgruppe* within this *Eingreifdivision*, consisting of the 2nd Battalion of our Regiment and one of our infantry regiments. We move into a camp near Lavannes, right behind the front; it is very full of troops, and strangely enough, has not yet been shelled at all. We have hardly settled in before along comes orders for us to move back to the Gentlemen's Camp after all. So the long march was all for nothing. Every conceivable kind of plan is being worked out, assuming every remotely possible way in which the enemy might be successful in breaking into our Corps sector. Everything is being staked on defence or counter-attack.

30 August: Move up to the front again to take bearings beyond Lavannes.

At the Gentlemen's Camp we are quartered in a hut; it could be quite comfortable if we weren't plagued by this awful unease and uncertainty all the time. There is a lot to remind us of that lovely camp at Marchais in summer 1917, except that the leafy forest is missing, and we aren't in the high spirits we were then, and so many of our comrades are missing: we were happy with them then, and today they are dead. And the autumn is coming on, the evenings are cool, and you get seized by a great fit of melancholy. Will peace ever come?

31 August: Another ride out to the front to take bearings with the Infantry gentlemen at the positions prepared for the counter-attack, if it materializes. Everything here has been worked out most expertly.

1 September: Big stand-to at 3 a.m.; my Battalion and the 19th I.R. stood to from 3.30 until 11 a.m., because Army fear an attack may be imminent. But nothing happens, and we are very tired, all the more because we had just had 30 to 40 kilometres of marching a day for two days. After that the stand-to was cancelled.

2 September: Another ride up to the prepared positions; I have a gigantic job with tactical problems.

Four years ago today I moved into the field, and now I really feel twenty years older. Bob* was standing at the barrack gate then, crying, and the soldiers were singing *In der Heimat, in der Heimat, da gibt's ein Wiedersehen!*—'We'll

* Friedl Schneider.—H.S.

see you again, at home, at home!' Many, many of those soldiers never saw home again.

The military communiqué of 3 *September* reports that on that day alone we shot down 55 enemy planes and 13 enemy captive balloons, of which the Loerzer Group brought down 26.

New regulations about anti-tank warfare are coming in every day; when a lot of regulations come in like that we call them *Goldkörner*, or 'pearls'.

In Moscow there has been an attempt to assassinate Lenin; he has been wounded and the man who was with him is dead.

In this sector our withdrawal is to go back to the Siegfried position, and only Ludendorff knows why. It's just very bitter that now we have to clear out of all the ground which we have conquered in those brilliant victories since 21 March: and we were already dreaming about being in Paris.

6 *September:* We keep receiving fresh instructions: our Division is now also an *Eingreifdivision* for the neighbouring corps on our left flank; each *Eingreifdivision* has several functions. A large-scale attack is expected from the direction of Rheims. In case the troops lying at the front line in prepared positions should be overrun, we have been designated to intercept the attack and to counter-attack: so there is no further question of taking a rest.

I rush up to the front nearly every day so as to be in the picture about everything.

Meanwhile the fearful battle is raging on between Arras and Soissons. The enemy are now attacking along a 150-kilometre front. It is a mobile, in fact a travelling battle; in brilliant tactical style we are pulling back and clearing the ground which we can no longer hold after destroying everything on it. Once again the enemy are sitting in the Siegfried desert as they were in March, 1917.

If it should stay quiet in our sector I shall be able to go on leave after all.

9 *September:* Captain Roser of the Reserve is here as acting Battalion Commander, and today, just by the way, he asked me if I knew his cousin who had been killed in action—Kurt Reinhardt! It gave me quite a turn! I had heard Kurt speak

so often about this Captain Roser, and now I'm so pleased to be able to talk about our dear, dead Kurt with this most good-natured and warm-hearted person.

2/Lt Reinhardt, who used to be my Battery C.O. in 1914 and 1915, is now in Petersburg.

11 September: 'Division ready to march.' The great attack is expected any hour now. I would actually have preferred to go on leave. In the evening the stand-to is cancelled again.

12 September: Another stand-to at 3.30; we move in a state of preparedness to the 'Blockhouse camp'. This stand-to finishes at 9 a.m. The generally nervous atmosphere is spreading. Let us hope that the French are having just the same fears that *we* are going to attack.

My leave has been approved. I have put everything in order and scribbled four pages of closely written notes for Seebach, my staff officer, so that he is up to date on all tactical and administrative details; I have also worked out everything for him in the future, so that I can go off with a good conscience. I have 21 days' leave and 4 days' travelling time. Hurray!

Before I went off, I walked once more through the camp in the wood, through stables and my men's huts. They all seemed actually quite cheerful and contented. They are really as comfortable here as could possibly be managed: decent food, good huts, warm stables for our valiant horses. It all looks really very homely!

12 September, night: My joy at going on leave is over, because we have just had orders: 'Division to prepared position East of Epoye.' So out we go again at 3 in the morning, into the black night; we take up the appointed position with the 19th Infantry Regiment; we are freezing cold, dog-tired and feel bad-tempered. Once again, the enemy do not attack. Back to camp in the afternoon. 2/Lt Seebach is back from leave, I hand everything over to him and would be able to proceed on leave, but leave seems to have been stopped because of the tense situation. I had been so much looking forward to my leave! In the night Regimental orders come in that I *can* go on leave.

14 September: After a night with a great deal of bombing, I went off at 6.30 in the little cart to Le Chatelet and then on by train. In the train I read about a new offensive in the Verdun sector. American troops have taken the advanced trench position known as the St Mihiel Bend, and for the first time in the German military communiqué, Austro-Hungarian troops have been named as being present on the Western Front. When the enemy Press are talking about General Foch's opponents, they still never mention anyone but Ludendorff.

I'm in Brussels at 2 a.m. and so, after a long time, sleep once more in a splendid bed. At this hotel I celebrate a completely unexpected reunion; the hotel porter recognizes me from the year 1903 at the Dutch seaside resort which I visited as a child. So this is the way you meet someone again after 15 years, and how the circumstances have changed! How little I dreamed back then of war and all the dreadful things that go with it! I spend the 15th in Brussels and see that things are still going along here as they were before, and that everything you could want is available in abundance.

The Austro-Hungarian Empire has addressed a letter to all nations of the world who are at war, inviting delegates to meet at a neutral place and to engage in the confidential discussion of mutually satisfactory conditions. Incredible! It would be incredible, in fact unbelievably splendid, but I fear that it is hopeless for us, since our opponents are at present in such a fanatical frenzy of victory.

17 September: At Cologne in the morning; I have a meeting there with Gustl Bähr, and in the afternoon travel on to Frankfurt. How splendid, a thousand times splendid, it is to travel along the Rhine! I have never enjoyed it as much as I did today. The sun was shining, and it was a marvellous autumn day, in this season which is so particularly beautiful on the Rhine. How heavenly my well-beloved Germany looked: the Rhine *is* Germany for me.

Arrived at Frankfurt in the evening; this time, the reunion was more tender than ever, because my people can hardly believe being able to see me alive after these last few weeks.

Lovely days of leave after that. One day I visit Frau Reinhardt, Professor Reinhardt's widow and Kurt's mother, she gave me the last photo taken of Kurt; the next day I went to see his grave, where he lies next to his father, who was also killed in action. I visit old acquaintances, and they are all beset by this heavy care, this dreadful worry—are we going to be all right? Food is scarce, and the whole economy is slanted towards war.

On 25 *September* I was in another air-raid—on Frankfurt this time. One morning I went with an old school friend, also on leave, to visit my old school. What a lot of happy childhood memories! What an innocent lot we were. It was here that we went to the Kaiser's Birthday parades, the masters who were reserve officers turned out in their uniforms, and there in front of us was the Garrison Church, with our own Regiment, the 81st, marching out of it to the parade, in their full-dress uniforms—this was where we got our first impression of soldiering—and now we are officers ourselves, old warriors.

On the Western Front there are terrible new battles in progress, and dreadful, highly alarming reports are coming in from Bulgaria, where Malinov* has offered the Entente an armistice without his Government's consent—or ours. Whether Bulgaria's defection can be prevented seems doubtful; one would not know how to go about it.

I had the depressing experience of meeting a soldier in the street who was very obvious about not saluting me. It really isn't my style to blow people up, but in this case I really lost my temper. If these stupid youths back at home make a show of letting discipline go to pieces, you have to do something about it! Why ever, if things work so well up at the front, does a thing like this happen to you at home? I go off on another trip or two into the Taunus, to the beauties of Wiesbaden and Königstein. I have applied for a bit of extra leave, but it isn't approved yet, so I'm going back to the front in any case. I travel on 29 *September*, along the Rhine once more; this time it is raining and a heavy sadness

* Aleksandr Malinov (1867–1938) was Premier of Bulgaria from 1908 to 1911, in 1918 and again in 1931. He it was who signed the armistice and offered the Bulgarian crown to Boris III.

is brooding, even over this landscape. A fine home leave is finished, and in a not entirely happy frame of mind, I go to face the new, gigantic battles. It's not the fighting which makes me unhappy, but the way the general situation has got worse.

Count Hertling has resigned. Who is going to want to be the Reich Chancellor? The situation is serious. In the Balkans the Entente are at the gates of Uskub, and in Syria the Turks have suffered a serious defeat. On the Western Front we have to endure the heaviest burden that is humanly possible.

1 October: I said good-bye to Gustl, and travelled through Aachen to Brussels.

Prince Max of Baden has become Reich Chancellor.

Universal suffrage has been brought in; a democratic government seems to be on the way. Perhaps this will help to iron out the internal squabbles.

Bulgaria is supposed to have surrendered unconditionally. Dreadful! But we've still got to remain masters of the situation.

The military communiqué of *2 October* reports that St Quentin has been occupied by the enemy. In Flanders and in the Champagne as well, we have moved to better positions further to the rear.

In the train to Brussels I have some conversation with a chief surgeon, who has a lot to say about the mess things are in at home. We also get round, of course, to the heroic way our men are fighting in the West, and are agreed that no other nation in the world could ever have endured pressure such as this; every single German soldier incorporates an act of heroism all on his own.

At Brussels I felt a blatant contrast to Frankfurt; this place is still dominated by the gay life, jollity and frivolity—in fact, the art of forgetting war.

4 October: I receive a telegram from home that my extra leave has been approved; I travel back at 2 o'clock and meet Flight Lieutenant Rolfes again; he comes from Frankfurt and is Udet's brother-in-law. Rolfes too has already scored 20 air victories. In the train for home I find myself travelling with a few engineers, who tell me that Bruges and Ostend are soon going to be evacuated. One can hardly imagine the way the disgusting Entente will crow over successes like this. The value of the equipment we're losing at Bruges and Ostend runs into millions.

The Czar of Bulgaria has abdicated.

5 October: At Cologne in the morning, and then on to Frankfurt.

In the evening extra editions come out, reporting that Prince Max of Baden, having taken office as Reich Chancellor, has despatched a note to President Wilson of America, accepting Wilson's earlier note as the basis for negotiations. And so we are moving with giant strides in the direction of peace.

The democratic Government has been formed, and practically all the Ministers come from the Left. Now every soldier at the Front must and will stand firm, so that the enemy get no further. Perhaps everything is going to be all right in the end! Perhaps the Great War will unite Germany, otherwise always so disunited, and perhaps the new Government, after an honourable peace, will restore Germany quickly to her old prosperity.

I spend a few more restful days in Frankfurt and then go to Munich for a few days, where I celebrate a reunion with several school friends.

Meanwhile a reply has arrived from Wilson; at first he asks a few questions, and demands the evacuation of the entire occupied territory before he opens negotiations with us. That would not be the worst thing that could happen; perhaps an honourable peace can in fact be achieved.

12 October: Our reply to Wilson states that we will comply with his request and evacuate the whole of the occupied territory. For us soldiers, who have fought victoriously for four years, this step is a hard and saddening one, but nevertheless—and perhaps it has to be like this—it is no use now racking our brains and considering all the possibilities; we have to look the bare facts in the face. Outnumbered in the West, Bulgaria's defection, the defeat of Turkey, internal chaos in Austria, shortage of food and clothing at home—all these factors oblige us to engage in the soberest reflection. But it is quite incredible that we might have been able to make peace on better terms in 1916.

Rumours of an armistice are already going the rounds. The people I am staying with invite me to remain with them a little longer.

15 October: Wilson's second reply has arrived. It is presumptuous and makes exorbitant demands. One can hardly find words to express the indignation with which every German must now be filled. They want to humiliate us to death! This hypocrite Wilson, this perverter of justice, this 'friend of peace' and 'idealist'. Whatever are we to do? How splendid, if we had the strength and the power, to say 'No', but that will hardly be possible. An official demand has been made for Kaiser Wilhelm to abdicate. A desperate situation, and the vilest trick imaginable to demand conditions of this nature from *us*, a nation which has fought so heroically for over four years, and stood firm against a whole world of enemies! An honourable opponent ought to show regard for us rather than humiliate us by bringing us to our knees.

Meanwhile fresh battles are raging in the West. The entire Western Front is rumbling and banging, but our line is still firm, even if the planned withdrawals cannot be concealed.

It is hard to say good-bye to my dear friends at Munich. I stay another day at Frankfurt. The burden of a terrible nightmare lies on everyone. Everybody's honour has been smirched, and the ignominy is too much to bear.

Lille, Bruges, Ostend and Roubaix are in enemy hands. Morale is frightful. Austria is supposed to be engaging in special negotiations. My God, who would have thought it would end like this? Undefeated! We must have made a lot of mistakes on the home front.

21 October: The note containing our reply to Wilson is on its way; U-Boat warfare is to be stopped, but we reject any attempt to bring discredit upon us or to impugn our honour.

I say good-bye to my people, good-bye after a leave that was pleasant all the same. I take the train to Charleville, where I am amiably received straight away, with a dose of bombs. At Charleville things look substantially different from the last time; the place is being evacuated, and the roll of guns is no longer very far away.

22 October: I travel on to Hirson and hear that our 9th Infantry Division has been withdrawn from the 1st Army and then, on the way to Flanders, re-assigned to the 18th Army; it is stationed between Solesmes and Le Cateau—once again, i.e. as usual, at the hottest part of the dreadful battle which is at present raging. We belong to Hutier's 18th Army once more —but how different the situation looks from what it was back then, when we were under the same command before 21 March.

At Hirson I just manage to find room in a mass billet, and hear most depressing news from fellow-officers of the progress being made by attempts to undermine Army morale: the men are being corrupted by reinforcements arriving from home.

23 October: It's almost impossible to get beyond Hirson, only a very small number of trains are running towards the front, and all you see is transports coming back; at last another officer and I manage to catch a transport which takes us to Avesnes.

24 October: Avesnes! My old military hospital station of February, 1917! This pleasant area, which was then right back in the rear, has now become a war area. How miserable it all looks! I push on to Le Trichou, where our supply column is stationed. Joyful reunion with the men there, and I'm glad to find that none of them are suffering from bad morale yet.

25 October: I've managed to get to my command post, back with Captain Knigge, 2/Lt von Seebach and my men. Thank God to be 'home' again! The command post is in the Ferme de Pavillon. The front runs through an area which so far has not been shelled, so our command post is undamaged, and looks really quite acceptable; but this position is still quite new, and this farm won't be standing long; we're barely east of La Neuville. The enemy line runs along the Oise–Aisne Canal, and our Divisional sector between Etreux and Tupigny.

There's nothing to be seen of any armistice here, although many officers feel gloomy about the news from home and the lack of discipline in the rear areas, whereas in our Division, I must say, morale is without exception quite wonderful.

In the evening an Artillery Order comes in, and I give here its first paragraph:

> After exhausting days and nights, the Artillery of the Division will once again be brought into action at a point which we shall hold, with our old and well-tried devotion to duty, as we have always done wherever we were needed. If every man, officer or gunner, is imbued with the idea that we were always unbeatable provided we handled our guns properly, then we shall be, here as everywhere, what is stated on our glorious guns: the *ultima ratio regis.*

As in the case of so many military orders, this one says everything very briefly, and much more can be read between the lines; it means, and promises, that here once again we shall have to withstand the fiercest French infantry attack imaginable; that we shall have to win or die for our King. The French are now going to try to score a military 'victory' as well; they already feel—mainly because of Wilson—in a position to be able to dictate, and they are going to try to break through in our sector, in order to be able to say that they chased the German Army out of France as well—but they will not be able to do that! For even if everything is turned upside down, we soldiers are not going to engage in revolution. We have done our duty for four years and three months; for four years and three months we have fought victorious actions, for four years and three months we have scored achievements which are completely unparalleled in history, and we shall hold on in the same spirit for longer still!

As in every German offensive and every defence battle, our Regiment is at the hottest place once again.

27 *October:* A telephone message comes in from the Crown Prince's Army Group, which I have to announce immediately to all five batteries under my command:

> It is of decisive significance to hold the present position. I ask that the troops should be left in no doubt whatever that the present position must be defended to the utmost.

234

I have passed this order on with an additional instruction that the contents are to be announced to all ranks immediately.

So now, while the people at home have already dropped out of the race, we chaps out here intend to show that the old power of resistance is still alive; and what a contrast there is between all this and what is going on at home.

In these dreadful times, one is prepared for anything, but a piece of news has come in today which really was too much and too unexpected: Ludendorff has gone; that greatest among commanders of armies, the man of iron energy, has been unceremoniously relieved of his post. And Kaiser Wilhelm is to follow him. For us fighting men of the front line, these are the two most terrible events which could possibly occur. Ludendorff was our idol, and the Kaiser our supreme commander in the field. Now it is really hard to preserve any confidence. Both these are going because Wilson has given the order for them to go: whatever is to happen now?

Wilson's new reply came in on the 23rd, but as before, he demands that the house of Hohenzollern should renounce the throne, and he does not wish to deal with the men who have governed Germany up till now.

Sapped of all will-power, German heroism seems to be sinking into ignominy.

28 October: At 6 o'clock the enemy attack the 18th I.D. and the 6th Bavarian I.D., on the left wing of our sector, and is repulsed. I really can't say much more about these little defence battles; it all seems such wasted effort; and what devotion to duty and what achievements by thousands of men are contained, once again, in that small word 'repulsed'! Oh, no one in the small-minded world at home has any idea of all that.

Our reply to Wilson has gone off again, and we are expecting an armistice. Some of the Kaiser's powers have been transferred to the popularly elected Government.

Crazy scenes in the Reichstag; we are on the shortest road to ruin, like Bulgaria and Austria. It is dreadful!

But here, and along the entire front, the spirit of German resistance is growing—a ray of light at last! As we expected, the enemy are attacking like mad along the entire Western Front. Once again, they will be throwing all their reserves into the firing line and staking everything on a chance of achieving a military defeat, but we shall also be staking everything on stopping them from doing so.

29 October: I am lying on my wooden bunk, with my telephone receiver in 'bed' beside me, and the buzzer gives the signal for Regiment: 'Second Lieutenant Sulzbach here!' 'Second Lieutenant Rubel speaking. Army expects large-scale attack tomorrow morning. Stand-to in highest state of preparedness for gas with effect from 5 a.m. Increased state of preparedness for battle action. Batteries are to put down harassing fire and waves of obliteration fire.'*

I give this order to all my five batteries and discuss the targets with them by telephone. Then we get some more sleep.

The attack came further to the left, not straight at our Divisional sector, and the enemy were repulsed as usual. That is still something which we take for granted in our Division, but now, when we have completed the operation successfully, we don't feel the same about it as we used to.

30 October: We leave this command post because it is too exposed, and move into a small, cellar-like vault, 100 metres away; we are stationed exactly level with our batteries.

In one newspaper we enjoy a British report, which reads as follows:

> German striking power has not suffered from any loss of energy caused by the recent withdrawals. The Germans are fighting on the Western Front as they have never fought before. Exceptionally heavy fighting is taking place on all sectors of the battle-front, as heavy as has ever occurred in the course of the War. The Germans are exerting all their strength in order to hold us back.†

2 November: The Austro-Hungarian Empire and Turkey have agreed to an armistice on all fronts. So now Germany faces the world alone, deserted by all her allies.

* *Vernichtungsfeuer.*
† This passage appears to be paraphrased from the *Daily News* of 2 October, 1918.

Count Tisza* has been assassinated at Budapest.

The Italian fleet has entered Fiume harbour.

3 November. Today I've been commissioned for two years, and yesterday I had been in the field for fifty months!

Austria and Hungary are Republics. The Emperor Charles was rightly called 'Charles the Last'.

Any comment on these wholly crazy items of news is super-fluous, for no words can express what is going on now in the heart of every soldier: despair, anger and indignation in the highest degree. What we are waiting for now is our death sentence.

The Austrians are supposed to have been attacking their own soldiers and officers and tearing the Imperial and Royal badge off their caps; they're said to be flying the Tricolor in Vienna; and what's happening to us?

3 November, 2 a.m.: Stand-to, in increased state of prepared-ness for battle.

4 November: At 6.45 a.m. the French began to lay down a bar-rage such as I haven't experienced in all these four years. It isn't a barrage any more, it isn't even a hurricane of fire, it's a typhoon of fire! The French are concentrating their fire from thousands and thousands of guns and shelling us with the most dreadful heavy-calibre stuff; nor is it, as you might expect, merely one or two divisional sectors in breadth—it is rumbling to the right and left just the same as it is in our sector. The enemy are firing a lot of smoke-shells too, and have shrouded our entire front in an impenetrable something-or-other, so that you haven't even got 50 metres of visibility—and they are going on and on with their barrage, so that there doesn't seem to be a square centimetre of earth left unchurned. The situation is damned serious. There is still a telephone line with some life in it, I try to get the Battery C.O.s on the line, and when that can't be done any more I send runners on a death-or-glory trip through all this fire, to get the batteries to lay down the most effective protecting fire that can possibly be organized. A few seconds later our own barrage starts rattling down on

* Ex-Premier of Hungary and one of the chief authors of the war. —R.T.

237

the Oise–Aisne Canal, and now the rumbling and thumping and banging are louder still, with our batteries putting up a crazy rate of rapid fire.

Meanwhile every means of communicating with the rear has been cut off, because the French have had our rear terrain so strongly under fire that there is naturally not a telephone line left intact. Up at the front we are thrown entirely on our own resources; we have to act on our own initiative and do some very quick thinking. Courageous mounted messengers are still galloping past through this terrible fire, it doesn't make any difference whether you are sitting up there on a horse or running on the ground—at least, it doesn't at these moments decisive! Now it's a matter of bringing up the limbers so as to save the guns in time, even if it means heavy casualties. We have had a day of large-scale fighting visited on us such as I have never seen before. What kind of shape are the infantry in? Nobody knows anything, and nobody knows either whether the enemy haven't perhaps got in behind us, because in this smoke-screen there's just nothing to be seen at all. Are our lines giving way? Has everyone been taken prisoner, and are we too going to be captured any minute? It's a dreadful situation! My batteries are still firing away like blazes, and so far, at least, no infantry have been driven back as far as my command post. Now here come the remaining gunners of No. 1 and No. 3 Batteries belonging to our 1st Battalion, carrying the essential parts of their guns in their hands. The guns have had to be abandoned, because the enemy have broken through just where the 1st Battalion were stationed. I stay at the command post. Captain Knigge tries to get through to the rear to reconnoitre for new positions.

More and more scattered other ranks collect at my post, and even moments like these are still really quite encouraging, particularly so, when parts of other units, and parts of my former No. 2 Battery, report to me and put themselves at my disposal. We wait here in our cellar—still not shot to pieces—for what may be in store for us, and take turns manning the observation post above the cellar. From my men of No. 2 Battery I hear that the French have advanced under a heavy curtain of fire and are now, some of them, actually between the batteries of our Regiment; a considerable part of our Division has been taken prisoner, and we have to try to keep up the defence from here. Of the 2nd Battalion, 19th Infantry Regiment, only one captain has come back, the only man out of the whole Battalion. Of my Regiment, five batteries are in enemy hands, but so far, my Battalion has had no casualties at all. What a mercy!

But we don't merely put up with these losses. Yes, today, even though it looks so different at home, we get together with a Bavarian regiment and put on a counter-attack in the afternoon, and all the Regiment's guns are safely found and brought back. That is the really wonderful thing—what *can* be done!

Nevertheless, our 1st Battalion has had terrible casualties: my old No. 2 Battery is completely out of action: the Battery Commander, 2/Lt Dopp (Lt Knauer's successor) has been killed in action, and so has our good-natured little 'Baby'! And many of our faithful gunners as well, and the third officer dangerously wounded. So today once again, my No. 2 Battery has lost all its officers. The courageous little 2/Lt Scholz-Babisch, whom we called 'Baby', fought desperately, with his Battery Commander, in his battery alongside his gunners, and put up a heroic resistance, revolver in hand, as the French stormed the battery. None of these heroes retreated so much as a step. They were lying, shot in the head, between their guns. As the men withdrew carrying the seriously wounded 2/Lt Wilde, the group received a direct hit, and most of them were killed. This is a brief description of today's action, and one day of large-scale fighting is made up of thousands, yes, hundreds of thousands of scenes like these. Four of our officers have been taken prisoner.

Today, 4 November, will remain unforgettable, if we ever get home in one piece, and will take its place among the many, many days of large-scale fighting—and it must have been the worst, with the terrible uncertainty added to everything else.

Evening is coming on. I have withdrawn my batteries, and orders to pull back are coming in by mounted messenger. Our

Division too is taking up new positions further to the rear, but not because of today's action, because here we have either held firm, or got everything back in our counter-attack!

The 2nd Army has been pushed back a bit, and Valenciennes has been lost. So now we are starting the large-scale withdrawal to the line of the Meuse: the new defence line. It will be a very big job, and very difficult, but we shall be able to manage it.

Each order comes hot on the heels of the one before; exhausted runners keep coming in, and I am kept hard at it adapting the orders for my Battalion and working out the details.

Meanwhile I am quite alone up at the front with my telephone operator and my runners and don't know whether there is any infantry left in front of me at all. The crazy fire we had yesterday has died down, but the enemy keep up a continuous searching and sweeping fire on the rear terrain, in order to disturb our withdrawal movements. At 10 p.m. I begin to withdraw, with another six men. (At first I intended to spend the night in this underground hole. If I had done so, I should have been captured, but we decided to go because of some vague feeling that it would be the best thing to do.) We kept off the roads and moved along hedges and across meadows, but even there we caught a bit of sweeping fire, so we had to keep chucking ourselves on the ground. It was a terrible night, pitch dark and raining, and after the preceding day our nerves were in a wretched state. This withdrawal was worse than getting back to Hartennes on 1 August. At last, well after midnight, we saw a light and made towards it after getting our bearings on the map. We landed in a Bavarian battery position, meaning that we had missed our way and got into the neighbouring divisional sector. We were dog-tired and were invited by these splendid chaps to spend the night at their position, which we were glad to do. My God, they still had convictions! They were filled with anger that anyone should dare to dictate peace terms like these to us. They have taken the very words out of my mouth: the Bavarians think like that, and our Silesians think so too, and so do all the chaps at the front. They think so today, and they'll go on thinking like this in the future. They lend us blankets, and we sleep with them in sixes in a hay-barn.

5 November: We were weakened by the new French barrage, but they were mainly laying it down on the positions we had abandoned. At 9 o'clock I managed to find Captain Knigge, who had been with Seebach, both very worried about me, because neither could imagine where I had spent the night.

My 2nd Battalion is now an *Eingreifstaffel,* or reserve detachment, with the 19th Infantry Regiment, so we are in the 2nd line with the 26th Reserve Corps.

The withdrawal proceeds the following night, starting at the delightful march-off time of 1 a.m. We ride through the pitch-black night; you can't see your hand in front of your face! The roads are soft after 24 hours of rain. The French are firing into the area with the vilest low-trajectory guns you could imagine, and at quite irregular intervals they put down sweeping fire with these heavy-calibre guns on all roads in the rear area. With our columns and our guns, however, we can't keep off the roads at all, and have to push on through this curtain fire; it was really dreadful, because our nerves were so bad from the day before, worse than they've been all these years. We have to put up obstacles too, to slow up the enemy, and once again every cross-roads behind us has to be blown up, heavy trees felled, and all bridges detonated. The hold-ups on the crowded roads are most disagreeable, as we are all eager to occupy our new positions. In spite of the darkness, the transmission of orders works as well as last time.

At 4 in the morning I directed concentrated fire on one particular village: a reprisal raid by all my batteries, 60 rounds from each battery, and felt enormous anger and indignation against the base, cowardly crime committed by the inhabitants, who shot two riflemen from our 154th Regiment in the back.

IX

1918

The End

On the night of the 5th to 6th we found passable quarters at Etroeungt. This was where we spent the night of 2 June, 1917, while we were moving back to Roisin in the rear. One shouldn't think back! Poor, wretched Germany! We found plentiful stores, and after the rough days we had been through, helped ourselves and ate our fill. We talked to the civilians, who knew perfectly well that we were on our final withdrawal, and that tomorrow their countrymen, French regiments, would be billeted here instead of ourselves. What a heavenly feeling that must be for these patriotic French! This time tomorrow they will be liberated—free after four and a quarter years! We can imagine how they must be feeling.

The white flag is flying high up on the church tower: I find this sign of our old-established chivalry most moving. We are showing the enemy that French civilian inhabitants from several villages have gathered here, so that they do not endanger the lives of their own civilians by artillery fire. We move on in the afternoon. I say farewell to the local civilians with the words '*Gardez un bon souvenir des Allemands!*'

Endless columns are rolling eastwards. A ride through a night like this is not at all agreeable. It is pouring with rain, the roads have been softened and churned up. The gunners and infantrymen are swearing and grumbling in the muck. All the troops are moving along in double column of route, with the heavily laden foot-soldiers wading through the mud; we are still going to be asked to put up a superhuman performance. But it's a piece of luck to have such a pitch-black night, and raining too, otherwise the French planes would be coming over in hundreds and dropping good-bye presents of bombs, and all these columns moving to the rear would be thrown into dreadful confusion.

6 November: In the evening at Semeries, a little place with 1,200 inhabitants, plus 1,700 evacuees, —and three divisions with mountains of luggage: you couldn't imagine a village being so busy! The other ranks, every conceivable branch of the service all mixed together, are literally lying on top of each other in the few forms of shelter available. We find one last floor and lie down on it, 100 men side by side, and ten elderly French civilians as well.

7 November. We receive maps as far as the A.–M. (Antwerp–Meuse) position; so this greatest of all withdrawals is proceeding in stages. This is another masterpiece of top-class strategy.

Now the danger from civilian snipers or *francs-tireurs* is increasing again, because the French civilians of course know perfectly well what is going on, and would dearly like to pot one or two more of us. One Army order has been drafted with this in mind, enjoining us to keep the strictest march discipline and to let no troops stray or lag behind. Nor, in future, may other ranks be sent out alone, or billeted alone, and no wounded man may be left even temporarily alone and unprotected. Corresponding regulations affecting civilians state that the latter have to keep indoors and that windows of houses must be kept shut.

We are now once again quite near Sains du Nord, and march on past it.

8 November: Stand-to in increased state of readiness: the enemy have pushed into Semoussies, so they are pressing exceptionally hard after us, more quickly than originally intended, and we have to hold certain positions a certain number of days, so that everything can be sorted out in the rear.

At mid-day we are brought forward and are therefore going into action once again.

We hear that yesterday our delegation travelled to France,

near La Capelle, to receive the conditions; the members are supposed to have been General von Gündel, General von Winterfeldt, and Admiral von Hintze. It's a splendid thought that it's all going to end some time, but we do hope for one thing: peace without humiliation!

I go with Major Nernst of the infantry to the command post, we get our batteries into position north of Felleries and lay down some solid fire, but it was what you might call a friendly action. It was in fact to be our last time in action in this World War.

At 5 p.m. we were pulled out again and moved on further in the divisional convoy through the pitch-black night. Once more endless ranks, column after column of marching troops; it is streaming with rain and we keep being held up on the crowded, rutted, boggy roads. At 3 a.m. we reach Beaumont and have crossed the Franco-Belgian border. And so, on 9 *November*, we have left France! We feel very sad.

The situation at home is perfectly dreadful; there are revolutionary movements at Kiel; Austria has disintegrated, and Serbs, Italians and others are to inherit the splendid fruits of centuries of ancient Austria's civilization!

9 November: The sun is out, and here come the groups of enemy planes to drop their bombs on Beaumont. Many are killed in this crowded little place. The ration dumps cannot be evacuated to the rear and are full of tinned food, which is being distributed to the troops marching past. The troops here —those we still come across in the rear areas—are completely infected with the mood that people have got into back home —quite demoralized; but as for our front-line troops, nothing will ever be able to wrest their wonderful spirit from them!

At Captain Knigge's billet there are also German women —an army auxiliary and her friend; they used to help here with various jobs when Beaumont was a lines of communication station. They ask us to take them with us on our march to the rear, and of course we agree, because otherwise the poor girls would have to stay behind. We entrust them to our baggage column, and it's a strange picture suddenly to see two women on the old baggage-waggon.

In the meanwhile, news from home is quite clear: there is no way out on the home front either, we are moving towards an inevitable finish, and a very terrible one: part of the Navy is in a state of revolt; a proper mutiny broke out on one ship of the line, the *König*, and her colours were hauled down and replaced with the red flag; the Captain was shot defending the old colours, on which he had taken his oath of allegiance.

Workers' Councils and Soldiers' Councils have been set up.

The Kaiser and the Crown Prince are supposed to have abdicated.

We are sitting at the bottom of the abyss, and our splendid Germany has fallen to pieces! In the evening a mounted messenger arrives, bringing hard facts to confirm the rumour that a genuine revolution has broken out at home.

Mail is stopped from home, and letters home as well.

The Kaiser and the Crown Prince have now in fact abdicated. Germany is a Republic. The new Government has been formed, with Ebert as Chancellor.

You don't know whether you are dreaming or stumbling through reality. The events have tumbled past in such a rush that you can't grasp them at all.

10 November: In the evening the following order comes in from Hindenburg:

> The armistice is to be concluded with all possible speed. This will put an end to the bloody struggle. The moment which we all long for is approaching, when each of us can go home to parents, wife and child, brothers and sisters. At the same time a radical political change is taking place at home. The men standing at the head of the new order have declared that peace and order are to be maintained in all circumstances. This applies to an increased degree to the Army; no man may leave his unit without orders. Every man has, as before, to obey orders given by his superior officer. It is only thus that an orderly withdrawal can take place back to the home country. The railway lines which are at present out of service must be put back into regular working order. The Supreme Military Command does not wish to shed fresh

245

blood or to unleash civil war. The Supreme Command wishes to collaborate with the new governmental authorities to preserve peace and security and to save our country from the worst that may befall. Armed force is only to be used against members of our own people in self-defence, or where an ordinary crime has taken place, or to prevent looting.

In the evening a further order comes in, of which I also give the text:

The Government has despatched the following telegram to the Supreme Army Command:
'To General-Field-Marshal von Hindenburg. We require orders to be given to all armies in the field to the effect that military discipline, peace and strict order are to be maintained in the Army in all circumstances; therefore, orders from each man's military superior are to be obeyed until he is discharged, and members of the Armed Forces are only to be discharged from the Forces by order of their military superiors. The superior officers of those discharged are to retain their arms and badges of rank. Where Soldiers' Councils or *Vertrauensräte*—shop stewards' committees—have been formed, these are to receive the unqualified support of officers in their work of maintaining good order and military discipline.

(signed) Ebert, Haase, Scheidemann, Landsberg, Barth.'

In contrast, Corps Orders of 9 November thank us for the successful action fought the previous day, the 8th: without our knowing the implications, we and the infantry deflected a dangerous enemy movement which was threatening the rear of the Corps. Semoussies, which the enemy had penetrated, was recaptured in a lively counter-thrust, and our Army's right wing thus made safe. Yes indeed, things of this kind were still being done out here long after it was all over at home.

At the same time, an order arrives from Hindenburg to us, reading as follows:

I stand as before at the head of the Supreme Army Command, in order to lead the troops back to our homeland in good order and in a resolute frame of mind. I expect all commanding authorities and officers to do their duty as before.

A further order by Hindenburg states that all action involving destruction on the roads is to cease forthwith.

You can't find words to express all the things you are feeling now, and so I add various important orders, copied from the original text:

The order issued by our Divisional Commander reads as follows:

Comrades! I turn to you in this gravest hour of all. A new democratic Government, under Deputy Ebert as Reich Chancellor, has been formed in Germany. Disorder has broken out in a number of German cities. The further course of this movement cannot be foreseen. One thing, however, is certain: our beloved country will only be able to emerge from the present revolutionary process without serious permanent damage if the movement develops in complete order and according to a strict plan.

It is therefore our first duty to our newly created Fatherland for every one of us, down to the youngest soldier, to pledge all his strength to the maintenance of peace and order—now, in the field, and later at home.

Comrades! An armistice and peace are coming very soon; but on the marches and the rail journeys home we shall have trials of strength and all kinds of difficulties to overcome. We shall only succeed in overcoming them by maintaining good order and holding firmly together.

Comrades! For years we have borne all the trials and sufferings of war, together. All units of the Division have done their duty honourably and can look back with justifiable pride on their war service. Let us all ensure that the 9th Division brings home unblemished the good name which it made in the war. We want to go home as good troops who have always held firmly together!

11 November, 1918: The order arrived in the morning:

Hostilities will cease as from 12 noon today.

This was the order which I had to read out to my men.

The war is over ... How we looked forward to *this* moment; how we used to picture it as the most splendid event of our lives; and here we are now, humbled, our souls torn and bleeding, and know that we've surrendered. Germany has surrendered to the Entente!

Apart from the Kaiser and the Crown Prince, all ruling princes of the German Federation have abdicated. Our Kaiser has transferred all his powers over the German Army to General-Field-Marshal von Hindenburg. Hindenburg is staying, out of love for his soldiers, who have achieved such an endless number of great deeds in four years and four months. In 14 days we must have evacuated the entire occupied area up to the Rhine, and this means that the millions of men, with all the huge stores of equipment and supplies held in the rear, must be transported back or abandoned to the enemy.

A few pages back I copied out Ebert's appeal for peace. Hindenburg warns his comrades:

You did not forget your Field-Marshal in battle—and from now on I rely on you in the same way!

It is a great, a really great, achievement, and a marvellous piece of self-control, that Hindenburg is not deserting us.

This very day I find a little poem in a magazine, entitled *Dem Letzten*—'To the Last Man'. It is for the last man who falls for his Fatherland. The last three lines read:

Er, der das Todestor verriegelt
mit seinem Tod den Frieden siegelt,
ein Auserwählter wird er sein ...

He who has locked the gates of Death
And sealed the peace with blood and breath,
He shall be one of the chosen ...

General von Hutier warns his 18th Army to expect a feeling of sadness, bitter tears in fact, when reading the words: 'Even if the war is lost ... you can be proud of your achievements!'

Then, in an order of some length, he writes:

> Undefeated by the enemy but forced to this by external circumstances, we have to abandon the territory which we occupied after so fierce a contest. Even if the armistice conditions prescribed by the enemy constitute a monstrous hardship for our nation, we can nevertheless march back to our beloved country with heads held high.

He goes on to utter a warning that order and discipline must be preserved, especially so that this great army's ration supplies should not be held up. He reminds us that feeding a single Army for one day requires five ration trains and 600 head of cattle. He reminds us further that four Armies are waiting along one railway track beyond Namur, that therefore at least 20 ration trains have to pull in if we are to be properly fed, so no interruptions in the railway service must be allowed to occur; further, that large numbers of the land forces will have to march home on foot. His appeal ends with the words:

> Keep the German Army's bright shield of honour clean to the last, and then, in spite of the unhappy way this war has ended, you will be able to look back full of pride, to the very end of your days, upon your heroic deeds.

The armistice conditions, which are not yet official, are supposed to be: surrender of 5,000 guns and all our U-Boats; release of all prisoners; occupation of Western Germany as far as the Rhine.—That would be more than a humiliated nation can bear.

Whereas our men still have the old front-line spirit in them, further to the rear one comes across undisciplined hordes.

What is this dispute over our oath to the colours really about? I took my oath to the black-white-and-red colours and to the Kaiser. But Ebert rightly says that at the present time we should disregard the details of our oath, continue to do our duty, and protect the Fatherland from destruction.

Shop stewards' committees are now being formed in all units, each consisting of one officer, one N.C.O. and two other ranks, with a small committee in addition. No one in the Regiment feels inclined for such things, but we are still ordered to have them.

12 November: To Sart Eustache: We did not find anything very pleasant there. The fanatical Belgians ran up the Belgian flag over our heads. The bells are ringing for the French marching in behind us. We have to keep calm and swallow this provocation.

13 November: On further to Sart-St Laurent.

We now keep meeting small or large parties of British or French prisoners moving west on their way home. What a splendid mood they must be in compared with us!

But then, now and again, you do get filled with a feeling of happiness to be going home for good, and an inexpressible thankfulness as well that in all these years, in those countless battles and actions, absolutely nothing has happened to me. I was stationed at the front four years and two months, and all but a fortnight of that in the murderous west. I believe now, as I believed from the first day of my service, in destiny and providence. I do not believe that there are many soldiers who were stationed at the front for fifty months and are coming home, as I am now, unwounded!

Our Regiment has to surrender five guns to the French. As late as 4 November, that frightful day of heavy fighting, we defended our guns like heroes and recovered and saved those which we lost. We did not lose a single gun to the enemy, and now we have to give them up!

We are now near Namur; the war is ending for me at the place where it started. Thus we come full circle after over four years, as though the beginning and the end were shaking hands. But you shouldn't think back to the strength we had in us at Namur in 1914, or remember how happy we were then, or compare all that with today.

In spite of it all, we can be proud of the performance we put up, and we shall always be proud of it. Never before has a nation, a single army, had the whole world against it and stood its ground against such overwhelming odds; had it been the other way round, this heroic performance could never

250

have been achieved by any other nation. We protected our homeland from her enemies—they never pushed as far as German territory.

Now comes the order which moved us most of all:

To my Armies!

Now that His Majesty the Kaiser has relinquished the Supreme Command, I too am forced by circumstances, now that hostilities have ceased, to resign the command of my Army Group.

As always in the past, I can today express most heartfelt thanks to my brave Armies, and to every single man, for their heroic courage, their spirit of self-sacrifice and self-denial with which they have looked all dangers in the eye and willingly endured all privations for the Fatherland both in good times and bad.

The Army Group has not been defeated by force of arms! We have been forced to this by hunger and bitter necessity! Proudly, and with heads held high, my Army Group may now leave that territory of France which was fought for and won with the best of German blood. Your shield, your soldiers' honour, is bright and unspotted. Let every single man take care that it remains so, here, and later, at home!

Four long years I was privileged to be with my Armies, in victory and adversity, four long years I belonged with a full heart, and my whole heart, to my faithful troops. Deeply moved, I take my leave of you today, bowing in respect to the overwhelming greatness of your deeds, those deeds which History shall one day make known in words of flame to later generations.

Now keep true, as before, to your leaders, until their orders can release you to return to wife and child, to hearth and home!

God be with you and with your German Fatherland!

The Commander-in-Chief
(signed) Wilhelm
Crown Prince of the German Reich
and of Prussia

Old soldier as I was, when I read this I could not help shedding bitter tears.

On *14 November* we had a rest day. The band of the 154th was playing in the village and everyone standing round to listen, officers, other ranks, civilians, exactly as it used to be when we were resting in the French rear areas after victorious battles.

15 November: It has gone bitterly cold, and we are moving across the Meuse. The villages and billets are very crowded.

16 November: It is freezing hard and we are marching towards the Eifel.

It's a really indescribable feeling to be getting near home in full Army formation; our spirits brighten, and we get our old optimism back again.

17 November: I ride beside the 19th I.R.; it's more pleasant to march with the band. On the march I have a lot to do and always have to work in billets in the evening.

The whole Army seems to be moving home along the endless roads of the Western Front in an exemplary fashion, making its way home with perfect discipline.

I have been elected to the shop stewards' committee and today I was elected to the small committee as well.

On the march I chatted with the riflemen of the 19th I.R. What a healthy attitude they have, what splendid character, every one of them! And how convinced they all are that Germany will never be beaten.

18 November: We march across bare, high ground as the first snow falls; it looks as though Nature, too, is laying her peaceful colour over blood-stained France and Belgium. We march on and on.

20 November: We reach the German border; before that we had a last rest with some nice Belgian farmers, and at 3 o'clock exactly I move across the piece of earth which they call a frontier.

After four and a quarter years the German Army is marching home.

The Eifel is bare and cold, and it takes an eternity to get from village to village.

21 November: We press on at a forced march, and have only another 70 kilometres to the Rhine. We have to put on a good pace to keep the roads clear, because the whole of the German forces from Flanders are coming along after us.

Clémenceau has arrived in Metz: Alsace-Lorraine is French!

We hear of bad goings-on at Cologne—officers are supposed to have had their epaulettes torn off.

22 November: Billeted at Vahlen after an exhausting march. The German people at our billets are very kind. They are proud of us and glad we are still in good spirits in spite of it all. It is touching to see what care they take of our horses, and they bring us butter, milk and meat. This evening we all sit together with our farm families, and for the first time let our troubled thoughts out into the open.

23 November: Rest day.

24 November: We move on through Münstereifel, a charming little town in a valley among the rough Eifel hills. Here the kindly farming people had decorated the whole town with garlands and flags, pennants and sprigs of fir, and as we marched through they pelted us with flowers and decorated our horses. This is what you would imagine the victorious march through the Brandenburg Gate* to have been like, but these good people gave us fresh courage and confidence. We've got another 28 kilometres to Bonn!

It looks bad again inside Germany, with the threat of Bolshevism about, and people are already talking about separating the Rhineland from the rest of Germany.

In the East, the Poles have marched into Posen. Can we really still be glad to be back home?

25 November: Rest day in Iversheim, really charming. All over the town the farm families have been baking cakes for us.

* The famous archway in Berlin at the start of Unter den Linden.—R.T.

26 November: March to just outside Bonn. We move into splendid billets at Schloss Annaberg, near Godesberg, the property of Count Westerholt. The most sumptuous billets we've had in the whole war. The kindly Countess Westerholt looked after us all in the most charming way.

27 November: Rest day: I took the opportunity to ride over to Bonn on my mare Tango Princess. On the way my trusty mount shied, never having seen an electric tram in her life, and took a tumble with me, which considering the hard road, was disagreeable for us both. Bonn has put out the flags for us splendidly, a real sea of flags and pine-branches. Discipline there is perfect.

On *28 November* we left our feudal and hospitable billet, where we had been received better than anywhere else in the whole war. In a fortnight the British will be in billets there—dreadful!

The march through Bonn itself was wonderful; we were the first front-line Division to pass through, the first of the 18th Army. The narrow streets were packed with civilians, who cheered us like anything. General Watter stood on the Rhine Bridge and took a march past. Meanwhile our guns had been hung with flags and wreaths of greenery, and our gunners sang as they marched behind the guns.

29 November: The march continues through the Siegtal to Dattenfeld, every village has been decorated and we get a joyous welcome everywhere, all the village children run after us and take us to the next village. No one at home had believed it would be possible for the front-line troops to march home with such splendid discipline. The bands play gay marches, and we are in very good spirits. At one village, though, we saw a heart-breaking scene: two mothers were looking on with laughing faces, but when the band suddenly began to play *I had a loving comrade,** they both began to cry miserably; they must have had sons or husbands killed in action.

We now have a march of nearly 350 kilometres behind us. At nearly every village the band plays the old soldiers'

* Traditionally played at every German soldier's funeral.—R.T.

254

song *In der Heimat, in der Heimat* [When we come home again]. The reception we are given gets warmer and more heartfelt the further we move inside Germany. We are given good billets everywhere, and everywhere the civilians are astonished, agreeably surprised, really overwhelmed by the morale of our troops. It is really marvellous—this whole march is wonderful, and our home country really seems to have understood that we are undefeated and unconquerable.

Now the demobilization orders keep coming in, which makes work for me, because the other ranks whose homes lie in this area are to be discharged here too. We move on through Dietzenhausen and Waldbröl. Again and again we find every little village, every little town, even tiny hamlets hung with wreaths and decorations. And what marvellous people they all are! Now and then you catch yourself thinking that this terrible end to the war is all nothing but a bad dream. The impression I got of that little place Waldbröl will always stay in my mind, a flash of light in troubled times, a glimpse of the best of German faith and true German constancy. Our drivers are not allowed to look after their horses themselves, the farmers take offence if we don't leave it to them, and they give the horses oats and hay and feed us too, although they have so little themselves. Yes, and another thing, they give us soap! And if they know we are going to stay the night or until mid-day the next day, they turn to straight away and bake us cakes. One old farmer tells me that nothing is too much trouble if it's for us. One could have burst into tears!

1 December: March to Hünsborn, we are already in Westphalia. On the *2nd* and *3rd* we move on as far as Dotzlar.

4 December: Rest day, and today finishes the longest chapter of my life: today I get my discharge from the Regiment!

Even though a thousand different kinds of hope have had to be given a pitiable burial, I do nevertheless feel, for myself and for the millions of others who served, that one has done what lay within one's power. I dread having to say good-bye to my men, and only wish the moment could be safely past.

I could not tell them, on *5 December*, what was in my

heart—I should like to have embraced every one of them. I said good-bye to my horse and to my faithful Fritz.* I took leave of my Regimental C.O., and I had the feeling that saying good-bye like this was much more terrible for each of us than a large-scale battle. I went over once again to my old No. 2 Battery and said good-bye to the few remaining faithfuls from the old days whom I still knew—and who were still alive.

In the evening, for the last time, I wrote my signature at the bottom of Battalion Orders, and then came the farewell which was of course the most difficult of all, from my faithful, well-beloved, courageous comrade Hans-Ado von Seebach.

I am travelling to Frankenberg, alone, and meanwhile feel I must mention something of particular interest: Corps of volunteers are being formed for the *Grenzschutz Ost*† to protect Germany against the Poles in the East; now just imagine this, soldiers who have been engaged in heavy fighting for years are volunteering straight away, thousands and thousands of them, and a large number of them from my Regiment. Could there be more splendid proof of spirit and conviction than this?

After a night spent with 15 soldiers in one compartment, I travelled through Marburg and arrived at Frankfurt on the morning of *7 December*, after four and one-third years! Alone and without my Regiment. Huge posters shouting appeals are no longer able to please me. I can't get used yet to the word 'Republic'. Well, here I am in the new Germany. I take my parents by surprise, but they expected me to arrive in the next few days anyway. They are very happy.

What does it all seem like to me now! Home at last, and not having to go away again!

On 8 December I went for a walk in my beloved uniform for the last time to report my discharge to the local military office, the *Bezirkskommando*.

I felt as though I were walking to my own funeral.

* My batman, Herrmann's successor.
† One of the post-Armistice formations of para-military volunteers formed in 1918.—R.T.